interpretation of how each of the new single-practice oriented schools of Buddhism arose, their teachings and role in the continuity of Buddhist development. It also reveals the inevitable cycle of dissension, corruption and decay each experience as they are drained of their vitality in the process of becoming affluent established institutions, making it clear that the foundation of Japanese Buddhism has never been and never will be a one-time endeavour—but rather a perpetual renewal.

This second volume completes the study by well-known Buddhist authors, that will be an essential textbook and reference work for students of Japanese Buddhism and intellectual history for many years to come.

The Authors

Who are outstanding authorities on Buddhism, noted for their many books and translations, presently reside in Japan. Daigan Matsunaga, former Professor of History at California State University Northridge, is President of the Eikyoji Institute of Buddhist Studies and head of the Eikyoji Temple complex. Alicia Matsunaga, former Professor of Oriental Languages at UCLA, is a Sapporo Director of Buddhist Books International.

FOUNDATION OF JAPANESE BUDDHISM

VOL. I

THE ARISTOCRATIC AGE

BY

DAIGAN MATSUNAGA Ph.D.

ALICIA MATSUNAGA Ph.D.

BUDDHIST BOOKS INTERNATIONAL

LOS ANGELES-TOKYO

Second Printing 1978

ISBN 0-914910-25-6
Library of Congress No. 74-83654
Printed by Kenkyusha Printing Co.

Tokyo, Japan

TO

ELVIRA & ORIS ENGBLOM

CONTENTS

CHAPTER FOUR: HEIAN BUDDHISM, DEVELOPMENT OF A NEW DIMENSION

CHAPTER I

INTRODUCTION

A. Pre-Buddhist Japan

From the dawn of culture, magico-religious cults played a dominant role in the lives of the early Japanese. The Mesolithic Jōmon culture, which commenced approximately four or five milleniums B.C., provides the first physical evidence of such beliefs in the form of *dogū* female figurines, indicative of fertility rites, phallic symbols, the *kussō* (fetal position) form of burial and filed teeth.[1] The Yayoi culture, which replaced the Jōmon in approximately the second century B.C., introduced a number of unusual bronze artifacts such as *dōtaku* (bells), mirrors, spears and other weapons too fragile to be functional, that must have been used symbolically in some form of religious rite. Although we cannot be certain of exactly what types of early religious beliefs existed, it is obvious that the indigenous faith conducted some form of magico-fertility rites, shamanism and disposal of the dead. The 297 A.D. account of Japan composed by Chinese from the Wei dynasty describes the existence of rites of purification, divination, and a shamanistic female ruler named Pimiko, who was buried in a massive tomb at the time of her death. Such a form of aristocratic burial was to characterize the third early Japanese society.

The *Kofun* (Tomb) or *Uji* (Clan) culture evolved during the third century A.D. and combined nearly all the religious elements subsequently mythologized in the earliest historical records of the eighth century. Continental influence played a significant role in the construction of large earthen tumuli over the tombs of Emperors and social leaders and the nascence of an ancestor worship honouring deceased heroes, and cultural leaders. The events of this era were projected into the past in the *Kojiki*

(Record of Ancient Matters) composed in 712 A.D. and the *Nihonshoki* or *Nihongi* (Chronological History of Japan) of 720, in an effort to emulate the antiquity of the Chinese Empire. The beginning of the Japanese nation was dated from the reign of Emperor Jimmu in 660 B.C. but in reality, the process of unifying the many semi-autonomous clans inhabiting the Japanese isles under the Yamato or Imperial clan only began in the fourth century A.D. and was still far from complete when Buddhism was officially introduced.

The Imperial clan, claiming descent from the Sun Goddess, Amaterasu Ō Mikami, was undoubtedly a vestigial remain of early shamanistic leadership and they played a dominant role in Japanese history of the eighth century. By this time they had been able to successfully extend their hegemony and surmount counter claims pressed by other powerful clans by reason of their superior shamanism coupled with diplomatic acumen and physical strength. Despite their assertion of divine descent, every other *uji* could boast a similar claim with respect to its own tutelary deity, the *ujigami*, who safeguarded and looked after the interests of the clan. It was only after the Imperial clan completed its process of federation that the myths and deities of the other clans could be woven into subservient roles in the prestigious *Kojiki* and *Nihonshoki*. These records stressed the antiquity of the nation in conjunction with the superiority and unbroken continuity of the Yamato clan; at the same time incorporating numerous imported myths and legends. In view of the fact that these first written accounts were not composed until after Buddhism had already received national recognition, it is impossible to imagine that they might present an untainted view of the indigenous Japanese faith. Not only were they influenced by Buddhism, but also by Confucian and Taoist thought that arrived in Japan simultaneously with the art of writing. Despite such obstacles, these works managed to unify, express and enforce the basic feelings of the early Japanese and with the exception of archeological findings, which pose unlimited problems of interpretation, the *Kojiki* and *Nihonshoki* are the most significant Japanese accounts of their early religious beliefs.

A primary concern of the *Kojiki* was to forge a relationship between the tutelar deities of the various clans and the ancestors of the Imperial family, while at the same time, encompassing local myths. Despite such a contrived task, considerable insight is offered into the early Japanese attitude towards life which can be described as a form of 'natural affirmation'. It was 'natural' in the sense that it was not a product of philosophical inquiry but resulted from an innate sensitivity and harmony with the world. Life was viewed as basically agreeable and as yet no sin nor evil was differentiated that ultimately could not be overcome. That which interfered with man's happiness was a temporary affliction or pollution capable of being expelled by lustration and rites of purification. Both man and the world in which he lived were deemed inherently beneficent and as yet there was no concept of a suffering that could shake worldly pleasures to their depths and lead to the questioning of existence itself.

Kami (sacred spirits or deities) abounded in the world of the early Japanese. Every existent was believed to have a spirit and a great number of these were considered worthy of veneration. Basically the *kami*, derived from shamanistic and animistic beliefs, were very vague in nature consisting of abstract notions such as the qualities of fertility and growth, natural phenomena and objects such as sun, wind, thunder, trees, mountains, and rocks; certain animals and human ancestral spirits were also included. On the whole, these spirits were benevolent, although capricious at times and quite capable of demonstrating human emotions. This humanism is particularly evident in the *Kojiki* myths of the violent Susanoo no Mikoto and his descendent Ōkuninushi no Kami, the kind-hearted somewhat foolish hero god, who always manages to be rescued from danger in order to achieve his goal. But even the noble Sun Goddess can display female emotions such as curiosity, love and wounded pride. The deities of the *Kojiki* on the whole, represent idealized human beings or personified aspects of nature rather than divine qualities.

The belief in the innate goodness of life itself made it impossible for the early Japanese to create an ideal supernatural world beyond the present, for such a creation would have necessitated the negation of the existing life. *Takamagahara*, the land of the gods, was an idealization of the Yamato country and the *kami* that dwelt there not only engaged in the same type of pursuits as their earthly counterparts but also frequently roamed among them. Even the land of the dead, *Yominokuni*, was envisioned as having a spatial relationship with the present world since it could be entered by means of a cave in the vicinity of Izumo and it was acceptable for the dead to wander at times back among the living. When Izanagi visits *Yominokuni* and shames his dead wife Izanami by striking a light and exposing her maggot infested body, she is perfectly capable of chasing him back into his own land until he sets a barrier in her pathway.

The *kami* primarily represented man's appreciation and harmony with the world in which he lived. In the early myths human sentiments are clearly projected upon natural phenomena and there is no disparity between the subjectivity of man and that attributed to nature. The loud crying of Susanoo, the Sun Goddess' naughty brother, parches the lands, while Ōkuninushi teaches the rabbit of Inaba, who was foolish enough to think he could trick the sharks to form a bridge for him on the pretext of counting them, how to restore the fur they ripped off when they learned of his deceit. In poetry, such an identity between the feelings of man and nature was expressed as follows:

> If in the age of the gods,
> Mt. Kagu could fight with Mt. Miminashi
> Over the fair hill of Unebi,
> Is it not natural that the men of today
> Should fight for a wife?
>
> Emperor Tenchi (626–671)
> *Mannyōshū* 13

The early Japanese viewed life as a unity between man and his environment and a strong desire existed to appreciate and comprehend the multiple aspects of nature that were so vividly expressed in the changing seasons. This extremely subjective emotional feeling for nature was a characteristic the Japanese people never lost and even today the spring cherry blossoms and fall moon invite excursions and viewing parties that are joined with the enjoyment of delicate foods created to match each changing season. Unlike the early Greek attitude towards nature, which bore many similarities to the Japanese, this feeling was never to lend itself to the dissecting knife of philosophical speculation. The Japanese passively accepted nature as an integral oneness in which they participated. This appreciation was to reach its most perfect forms of expression blended with Buddhist philosophy, in poetry and the arts, whereby man could unite with nature. But even in such forms, the appreciation for the whole prevailed over the natural human tendency to draw out and idealize a single aspect at the expense of the rest.

B. Fertile Soil for Buddhism

The question arises how the Japanese people could accept Buddhism, an alien religion, when they already had an indigenous faith that apparently satisfied their needs? The answer is that from the beginning the two religions had a great deal in common. First, the indigenous faith can scarcely be termed a religion in the narrow definition of that term. It was rather a loose combination of various shamanistic and animistic beliefs varying regionally that were not joined together until the introduction of Buddhism and Chinese civilization. The native faith more closely approximated a psychological attitude than a religion, since it represented the closeness of the people to the land they loved and the deities venerated were the personifications of that land in the form of its stones, earth, trees and mountains. Until the arrival of Buddhism, the autochthonous faith did not even have a name; it was only designated the 'way of the gods' (Shintō) in contrast to the new foreign religion. At that stage of development it could have become compatible with almost any religion, providing the new faith met certain necessary conditions. One of these prerequisites was a non-exclusive nature.

Since the indigenous faith embraced almost everything within its fold and had multiple varieties of *kami*, it was not capable of forsaking these for a monotheistic religion that would deny the enchorial deities their due veneration. In fact, the fear was expressed when Buddhism was introduced that the native gods would be neglected and thus wreak havoc upon the land; but such a concern was unfounded. Buddhism was a religion with a

1.0 + 35 + 40 + 60 = 2.35

long history of assimilating alien beliefs and divinities and found the acceptance of the Japanese *kami* to pose no problem. It very soon was able to find a proper place for them in its pantheon where they could be utilized as *upāya* (adapted teachings) to lead the laity into the acceptance of basic Buddhist doctrines. Actually it was necessary for Buddhism to assimilate the native deities since this was the historical method of propagation.

Not only was Buddhism amiable towards the indigenous *kami*, but it also provided multiple varieties of new divinities compatible to them. In India, the Buddhists had assimilated the autochthonous *deva* (heavenly spirits) into their pantheon as guardians and protectors. These deities were brought to Japan in accompaniment with many varieties of bodhisattvas and Buddhas developed in Mahāyāna Buddhism to symbolize abstract philosophical concepts. The early Japanese soon found that the new religion offered not merely one new deity for veneration but literally hundreds suited more appropriately to the needs of advanced civilization than the indigenous *kami*. For example, the Indian *deva* Śrī-Lakṣmī became Kisshōten, patroness of virtue, while Sarasvatī transformed into the popular Benzaiten, goddess of fortune, eliminator of calamities and popular patroness of musicians; both still enjoy appeal in modern Japan. In this respect, Buddhism complemented the native faith. Not merely did it introduce many new and practical forms of divinities but it also brought iconographic representations of them, an aspect the native faith lacked. This made the new gods seem far more tangible and approachable.

Without scriptures or systematization, the indigenous faith could not provide a philosophical challenge to Buddhism. It did offer some similarities in attitude however, to Buddhist philosophical goals. The native feeling of unity with nature had much in common with the Buddhist concept of interrelatedness, with the difference of course, that the Buddhists arrived at their concept by means of a logical process that ultimately was denied in favour of intuition. The Buddhist method necessitated the introduction of philosophical negation, since it clearly recognized the existential plight of man and the imperfections of the world in which he lived. It was a process that entailed a great deal of self-awareness and introspection. The early Japanese 'natural affirmation' of life was pre-logical and dependent upon the native intuitive faculties that had not yet begun to delve into such problems as impermanence, the inevitability of death and the abyss of frustrations caused by the individual ego in its attempt to colour the world in accordance to its own liking. With the advance of civilization the early Japanese attitude of 'natural affirmation' was forced to yield, since as man intellectually progresses he becomes more self-aware until ideally, he reaches the stage where he can shed self-consciousness and learn to accept himself, while still keeping in mind the discovery of his own frailty. In Buddhism, this realization was considered to be a product of Enlightenment. The native Japanese attitude offered fecund soil that eventually, after being swept by the bleak wintry gales of suffering and self-awareness that accompanied the new nation's growing pains, was ready for the planting of the Buddhist seeds of Enlightenment. There could be no quarrel between the two religions in this area as the native faith was receptive to a developed philosophical system.

Certain other attitudes of the indigenous belief were also compatible with Buddhism. For example, the early Japanese did not believe in the existence of an absolute form of evil. This naturally made it difficult to believe that a foreign religion could be wholly bad. Also their innate faith in the goodness of man made it difficult for them to accept any form of religion that advocated the existence of absolute evil or eternal damnation. The Buddhists had hells, which at the philosophical level represented psychological states of mind in the present life, and were taught symbolically to the laity as possible abodes of future suffering in order to induce the practice of virtue. Yet even at the symbolic level, deliverance was always possible as soon as the individual had exhausted his evil karma. The Buddhists considered evil as suffering, which could be overcome by personal effort, and in this respect shared the optimism of the native faith.

Both beliefs also displayed an interest in magical or mystical rituals. In Buddhism this was epitomized in Tantrism, which eventually mingled with the native faith to form the unique Japanese phenomenon known as

Shugendō. The more purely Japanese forms of Buddhism were generally to discard this interest during their development in the Kamakura period, but it was initially an important meeting point and offered Buddhism a natural entrée into Japanese society.

Finally, one other aspect of the early Japanese society that made it capable of receiving a new religion was its authoritarian nature. Once the Imperial family and leaders of the great clans came to a decision to accept the new religion, the common people out of force of habit followed their lead. It was not necessary for the Buddhists to convert the masses in order to become a national religion, merely the leaders, who were predominantly more interested in the pragmatic benefits of a religion than its spiritual aims. The Yamato leaders were eventually to decide that Buddhism, the faith of advanced continental nations, had a great deal to offer Japan and this important factor was to allow Buddhism a prestigious place in Japanese society and vast sums for temple building at a time when the masses were as yet scarcely aware of its existence. With such a foothold, so easily acquired, the conversion of the masses could be postponed.

In brief, early Japanese society offered an ideal soil for any developed and organized religion that could prove compatible with the psychological attitude of the Japanese people, which was in effect the native faith. This was the key to the Buddhist success in Japan.

CHAPTER II

INCEPTION OF BUDDHISM

A. Official Transmission and the Socio-political Milieu

Traditionally, the *Nihonshoki* lists 552 A.D. as the date of the official introduction of Buddhism to Japan by the leader of the Korean Kingdom of Paekche (Jap. Kudara), who presented a gilt-bronze Buddha image and sutras to the Yamato court in an effort to foster a political alliance with Japan against the neighboring Korean states of Silla and Koguryŏ. The accuracy of the *Shoki's* date for this event has long been disputed and from earliest periods the year 538 has been considered more precise. In any event, the formal introduction of Buddhism did not represent the first contact of the Japanese with the new faith. Undoubtedly, traders and merchants had brought the teachings with them generations earlier and it was also the dominant faith of most continental immigrants settling in Japan. Among these, there is no question that the large colonies of Koreans already had priests among them. As early as 522, it is recorded that a monk of Chinese ancestry known in Japan as Shiba Tachito, had constructed a temple.[1] This priest, who later reverted to the lay state, was to play an important role in Asuka Buddhism.

The formal introduction of the alien religion to the Japanese court necessitated an official position regarding its acceptability and this was a difficult task for the Emperor to face. As the leader of what had now become a loosely federated native cult, charged with its protection and the conduct of its rituals, the Emperor had to be extremely careful in accepting a new religion The early Yamato state was a theocracy and in classical Japanese the term *matsurigoto* literally combined both religious rites and civil administration. For the Emperor to consider conversion to an alien faith at that period could pose a threat to the very basis of his power, which as yet was far from being solidified. It also presented problems in dealing with the *uji*, many of whom had only recently been willing to accept the supremacy of Imperial spiritual leadership. To make matters worse, the introduction of Buddhism by the King of Paekche demanded a decision regarding a foreign alliance that already had become an issue among the leading clans.

For some time competition had been waged between the Soga and Mononobe clans, the two most powerful survivors of the more aristocratic type of *uji*. At this period the clans could be divided into three categories: the *shimbetsu* or those who claimed descent similar to the Imperial family from the gods of *Takamagahara* and the descendents of gods dating prior to Emperor Jimmu, the *kōbetsu* or those of Imperial descent after the time of Emperor Jimmu and lastly, the *bambetsu* or powerful *uji* of foreign descent. The Mononobe were a strong military *uji* belonging to the *shimbetsu*, which were more conservative in nature with an older tradition. In contrast, the Soga belonged to the *kōbetsu*, claiming closer ties to the Imperial family and more liberal. The Soga, who acted as managers of the Imperial estates, which relied heavily upon the settling of foreign immigrants and utilization of their skills, believed that Japan should import the superior civilization and organized form of government found on the continent. In opposition, the conservative Mononobe were joined by a lesser *shimbetsu uji*, the Nakatomi, hereditary ritualists with a vested interest in the indigenous faith, and insisted upon a continuation of the old order. The adoption of Buddhism was not the only issue in the battle between these clans that eventually led to military confrontation, but it added additional fuel to the fire. Emperor Kimmei (531–571)[2], caught between the two groups and his own qualms about the desirability of accepting a foreign religion, decided as a compromise to allow the Soga clan to embrace Buddhism.

The Soga acceptance of Buddhism was far from a conversion in our ordinary sense of the term. They had no philosophical understanding of the new religion and merely regarded it as a possible superior form of magic long practiced by the advanced civilizations they respected and sought to emulate. Undoubtedly, they still must have faced the simple question that confronted all Japanese on their first encounter with the alien religion; namely, would it anger the native gods? This problem had to be solved before Buddhism could ever be properly welcomed in Japan. The Soga were opportunistic enough to risk the chance and perhaps confident enough in their belief in foreign supremacy. Still this general uneasiness regarding the feelings of the native gods is clearly expressed in legends of the time recorded in the *Nihonshoki*.

According to one account, the new faith was proscribed by the Emperor shortly after the Soga accepted it in the belief that the native gods had been offended and caused an outbreak of plague; the Buddha image was subsequently thrown into the Naniwa canal (*Nihonshoki*: Kimmei, 13th year, 10th month). A similar story is alleged to have occurred during the reign of Emperor Bidatsu (572–585), who allowed the image to be restored in hopes of curing the illness of Soga no Umako, leader of the clan. (Bidatsu, 14th year 3rd month, 30th day). Although the credibility of these accounts is extremely weak, they perhaps represented the swaying tensions in the Soga-Mononobe struggle for power as well as the widespread mixed feelings concerning the new faith.

The first Emperor to actually espouse Buddhism was Yōmei (585–587), whose mother had been a Soga. He took up the new faith when he became gravely ill and requested that an image of Yakushi (Bhaiṣajyaguru), the healing Buddha, be made in hopes of aiding his recovery. The *Nihonshoki* chronicler wrote concerning this, that "the Emperor Yōmei believed in the teaching of Buddha and respected the way of the gods."[3] The Emperor did not live long enough to see the Yakushi image completed and his sister, Empress Suiko (592–628) finished the project twenty years later and enshrined it in the Hōryūji temple.

In the succession dispute that followed the death of Yōmei in 587, the Soga went to war against the Mononobe and Nakatomi, winning a decisive victory that permitted them to freely engage in the importation of continental civilization and the establishment of Buddhism as a state religion. This new policy was actively initiated under Empress Suiko and her regent, Prince Shōtoku, the son of Yōmei.

B. Prince Shōtoku and Buddhism

Traditionally Prince Shōtoku has been regarded as a renowned statesman and the father of Japanese Buddhism. There is no question that with the passage of time he was legendized to such a degree that the character of the actual man has been lost. As early as the *Nihonshoki* (Suiko, 1st year, 4th month, 10th day), he is described as being able to speak the moment he was born and proved to have such wisdom as an adult that he could attend to the claims of ten men at once and decide them all without error. He was also supposedly gifted with a foreknowledge of future events. Modern critics have gone to the opposite extreme in an attempt to demythologize the Prince without being able to present any more concrete evidence. The true character of Shōtoku Taishi must still lie illusively between the extremes of legend and so-called modern criticism.

Although it is difficult to believe that Prince Shōtoku could have been the intellectual giant portrayed in popular legend, we certainly cannot dismiss him as an illiterate. As the son of the first Buddhist Emperor, Yōmei, it is most likely that when he was appointed regent in 592 at the age of 19, that he had already received considerable education in Buddhism and Chinese culture. Five years had elapsed between the conversion and death of his father and his own appointment, it is logical to presume that a great portion of that time was devoted to education. He was later to enjoy the reputation of a scholar both among his contemporaries and following generations. It is most likely that there is a solid core of truth ingrained in the popular legends, for certainly someone was responsible for directing the nation along a new pathway at that crucial period and Shōtoku Taishi is the logical choice. If he was an individual gifted with foresight and vision in the age of social formulation, it would be quite natural to make him a cultural hero.

The Prince's personal attitude towards Buddhism is best symbolized by his alleged deathbed quotation from the *Dhammapada* to his followers:

> Avoid evil, undertake good, purify the mind:
> this is the teaching of the Buddhas.
>
> Verse 183

This statement contains the essence of Buddhist morality and is one of the most perfect summations of the entire teaching. 'To avoid evil' and 'undertake good' is a commonplace moral injunction that might be advocated by any religion, but the specific goal of Buddhism lies in the purification of the mind; for without a pure mind, the practice of goodness and avoidance of evil can degenerate into mere self-righteous conduct. The emphasis upon mental purification resulting from proper conduct has given this verse a significant role in Japanese Buddhism to the present date.

The last testament of the Prince to his wife, stating: "this world [for the unenlightened] is illusion, the Buddha alone is true", displays a knowledge of Buddhism far advanced beyond his contemporaries.[4] The idea that common man's view of the world might be an illusion did not properly invade Japanese thought until generations later; during the Heian period it became a dominant theme pervading almost every area of literature. It is quite likely that Prince Shōtoku's comprehension of the transitory and illusory nature of the present world was a conviction derived from personal experience. He must have often been an isolated and lonely figure during his long thirty year regency, living amongst corrupt relatives in a new nation filled with dissent, intrigue and political rivalry. The native faith could hardly have offered him a solution since the sufferings he experienced as the leader of a nation in the throes of adapting an advanced civilization could not easily be removed. He grappled not merely with simple problems generated by physical and ritual impurity but rather the complexities of human greed and ambition that feed upon wealth and power. The path to achieving such an advanced civilization entailed sufferings that the early *uji* chiefs had little imagined, for when man has to struggle for his daily survival he does not have the leisure to indulge in seeking the goals of personal ambition and thereby perpetrating countless subtle inhumanities against his fellow man that the so-called more civilized individual possesses. The native natural affirmation was not capable of coping with the complex problems of a world that increasingly defied common sense reality.

Whether Prince Shōtoku assumed complete administrative control of the fledgling nation when he became regent at the age of 19 is debatable although not improbable. In any event, there was no discrepancy between Imperial interests and the interests of the Soga clan, who by then had successfully managed to integrate into the Imperial family by marriage; both Empress Suiko and Prince Shōtoku were of Soga blood.

One of the most crucial developments in Japanese Buddhism that can be directly attributed to Prince Shōtoku was the beginning of official embassies to China in 607. These missions played an essential role in the development of Buddhism and Japanese culture. Students and priests who went to China brought back new ideas for centralized government that ultimately led to the Ritsuryō reform movement, while the encounter with the purer forms of Chinese Buddhism brought with it a more profound knowledge of the sutras and in time, the Chinese sects of Buddhism to Japan. This initial contact of Japanese students with Chinese Buddhism was to set the pathway for the development of Japanese Buddhism for the next several centuries. Certain other alleged accomplishments of the Prince are more questionable.

According to tradition, Shōtoku Taishi composed a 'Seventeen-article Constitution' in 604 and also wrote commentaries upon three important Buddhist sutras of the day; the *Shōmangyō* (*Śrīmālā siṃhanāda sūtra*), *Yuimagyō* (*Vimalakīrti nirdeśa sūtra*) and *Hokekyō* (*Saddharma puṇḍarīka sūtra*). Of these accomplishments, the so-called constitution is most controversial. It is quite possible that it may have been composed a generation or more after the Prince's death as a tribute to his memory rather than by Shōtoku Taishi himself. In any event, the 'constitution' represents a set of moral injunctions rather than a body of law. Insofar as they advocated a centralized government and bureaucracy of merit rather than heredity, they did represent a radical innovation for Japan. This was the essence of the Taika reform initiated in 645, almost a quarter of a century after the death of Prince Shōtoku. It is not inconceivable that the Prince originated the idea since it was a logical step in the assimilation of the Chinese cultural-political system, and certainly must have been considered well in advance of the Taika reform.

The three commentaries on Buddhist sutras (*Sangyōgisho*) attributed to Shōtoku Taishi display a considerable knowledge of Buddhist philosophy. There is no definitive proof that Shōtoku Taishi actually wrote them and some critics maintain they were probably written by a Chinese priest.[5] From the content however, it appears that the commentaries are composed in a Japanese form of Chinese rather than pure Chinese and references to other sutras are limited to those introduced to Japan during Shōtoku's period. Such evidence has led some contemporary Buddhist scholars to still affirm Shōtoku Taishi was the author.[6]

Tradition also maintains that Prince Shōtoku was responsible for building some of the great temples of the Asuka period such as the Hōryūji and Shitennōji. Although the Prince cannot be credited with personally constructing temples as some legends imply, it is clear that this was an important era of temple building. According to the census taken two years after Shōtoku's death, Japan had acquired 46 temples. Most likely Korean immigrants contributed a great deal to their construction since they were designed following the style of Paekche, but they could not have been built without official sponsorship and that had to be provided by Prince Shōtoku and the Soga clan.

Historically, the Hōryūji temple is most closely associated with the Prince since it adjoined his Ikaruga palace and was supposedly built in order to house the Yakushi image created for the benefit of his father, Emperor Yōmei. In this temple the famous Yumedono is presently found where, according to legend the Prince was believed to have spent his periods of contemplation. Actually, the present Hōryūji is a restoration built on a slightly different location after the fire of 670.

The Shitennōji, according to legend, was built by Prince Shōtoku and the Soga family as a fulfilment of a vow to the Four Deva Kings (Shitennō), guardians of the directions and protectors of Buddhism, for the 587 Soga victory over the Mononobe. It is somewhat questionable however, whether the temple was actually known as the Shitennōji at the time of its construction and in early periods it was generally referred to by its regional name, Arahakadera (Deserted Tomb Temple). It is also doubtful whether the Four Deva Kings were even the principal images of veneration during the earliest days of the temple. Despite the question of this temple's original name, it is clear that it was built in Naniwa during the regency of Prince Shōtoku. At the time of the excavation following the destruction of the pagoda by a typhoon in 1934, it was ascertained that the foundation stone of the original was similar to those of the Asukadera and Hōryūji, the roof tiles also proved to be of a proximate date.[7] The *Nihonshoki* date of 593 (Suiko 1st year 9th month) for the beginning of construction must be nearly reliable.

Another great temple reportedly built by the Soga clan in fulfilment of a vow for their victory over the Mononobe was the Asukadera (Hōkōji) completed according to the *Nihonshoki*, in 596 (Suiko 4th year, 11th month). This was one of the earliest temples to have a systematic arrangement with a somewhat unusual style; a center pagoda with three *Kondō* (halls); a similar arrangement has since been discovered near Pyongyang, the ancient capital of Koguryŏ.[8] Apparently this temple represents a close link with the Korean influenced tomb culture, for in the excavations between 1956–57 it was discovered that beneath the pagoda, jade, *magatama*, swords and other objects frequently found in the ancient tombs were buried in accompaniment with Buddhist relics. Traditionally, the Asukadera was the main temple of the Soga clan and therefore extremely important during the Asuka period. In later years it became known as the Gangōji and when the court moved to Nara, a new temple (Shingangōji) was constructed in that city in 716.

Although we cannot directly attribute the construction of 46 temples during his lifetime to Shōtoku Taishi, we can safely state that the majority of these temples were built under Imperial sponsorship or the patronage of the Soga clan, in which case Prince Shōtoku was either directly or indirectly responsible.

Sufficient changes occurred in the evolution of Japanese Buddhism during the regency of Prince Shōtoku to consider him the sponsor, and by extenuation, father of Japanese Buddhism. Even if we do not accept the authenticity of the writings attributed to him, we have to conclude that he became the symbol of a new direction in the development of Buddhism, a movement away from the theurgic concerns of his contemporaries towards a proper understanding of the teachings. This movement remained merely an undercurrent during the subsequent Nara period, in which thaumaturgy dominated, and did not begin to gain momentum until future generations decided to create a truly Japanese form of Buddhism.

C. Characteristics of Asuka Buddhism

For all practical purposes, Asuka Buddhism functioned as a mundane instrument of the ruling classes. In other words, it was utilized as a superior form of magic and shamanism to enforce the roles of the Imperial family and aristocracy. Prior to the introduction of Buddhism, the indigenous faith had used prayers, divination and other practices as a means of relating to the powers of nature believed to be *kami*. When Buddhism entered the early society it was immediately viewed as another form of theurgy, in fact a more potent variety in view of its acceptance by Japan's powerful civilized continental neighbors. The Buddhist images, having no counterpart in the native faith, were regarded with awe and gained popularity among certain court factions as having powerful efficacy in promoting material prosperity, the cure of illness and aversion of calamities. At the earliest stage the various Buddhas and bodhisattvas were not even clearly differentiated. For instance, the Yakushi (Bhaiṣajyaguru) image of the Hōryūji main hall bears no real difference in appearance from the Shaka (Śākyamuni) image and the two can only be differentiated by means of their carved inscriptions. Even in this area a confusion exists since the inscription on the Shaka image refers to his vow to cure illness and grant prosperity, which are normally attributes of Yakushi. At this period the image itself was believed to possess powers and the philosophical significance tended to be disregarded.

1. The Healing Cults

As one of the first devotions embraced by an Emperor, the cult to Yakushi Nyorai enjoyed immense popularity in Early Japan and typifies the interest in theurgic healing rites. Although not much is known regarding the origin of Bhaiṣajyaguru Buddha in India, his prototype

Bhaiṣajyarāja bodhisattva (Yakuō) plays a significant role in the *Lotus Sutra* as a healing bodhisattva. It is quite likely that Bhaiṣajyaguru was derived from the concept of the historical Buddha as a healer or physician who could cure the ills of the mind, source of human suffering. The concept of Amitābha and his Western Pure Land apparently influenced the development of Bhaiṣajyaguru and an Eastern Buddha land. But it would appear that Bhaiṣajyaguru's Buddha land was regarded by his devotees as a type of *deva* heaven and not as a realm of final liberation, for unlike Amitābha, Bhaiṣajyaguru predominately dispensed mundane benefits.[9]

Bhaiṣajyaguru does not appear to have ever enjoyed the degree of popularity in India that he achieved in Japan. In his course of development he became closely associated with Indian Tantrism and eventually this aspect was popularized in Japan during the Heian period. The Yakushi image constructed for the recovery of Emperor Yōmei was completed in 607. The famous Yakushiji temple was begun in 680 as the result of a vow made by Emperor Temmu to obtain the cure of his consort, Empress Jitō. This temple houses the Yakushi triad, one of the earliest and most celebrated examples of T'ang sculpture in Japan.[10]

Throughout the seventh century various devotions were held in honour of Yakushi to revive dying Emperors or members of their family, to ensure longevity, to assist the dead and even to ward off such calamities as drought, famine and plague.[11] These practices easily mingled with native beliefs and won acceptance. The devotion to Yakushi also began to encompass the practice of various transformed ethical rites utilized for the same goals.

2. Keka, Ango, Hōjō-e and Sai-e

The *keka* (Rite of Repentance) in India was a ceremony related to the public confession of the transgression of Buddhist moral laws and was later observed as such by the Ritsu sect in Japan. But already in China this particular practice had been transformed by various Chinese sects into a ceremony held in honour of a popular Buddha or bodhisattva. Such a metamorphis had both desirable and undesirable features. The monastic chapter of faults, advantageous in preserving the spirit of monastic life and perhaps beneficial in promoting individual humility, could also lead to an attachment to trivialities and deviation from the spirit of self-reliance or personal responsibility set forth in Early Buddhism. With the proper attitude, penitential rites centered around a Buddha or bodhisattva, understood to be merely a mythical projection, could be more constructive unless they happened to degenerate into a form of deity worship. The latter tended to be the case in early Japan where the devotional rites of repentance were utilized, much in the manner of the Shintō purification rituals and harvest rites, as means to gain material benefit. *Keka* were held in honour of Yakushi to heal the sick, overcome calamities, purify the nation and grant longevity. In this respect Buddhist penitential rites transformed into an asset for the nation but in the process lost their significance for the individual.

The *ango* or retreat met a similar fate. Originally in the Indian Buddhist sangha rainy season retreats were held, during which rites of repentance as well as periods of instruction and study for the clergy were offered. This was the time during the year when the monks, unable to travel, would gather together to advance their learning and understanding of the Dharma. In Japan, priests and nuns were often invited to the palace or met in the great temples during the *ango* and held lectures on the various sutras. Members of the aristocracy attended in all their pomp and splendour and perhaps the instructions did benefit them, but the initial intention was once again a quest for mundane benefits. The modern summer *ango* held by the clergy of various sects is a vestige of this ancient custom.

The *hōjō-e* or 'gathering to liberate captive creatures' was an outgrowth of the Mahāyāna respect for all forms of life. In Japan this notion was extended to granting amnesties for prisoners on such occasions as thanksgiving for an Empress-consort's recovery and during periods of drought, flood and various other calamities. Official ceremonies would also be held to release captured animals and although the practice was often abused, since fishermen and hunters would deliberately capture creatures for the aristocracy to playfully release, it did increase the sensitivity of the Japanese against wanton killing for sport. Prior to the advent of Buddhism, the Japanese had been very fond of hunting, a favourite pastime of the aristocracy, but from this time onward it declined. Even the Shintō shrines, who had long discriminated against bloody offerings, found the Buddhist reverence for life readily acceptable. The concept further became related to the development of Japanese vegetarianism.

The *sai-e* or 'vegetarian repast' was derived from the Indian Buddhist days of abstinence for laymen. The practice was not initially vegetarian and the laymen simply followed the example of the monks, refraining from eating after noon. The meetings also observed the rule against the taking of life and as a result vegetarianism gradually evolved which became popular under Mahāyāna influence. In China the vegetarian repasts were first offered to gain personal merit and then came under the strong influence of Taoism, being later offered for theurgic purposes as well as on such special occasions as the birthday of the Emperor.

The *sai-e* in Japan were held in accompaniment with the *keka* and *ango* as special devotions to bring national prosperity. The practice greatly influenced Japanese culture and the habit of meat eating, which had been a common custom in pre-Buddhist Japan, did not regain influence until the late 19th century. An entire form of vegetarian cooking evolved as a result of these repasts that still enjoys popularity and modern Buddhists observe vegetarianism on days of memorial services.

Such devotions as the foregoing did little to advance the understanding of the common people during the Nara period, although they played an important role in the long process of molding public attitudes. The Ritsuryō government was not interested in the spiritual advancement of the masses, merely their control. In fact by the eighth century legal restrictions were even placed against the teaching of Buddhism to commoners on the grounds that it might tempt them to cause dissension. One of the first to fall victim to the restriction against preaching was En no Gyōja, the hermit of Mt. Katsuragi. In the year 699 he was exiled by Imperial decree to Izu on the charge of sorcery. As far as the government was concerned, Buddhism was beneficial only in the hands of the ruling class; disseminated among the populace, it could pose a threat. Firm control had to be exercised both over what was taught and the teachers themselves.

3. Buddhism and the Establishment of the Ritsuryō Government

After the death of Prince Shōtoku in 622, the Soga clan under the leadership of Emishi and his son Iruka, devoted themselves to the advancement of their personal ambitions, alienating other members of the court. In 643 they even put Prince Shōtoku's heir to death and gradually began to usurp prerogatives of the Emperor. This situation became increasingly unbearable for the other clans. Finally in the year 644, the Nakatomi clan conspired with Prince Naka no Ōe (the future Emperor Tenchi) and a dissatisfied branch of the Soga clan to stage a successful *coup d'etat.* The Soga leaders were killed and in 645, with the accession to the throne by Emperor Kōtoku, the Taika Reform movement was initiated. Under the guidance of Prince Naka no Ōe and the Nakatomi clan leader (subsequently known as Fujiwara Kamatari), the plan for a new centralized government was inaugurated modeled after the style of T'ang China. In theory, private landholdings were abolished, provincial governments and bureaucratic offices established and a system of equal land distribution and taxation put into practice. It was actually something of a fifty year plan since the Ritsuryō codes were not formulated until 701. Idealistically, this movement offered a solution to Japan's problems with the creation of a strong centralized government, but its inexperienced founders were not aware of the tenacity of the *uji* system. Aristocrats, temples and shrines were soon to gain tax-free privileges that eventually undermined the system and led to its downfall.

Buddhism was significantly affected by the new reform policy. Shortly after the death of Prince Shōtoku the need had become apparent for the regulation of monks and nuns. According to the *Nihonshoki* (Suiko, 42nd year, 4th month), a priest's hatchet murder of his grandfather became an important political issue. At that time the government census reported that the 46 temples in Japan housed 816 monks and 569 nuns.

Most of the clergy were under the personal control of the Soga clan. In fact in the year 614, one thousand had reportedly been ordained to effect the cure of Soga no Umako. Empress Suiko, in an attempt to handle the growing problem created a governing board of priests, while admonishing Umako to control their behaviour.[12]

Immediately after the 645 *coup d'etat*, an Imperial envoy was sent to the Asukadera to announce a new policy of government control of the clergy. Although the authenticity of the wording of this edict is disputable, it appears to have been an effort to remove Buddhism from Soga domination and display the power of the new government.[13] In line with this action, the Kudara daiji temple (later known as the Daian-ji), founded by priests returning from study in China, was made an official temple symbolizing the new direction of Buddhism under the Ritsuryō government. Just as a conscious policy existed to adopt the Chinese political system, the implementation of Chinese Buddhism now seemed more desirable than Soga domination. In emulation of the T'ang Chinese practice of appointing Ten Masters in charge of Buddhist education, the Ritsuryō government initiated a similar plan and four of the nominees were monks who had studied in China. This represented significant government recognition of their importance and future role in guiding the destiny of Nara Buddhism.

The Ritsuryō government further moved to make the Emperor the supreme leader of the Buddhist faith. This was one method of resolving the problem of how to reconcile the new religion with the Imperial role. Since Emperor Kōtoku personally believed in Buddhism, the plan was able to develop quite naturally. Buddhist festivals such as the *Urabon-e* (Festival of the Dead) and *Kambutsu-e* (Buddha's Birth Festival) came to hold importance equal to great state functions. During the period from the initiation of the Taika reform in 645 to the beginning of the Nara period in 710, the most noticeable advancement in Buddhism was in the increase of court rituals. The Taika reformers were content in placing the religion under Imperial control and the monks and nuns under supervision; they did not involve themselves further in Buddhist affairs. Developments during this era largely resulted from the personal devotion of individual emperors and their desire to obtain mundane benefits.

Emperor Temmu (673–686) was one of the most devout sovereigns, even becoming for a brief period a Buddhist priest. He increased Buddhist ceremonies and rituals held at the palace and sponsored the Daianji temple as a center for the propagation of Buddhism. He also decreed that sutras such as the *Konkōmyōkyō* (*Suvarṇaprabhāsa sūtra*) be recited for the nation. In 685, he set forth an edict that Buddhist shrines be built in 'every house' in the provinces (*Nihonshoki:* Temmu 14th year, 3rd month, 27th day). Although the exact meaning of 'every house' has been disputed by historians to date, it most likely referred to the homes of the aristocrats living in the provinces. This effort to promulgate Buddhism was clearly the antecedent of the *kokubunji* (National temple) system that was to come into being in 741 under Emperor Shōmu.

In conclusion, in examining Buddhism during this period we have to state that it was primarily concerned with exterior aspects rather than the inner life of man. Rituals and temple building were the order of the day; the aristocracy, with the exception of Prince Shōtoku, were not yet ready to apply the philosophy to the problems of human life for they were far too enchanted with the brilliance of the rapidly developing court life.

CHAPTER III

NARA BUDDHISM (710–794): THE FOUNDATION STONE

In the year 710, a dramatic change occurred in court life with the completion of the first permanent capital of Japan in the city of Heijōkyō (Nara). Prior to this, the court had usually been held at the individual palace of the Emperor and changed whenever a new Emperor succeeded to the throne. Probably this early system was influenced by the Shintō belief in the defilement of death as well as the lack of necessary technology to construct a permanent capital.

The Taika reform of 645 had visualized the need for a permanent capital but it took some time to be constructed. When the city of Nara was completed, it was a small-scale duplication of Ch'ang-an, the great capital of T'ang China, and served as a symbol of the entired Ritsuryō government borrowed from China. Another aspect of Nara, one that its founders never imagined, came to be the dominant influence upon government of the Six Sects of Nara Buddhism. And if the Nara period is thought of today, the image conveyed is predominantly of the development of Buddhist learning and culture coincident with the role of the Six Nara sects in politics and aristocratic society.

For the Japanese, the importation of these Six Sects brought together nearly all the major elements of over one thousand years of Buddhist development in India and China. At the same time it represented their first exposure to theology and systematized schools of philosophy. Naturally such a tremendous store of knowledge could not be immediately digested but rather had to be gradually sampled and savoured over the ensuing generations. But the Japanese were anxious and eager to learn, a trait that they have repeatedly displayed when facing superior foreign culture or technology. By the close of the Nara period, very little of the great knowledge locked within the Six Sects had managed to seep out among the general populace but Japan had developed scholars and leaders, the backbone of future Buddhist development. The constant flow of ideas from China during this period stimulated a rapid cultural progress that must have been nearly equivalent to Japan's leap into technology and industrialization in modern times.

With the sudden acquisition of the major ingredients of over one thousand years of Buddhist development, the Japanese had the opportunity to experiment, select and remold Buddhist philosophy to meet their needs. The golden age of Japanese Buddhism was not to come into being until the Kamakura period, when the assimilation, digestion and experimentation had been completed but the philosophy of Nara Buddhism formed the foundation of Kamakura thought. As we shall see, all the elements were already present at this early stage. By the close of the early Heian period the assimilation of new ideas came to a halt with the virtual collapse of the T'ang empire and growing Japanese self-confidence. The remainder of the era was devoted to philosophical digestion, experimentation and remolding, as well as empirical application. This makes the Nara period the most crucial time of assimilation in Japanese Buddhist history.

A. The Six Nara 'Sects', Scholastic Buddhism

For the first three-quarters of a century after its official introduction to Japan, Buddhism was non-sectarian in nature. The Sanron and Jōjitsu schools officially arrived in 625 and were followed by the Kusha, Hossō, Kegon and Ritsu. What became known as the Six Sects of Nara Buddhism are traditionally believed to have been established between 747–751.

One of the first problems encountered in the study of these schools of thought is a proper understanding of the term 'sect' (*shū* 宗) in Japanese. During the Nara period, *shū* refers to a group of scholars gathered together to study one tradition, but this does not necessarily mean that an individual or temple was restricted to a single tradition. Just as in Indian Buddhism, adherents of Mahāyāna and Hīnayāna schools could study together within the same monastery, so in Japan, a single temple could house more than one 'sect'. In fact an alternate Chinese character *shū* 衆 denoting 'community' or 'gathering' was frequently used during the early stages. For a long period, all Six Sects of Nara were housed simultaneously at the Tōdaiji temple. If there had been any drastic theological differences this would not have been possible, nor could ordination have remained the prerogative of the Ritsu sect for such a long time. Later, Japanese sectarian movements did evolve but the Japanese concept of 'sect' has never denoted the type of doctrinal differences associated with that term in other great religions; they function much closer to the medieval concept of a religious order.

Besides the so-called Six Sects of Nara, other schools did exist but there were usually variations such as the Shutara (*Sūtra*) sect based upon the study of the *Mahāprajñāpāramitā sūtras* (*Daihannyakyō*), the new Sanron derived from the teachings of Bhāvaviveka (490–570), the Shōron, which was an early form of Yogācāra that began prior to the introduction of the Hossō school and so on. These were ultimately either absorbed or disappeared as the Six Sects gained in popularity. The Six Sects themselves also carried elements of other schools of thought within their transmission such as the Tendai and Zen propagated among Ritsu scholars and the Pure Land devotions of certain Sanron priests.

If we examine the historical contribution of the Six Sects of Nara, we will find their major role was the introduction of the academic study of Buddhism to Japan. As centers of propagation among the masses they were not successful. In fact two of them, the Kusha and Jōjitsu, remained merely schools of thought never attracting individual adherents. The Sanron, Hossō, Kegon and Ritsu attracted members of the aristocracy but virtually made little effort to appeal to the Japanese masses. In fact, such an appeal would have been contrary to the policy of their major sponsor, the Ritsuryō government. Their purpose in the eyes of the government was still very much the same as what had been expected of Buddhism during the previous period, to conduct rites and services for the protection of the nation, the Imperial family and aristocracy and to promote culture and study. Although some individual priests such as Gyōgi of the Hossō sect personally believed that as Buddhists they were obliged to teach and help the masses, the majority yielded to government restrictions and were content to either cater to the aristocrats, become petty government officials or else avoid worldly involvement and devote themselves to study. In this manner, Nara Buddhism remained very foreign and alienated from the Japanese people; that is the reason why today when we think of the Nara period, the image of magnificent temples and art works come foremost to mind coupled with the notion of political corruption. The Nara sects tend to be dismissed as sterile scholastic movements, exerting little influence upon the course of history. Such an image is false but it exists because, outside of Buddhist institutions of higher learning, very little is known about the nature and philosophy of these sects nor their subsequent role in the development of Japanese Buddhism. Today the doctrines of these early schools still form an essential part of the curriculum of Japanese Buddhist universities; for to attempt to study Zen, Nichiren or Pure Land thought without comprehending the philosophical foundation provided by the doctrines of the Six Sects of Nara, is in effect a study of the branches of the tree that ignores its roots. The Kamakura Buddhist developments were a by-product of this historical groundwork. We thus will present the background, textual basis and major philosophical doctrines of each of the Six Nara Sects.

1. KUSHA SHŪ (Abhidharmakośa sect), *The Philosophy of Analysis*

This school is based upon the *Abhidharmakośa*, a treatise written in India during the fifth century A.D. by Vasubandhu and generally classified as belonging to the Sarvāstivāda school of Buddhism, since it represents the most complete systematization of that sect's doctrine. The Sarvāstivāda (lit. 'all exists') school came into being during approximately the middle of the third century B.C., when it separated from the Sthaviravāda tradition. It was mainly concentrated in northwestern India in the area of Gandhāra and Kaśmīra, although it spread throughout the country and eventually entered central and Southeast Asia and China.

The Sarvāstivādins are numbered among the 18–21 Abhidharma schools, a variety of scholastic Buddhism devoted to the analysis and elucidation of the Dharma, which were dominant in India from the fourth century B.C. to the rise of Mahāyāna. According to tradition, Vasubandhu, the author of the *Abhidharmakośa*, first belonged to the Sarvāstivāda school but later adopted the more progressive views of the Sautrāntika, a branch of the Sarvāstivāda that formed an independent school during approximately the third century A.D. and opposed what they considered to be the 'realistic' approach of the Sarvāstivādins. The *Abhidharmakośa*, written from the latter viewpoint, so clearly systematized Sarvāstivādin doctrine that adherents of that sect initially took it to be an important elucidation of their views rather than a criticism. This brilliant treatise came to play a significant role in the history of Sarvāstivādin literature and an extensive number of commentaries grew up around it; the best known refutation was composed by Saṃghabadhra during the fifth century.

Tradition maintains that the Vasubandhu who wrote this text was later converted to Mahāyāna and became a founder of the Vijñānavāda school. In modern times it is questioned whether these two Vasubandhus are indeed the same person.[1] In any event, the *Abhidharmakośa* provides an ideal forerunner for Vijñānavādin philosophy and undoubtedly this is one of the principal reasons why the Kusha school was brought to Japan in conjunction with the Hossō (Vijñānavāda), becoming a permanent appendage of that sect in 793.

a. *Historical Transmission*

The *Abhidharmakośa* was first translated into Chinese by Paramārtha (Chen-ti) between 563–67 and quickly became the main object of study for the already existing Abhidharma school. Not long thereafter a new sect, the *Kośa* (Chu-she) arose based solely upon this text which offered the most tangible detailed psychological approach to the analysis of the dharmas (factors of existence). Between 651–54, a new translation was made by Hsüan-tsang and his version became the official translation of the school. The *Kośa* sect was first introduced to Japan during the mid-seventh century by Japanese scholars who had studied directly under Hsüan-tsang's disciples. The exact order of Japanese transmission is unclear but the names most frequently associated with it are Dōshō (638–700), Jōe (644–714), Chitsū (dates unknown) and Chitatsu (dates unknown). Gembō (?–746) was credited with a later transmission.

b. View of Existence

The Sarvāstivāda school had the soteriological aim of proving the non-self (*anātman*) nature of all existents and setting forth a method to reduce and exterminate clinging and other psychological attitudes that served as obstructions on the pathway to Enlightenment. In the tradition of Early Buddhism it clearly associated the concept of non-self with impermanence (*anitya*). Since all phenomena (*dharma*) lack an independent, self-subsisting core or essence, they are considered to be subject to change. The basis of this concept was clearly elucidated by the historical Buddha in the first of the Four Noble Truths, which explained the existence of suffering (*duḥkha*), as attributed to the impermanent and empty nature of human existence. The relationship between non-self and impermanence also played an essential role in the doctrine of Interdependent Origination (*pratītya-samutpāda*), the beginningless and endless cycle of cause and effect.

The Sarvāstivādins sought to present the theories of non-self and impermanence in a tangible manner by analyzing the nature of human existence and the relationship between man and his container world. Their ultimate aim was to lead to the understanding of how Enlightenment could be achieved but in the process they developed an advanced form of psychological study. They are primarily known today for their systematic classification of the *dharma* (factors or elements) of existence. Their philosophy influenced the development of many other schools of Buddhist thought and the Mahāyāna movement initially crystallized as a reaction against what were believed to be the Sarvāstivādin 'realistic' extremes.

c. Five Categories and Seventy-five Dharmas

In keeping with many other schools of the Abhidharma tradition, the Sarvāstivādins divided phenomena into two major categories of conditioned (*saṃskṛta*) and unconditioned (*asaṃskṛta*) factors or elements. The conditioned factors consisted of four categories comprising a total of seventy-two dharmas of phenomenal existence brought into being by a combination of direct and indirect causes. The unconditioned factors consisted of a single category composed of three unchangeable dharmas; incomprehensible space as the container of the conditioned elements, and two means by which a conditioned element could attain extinction:

FIVE CATEGORIES and 75 DHARMAS

CONDITIONED DHARMAS (*saṃskṛta dharma*)
- I. Material (*rūpa*) .... 11 dharmas
- II. Mind (*citta*) .... 1 dharma
- III. Attendant Mental Faculties ...46 dharmas (*citta samprayukta saṃskāra*)
- IV. Disassociated Elements.........14 dharmas (*citta viprayukta saṃskāra*)

UNCONDITIONED, DHARMAS
- V. (*asaṃskṛta dharma*) .... 3 dharmas

The following presents a description of the contents of the five categories:[2]

I. Material (rūpa)

Embracing ten dharmas that can be destroyed, suffer change and are tangible (composed of the basic elements representing solidity, motion, warmth and fluidity).

SENSE ORGANS		SENSE OBJECTS
1) eye	....	6) form
2) ear	....	7) sound
3) nose	....	8) smell
4) tongue	....	9) taste
5) body	....	10) touch

These dharmas interact mutually interdependent in a subject-object relationship but are capable of being differentiated by the human mind.

The eleventh dharma in this category can be defined as composed of factors that are mutually exclusive, in that they cannot share the same locus.

11) Dharma without manifestation (*avijñapti*)

These dharmas produce some form of material change within the individual that can have both immediate and future effects. Examples most frequently presented are the immaterial changes occuring in a person after he has received ordination (good cause → good effect) or upon committing an evil action such as murder (evil cause → evil effect). In both cases a change immediately occurs at the time of commission. Ordination reflects an inner transformation, the sense of actualizing religious commitment and leads to future good actions, while a murder creates a moral induration within the conscience of the perpetrator that leads to further improper actions. This can also be discussed in terms of manifest (*vijñapti*) and unmanifested (*avijñapti*) karma. Manifested karma (actions) are clearly visible to others, but more morally significant are the unmanifested karma which can be divided into three categories: 1) karma produced as a result of discipline arising from the acceptance of the *śīla* and the practice of meditation (invisible good effects), 2) the results of habitual premeditated evil actions (invisible evil results) and 3) involuntary results depending upon the opportunity or time that may or may not bring forth a good or bad result (the invisible result of unintended actions that according to the time and place bring about either good or bad results in one's own life or the lives of others).

It is obvious with the inclusion of this last dharma under the category of matter that the Sarvāstivādins were not seeking to develop a metaphysical world view but rather to analyze the psychological states and ethical actions conducive to Enlightenment.

II. Mind (*citta*)

12) Master of the Mind

An allegorical manner of expressing the central organizing role of the six consciousnesses as leader of the mental functions (categories III and

IV). The six consciousnesses consist of visual, audial, olfactory, taste and tactile consciousnesses as well as the mind consciousness, which acts as a unifier.

III. Attendant Mental Faculties (citta samprayukta saṃskāra)

In order to analyze all the psychological functions of man, six mental sub-categories were devised consisting of forty-six dharmas.

A. Basic Functions (mahābhūmikā)

13) Sensation (*vedanā*) initial involuntary mental response to contact with the objective world.
14) Idea (*samjñā*) conceptualization of response.
15) Volition (*cetanā*) voluntary response.
16) Contact (*sparśa*) simultaneous coordination of organ, object and mind.
17) Desire (*chanda*) wish to act.
18) Intellect (*mati*) accumulation of information, discrimination.
19) Memory (*smṛti*) remembrance.
20) Attention (*manaskāra*) arouses consciousness.
21) Judgement (*adhimokṣa*) inclination or determination.
22) Concentration (*samādhi*) focusing of mind.

B. *Basic Good Functions (kuśala mahābhūmikā)*

These arise when a virtuous state of mind exists.

23) Faith (*śraddhā*)
24) Diligence (*apramāda*)
25) Flexibility of mind and body (*prasrabdhi*)
26) Equanimity (*upekṣā*)
27) Shame (*hrī*) self-reflection.
28) Modesty (*apatrāpya*) shame toward others.
29) Non-covetousness (*alobha*) selflessness.
30) Non-malevolence (*adveṣa*)
31) Non-violence (*ahiṃsā*)
32) Endeavour (*vīrya*)

C. Basic Defiled Functions (kleśa mahābhūmikā)

These arise from a tainted state of mind.

33) Ignorance (*moha*)
34) Negligence (*pramāda*)
35) Indolence (*kausīdya*)
36) Disbelief (*āśraddhya*)

37) Depression (*styāna*)
38) Restlessness (*auddhatya*)

D. Basic Evil Functions (akuśala mahābhūmikā)

Evil mental functions that are volitional.

39) Shamelessness (*āhrīkya*) lack of self-reflection.
40) Lack of modesty (*anapatrāpya*)

E. Lesser Functions of Defilement (upakleśa bhūmikā)

These functions can arise with a fragmental consciousness independent of the totality of the mind (Master of the mind). In other words, they can be indeliberate and uncontrolled and are capable of being eliminated by self-culture.

41) Anger (*krodha*)
42) Rationalization of conduct (*mrakṣa*)
43) Parsimony (*mātsarya*) clinging to one's possessions.
44) Jealousy (*īrṣyā*)
45) Worry (*pradāsa*)
46) To cause injury (*vihiṃsā*)
47) Enmity (*upanāha*) hatred.
48) Deceit (*māyā*) to create an illusion.
49) Fraudulence (*śāṭhya*)
50) Arrogance (*mada*) pride of possessions.

F. Irregular Functions (aniyata bhūmika)

These cannot be classified into the preceding five subdivisions.

51) Reflection (*vitarka*) conjecture
52) Careful investigation (*vicāra*)
53) Drowsiness (*middha*) absent-mindedness, torpor.
54) Regret (*kaukrtya*) repentance.
55) Longing (*rāga*)
56) Instinctive resistance (*pratigha*)
57) Varieties of pride (*māna*)
58) Doubt of the teachings (*vicikitsā*)

IV. Disassociated Elements (citta viprayukta saṃskāra)

The former fifty-eight dharmas of the first three categories function interdependently. The elements in this classification consist of non-material and non-psychological dharmas that were not classified in terms of the mind.

59) Acquisition (*prāpti*) concept of possession as a determined

attribute of a certain individual but not necessarily of all beings. For instance, a dog possesses a tail while a man does not but a man has the ability to read, write and speak. These refer to physical and psychological attributes.

60) Non-acquisition (*aprāpti*). Inability to possess certain physical and psychological attributes.

61) Communionship (*sabhāgatā*). Qualities shared by species of sentient beings.

62) Attainment of the fourth stage of *Rūpadhātu* (*āsaṃjñika*). State of meditation that causes all mental functions to cease.

63) Thoughtless trance (*asaṃjñi samāpatti*). State reached by non-Buddhists thinking they have attained Nirvana.

64) Annihilation trance (*nirodha samāpatti*). Hermit meditation that arrives at the state of the cessation of mental functions.

65) Life (*jīvita*) strength of vital power

66) Birth (*jāti*) 67) Subsistence (*sthiti*) 68) Decay (*jarā*) 69) Impermanence (*anityatā*)	Symbolic expression of the impermanence of all dharmas. These four dharmas complete their cycle every 'second' (*kṣaṇa*)
70) Character or letter (*vyañjana kāya*) 71) Name (*nāma kāya*) 72) Phrase (*pada kāya*)	Symbolize the function of human communication

UNCONDITIONED DHARMAS (*asaṃskṛta dharma*)

In contrast to the empirical existence of the foregoing dharmas which are conditioned by the laws of Interdependent Origination (*pratītya-samutpāda*), these dharmas are permanent and unchangeable.

73) Space (*ākāśa*). The limitless container for the material world.

74) Extinction through intellectual power (*pratisaṃkhyā nirodha*) The ability to destroy all defiled dharmas by the power of wisdom. In Sarvāstivāda, the defiled dharmas such as ignorance, sloth, shamelessness, etc. are destroyed one by one on the path to Enlightenment until the extinction (*nirvāṇa*) of all is attained.

75) Extinction due to lack of a productive cause (*apratisamkhyā nirodha*) This form of annihilation of dharmas is not based on spiritual wisdom but simple due to the fact that direct and indirect causes fail to exist.

d. *Theory of Causation*

In correspondence with the concept of seventy-five dharmas of existence divided into five categories, the Sarvāstivādins also believed in the existence of six direct and four indirect causes responsible for the rise of the conditioned dharmas. It must be noted that all Buddhist theories of causation deny the existence of any form of original entity or beginning, which contradicts the endless cycle of Interdependent Origination. The Sarvāstivādins postulated the following ten varieties of causation:

DIRECT CAUSES

1) Active cause (*kāraṇa hetu*). The principal factor in the production of an effect.
2) Co-existent cause (*sahabhū hetu*). More than two factors mutually cooperating to produce a cause.
3) Similar variety cause (*sabhāga hetu*). A cause assisting other causes of its kind to produce a continuity.
4) Attendant cause (*samprayukta hetu*). Related to mind and its objects. This cause has the same characteristic as #2 but relates to psychological aspects.
5) All prevalent cause (*sarvatraga hetu*). A cause among #3 that is always connected with the ignorant desires of man.
6) Ripening cause (*vipāka hetu*). A cause that has incompleted or neutral present results.

INDIRECT CAUSES

1) Direct indirect causes (*hetu pratyaya*). This consists of any one of the foregoing causes with the exception of the first.
2) Immediate indirect cause (*samanantara pratyaya*). The moment of union between mind and its function, which proceeds to produce further consequences.
3) Objective indirect cause (*ālambana pratyaya*). External world acts as the indirect cause conditioning the rising of the mind.
4) Dominating indirect cause (*adhipati pratyaya*). In Sarvāstivāda philosophy, this is defined as equivalent to the active direct cause for a single dharma.

e. *Eternal Existence of the Dharmas in the Three Worlds*

This theory represents one of the most unique and controversial aspects of Sarvāstivādin doctrine. In light of the fundamental Buddhist philosophy of Interdependent Origination, coupled with the theories of impermanence and non-self, the manner of the existence of the dharmas became a natural concern of many of the Abhidharma schools. The Sarvāstivādins strictly interpreting the nature of the existence of the dharmas as impermanent, maintained the theory of instantaneous being, but at the same time they also asserted the controversial notion of the reality of the dharmas in the three worlds of past, present and future. To their opponents, this appeared to be a contradiction of the orthodox teachings of impermanence and Interdependent Origination, as well as a denial of the traditional Buddhist emphasis upon the present. The Sthaviravādins, from whom the Sarvāstivādins had initially seceded, maintained that the only past phenomena that could be attributed with a form of 'existence' were those actions which had not yet produced results. This 'existence' however, could not be regarded in the same light as the existence of present phenomena. Because of the Sarvāstivādin deviation, many philosophers viewed their position as an effort to still cling to some form of permanent substance (*ātman*) and they were labeled 'eternalists' and even classified as 'unorthodox'.[3]

The Sarvāstivādins contended that the past and future were real, since the present has its causes in the past and its effects in the future.[4] They conceived of the elements (dharmas) as moving from the future to their momentary position in the present and as a result of the proper union of direct and indirect causes, then proceeding on into the past where they still exist. For example, according to this view, a rose that was in a vase on the table five minutes ago is not the same rose that is there now despite the fact that to the naked eye, its physical qualities have not changed. The Sarvāstivādins would contend that its dharma body or combination of elements has changed; in other words, its freshness has diminished and its petals undergone a subtle movement. Even after the rose has ceased to exist as a rose, the factors composing it continue to endure in altered and continuously changing form; the petals decay to create humus, the moisture enters into the atmosphere. Such a viewpoint has caused the Sarvāstivādins to receive the label of 'realist', although it can be debated whether such a term can be properly applied to any school of Buddhist thought without qualification.

Modern Japanese Kusha scholars do not see any contradiction between the Sarvāstivādin concept of the eternal existence of the dharmas and the orthodox Buddhist interpretation of impermanence.[5] They contend that the Sarvāstivādins main intention was to present an elucidation of the theory of impermanence. Thus, when the Sarvāstivādins speak of the existence of the dharmas in the three worlds (future, present and past) they are not looking at these time periods horizontally in a chronological manner but rather as the contents of this precise moment; exactly like capturing a single picture frame of a movie.

Normally, when we view a film, the eye perceives the picture frames in a chronological sequence whereby the actions of the past influence the present, which in turn move into the future. Such a unilateral past to future order is commonly set forth in conventional explanations of the Buddhist cause and effect theory, but it does not represent the entire situation. From the standpoint of the projectionist of the film, the chronological sequence is reversed, with the future running into the present and away into the past. In other words, the Sarvāstivādins locked potentiality as well as past effects into their eternally moving moment. From this point of view, the existence of the present egg is not merely the result of the chicken's former action but equally due to the chicken's inherent potentiality as a chicken to produce an egg. It is obvious that the cause conditions the effect, but without an effect, there could be no cause. This view was analogous to their investigation of chronological time.

In normal human comprehension, time is viewed as though it consists of independent static elements capable of being stopped, isolated and analyzed. Actually such a notion is an intellectual abstraction created by humans for the convenience of daily life and viewed by all schools of Buddhism as a figment of imagination. The true moment is eternal, boundless and ever-flowing. In light of their comprehension of such a transcendental moment, the Sarvāstivādins attempted to explain its briefness in relative terms by the analogy of the snap of the fingers. One quick adult snap of the fingers could be divided into 65 parts or 'seconds' (*kṣaṇa*) and just one of these 'seconds' comprise the fleeting but all-embracing moment.[6] Within each of these infinitesimal divisions occurs a constant cycle of arise (*utpāda*), stability (*sthiti*), decay (*jarā*) and destruction (*anityata*) just as illusive to the human eye as the inability to distinguish the slight changes that occur within three or four film frames.

In their view of the progression of time, the Sarvāstivādins clearly distinguished two forms of order: past → future and future → past. Whenever they spoke of the impermanence of the dharmas, they dis-discussed it in the conventional past → future sequence but when they spoke of the 'eternal existence of the dharmas in the three worlds' they always viewed the chronological process from the standpoint of the film projectionist, moving from the future to the present and into the past.[7] This means that ultimately, just as the projectionist, they visualized the existence of the whole film at the same time or the reality of past cause and future potentiality locked into the present moment.

f. Atom Theory

In order to further emphasize the imperceptible process of change, the Sarvāstivādins developed an atom theory. The problem had arisen in the analysis of the seventy-five dharmas, of how to explain the fact that the material existents of Category I (*rūpa*) could occupy space, if composed of the abstract qualities associated with form, sound, smell, taste and touch. The Sarvāstivādin atom theory represented a quantitative view of existence, as opposed to the qualitative approach of the seventy-five dharmas. It appears that the theory did not arise until quite late in Sarvāstivādin development and was probably derived from the Jains or Vaiśeṣika.[8] The Sarvāstivādins failed to successfully perfect it, their main difficulty arising from the attempt to analyze the psychological dharmas in the quantitative terms of atoms.

Eight atoms were postulated by the Japanese Kusha school, each composed successively of seven of its predecessors arranged in a circle of six gathered around a centre atom:

1) Finest atom (*paramāṇu*)
2) Form atom (*aṇu raja*)

3) Fine metal dust atom (*loha raja*)
4) Water dust atom (*ab raja*)
5) Rabbit hair dust atom (*śaśa raja*)
6) Sheep hair dust atom (*avi raja*)
7) Cow hair dust atom (*go raja*)
8) A single dust particle that can be caught in the light of the sun (*vātāyanacchidra*)[9]

The purpose of this theory was to demonstrate the infinitesmal factors that form the basis of existence. For instance #3, the metal dust atom and #4 the fine water dust atom, were believed to be small factors capable of moving in the invisible to the human eye spaces existing in metal and water. Such a theory was highly scientific considering the age of its development. The rabbit, sheep and cow hair dust atoms were conceived of as being the size of the tip of an individual hair of each of these species. The atoms were considered to be conditioned dharmas themselves, incapable of self subsistence, rising and disappearing within a fraction of a second. Although the human eye might not perceive a change, at every moment constant movement occurs.

The purpose of this analysis was to intellectually demonstrate the error in conceiving of the self or an existent as a solid permanent entity. Even the human body was hyperbolically described as having 84,000 hair pores, in each of which 900 million bacteria resided. In this respect, the Sarvāstivādin teachings could be interpreted as perfectly harmonizing with the doctrines of impermanence and non-self. Other Abhidharma schools, such as the Sautrāntika offered differing methods of explanation that they believed reflected the situation more accurately but the difference in basic concepts was not as great as might be imagined. Each school naturally had the tendency to interpret its opponents in the most unfavourable and extreme manner. The Sarvāstivādins might be accused, in conjunction with the other Abhidharma scholastic schools, of devoting too much effort to the means, but they did create a wealth of psychological knowledge and method of analysis that paved the way for future Buddhist developments.

2. *JŌJITSU SHŪ* (*Satyasiddi śāstra*), *The Investigation of 'Truth'*

This school is centered around the *Satyasiddhi śāstra* (Establishment of Truth) written by Harivarman during the third century. The author according to legendary biographies, once studied under a Sarvāstivādin master and dissatisfied with those teachings, sought to create a more perfect doctrine encompassing the best aspects of all the existing Abhidharma schools into one system. The work clearly represents a criticism of Sarvāstivādin thought but scholars have never been able to agree under what Indian sect to classify it, since materials relating to it are exiguous. To date, four theories regarding its affiliation are dominant: 1) the work is eclectic and therefore does not belong to any single school, 2) it is a product of the Dharmaguptaka school (this is the traditional Japanese view), 3) it belongs to the Sutra or Sautrāntika sect, and 4) it belongs to the Bahuśrutīya school.[10] There are no existing records to prove that the text was popular in India and the Sanskrit version is no longer extant.

a. Historical Transmission

The *Satyasiddhi śāstra* was translated into Chinese between 411–12 by Kumārajīva and managed to stir up considerable interest in China primarily due to its similarity to Mahāyāna thought; it was obvious that the author had studied Mahāyāna. A number of Chinese scholars classified it as Mahāyāna but this opinion never became dominant. Two of Kumārajīva's disciples, Seng-tao and Seng-sung became masters of the teaching and established different branches of the schoo. in China.

The first transmission of Satyasiddhi to Japan is usually believed to have been made by Ekan (Kor. Hyegwan), from Koguryŏ; it is believed that he transmitted Jōjitsu teachings in accompaniment with Sanron. Prince Shōtoku's tutor, Eji was also known to have been a Sanron and Jōjitsu scholar. Throughout Japanese history the Jōjitsu has been linked to the Sanron sect, with the exception of during the early part of the eighth century when Jōjitsu managed to maintain a degree of independence by having its own official shrines and images for veneration. By the year 806, in the official assignment of *nembundosha* (annual priests), the Jōjitsu quota was listed as incorporated within the Sanron; it appears that from that time onward they were considered to be an appendage of the Sanron school.

b. Quest for 'Truth'

The major objective of this sect is contained within its title Jōjitsu (Satyasiddhi), which literally means, "The Establishment of the Truth."[11] In this instance, Harivarman understood 'truth' to refer to the doctrine of the Four Noble Truths, which he termed 'the essence of the *Tripiṭaka*.' His goal in writing the *Satyasiddhi śāstra*, as he explained in the thirty-sixth chapter, was to clarify the meaning of the Four Noble Truths as a path to attain Enlightenment. The development of his understanding proved to be quite revolutionary for its day and imbued with the spirit of Mahāyāna.

Previously the Abhidharma sects, in particular the Sarvāstivāda, had devoted considerable time to the conceptual analysis of the doctrine of the Four Noble Truths, which they recognized as the major practice leading to Enlightenment. In the process of their detailed categorization, the dynamic quality of the doctrine tended to disappear and many critics in the budding Mahāyāna movement felt that they had lost the spirit of the Four Noble Truths by reducing them to mere classifications of terminology. Harivarman was one such critic of traditional Abhidharma methodology and he sought to unveil the spirit of the Four Noble Truths by emphasizing one single truth, *nirodha satya* (cessation) or Nirvana and its attainment. He thus initiated a new movement, placing emphasis upon philosophical interpretation as opposed to traditional categorization and this spirit was further developed in Mahāyāna with the evolution of the three, two and one truth theories, each attempting to capture the dynamic essence of the teachings. Harivarman's goal was the attainment of cessation (*nirodha*) and because of his emphasis upon what appears to be a negative end and the doctrine of emptiness, this school has often been termed 'nihilistic'. Such a classification is inaccurate since even though the Jōjitsu sought to transcend the conventional world, they displayed an obvious concern for its sociological aspects, as displayed in their analysis of the eighty-four temporary dharmas of existence. This school can be better understood as a logical step beyond Sarvāstivādin teaching, which had proven the non-existence of the self but failed, at least in the eyes of their opponents, to clearly demonstrate the non-existence of the dharmas.

c. Twofold Emptiness and the Middle Way of the Two Levels of Truth

In line with its emphasis upon *nirodha satya*, the *Satyasiddhi* school stressed the empty (*śūnya*) nature of both self (*pudgala nairātmya*) and the dharmas (*dharma nairātmya*). Although maintaining such a concept of twofold emptiness, they believed that they had achieved a middle way between the errors of eternalism or 'all-exists' and complete nihilism. Their position of the middle way was explained by the two levels of truth, a doctrine, which from the time of Nāgārjuna, played a prominent position in Mahāyāna Buddhism. At the level of conventional or 'covered' truth (*saṃvṛti satya*), they admitted the temporal existence of the individual composed of five psycho-physical factors (form, feeling, notion, activities and consciousness) as well as the eighty-four dharmas of existence. But ultimately, from the viewpoint of Absolute truth (*paramārtha satya*), these were considered to be empty containers possessing no permanent essence or substance.

Later critics were to maintain that the Jōjitsu did not actually attain their middle way goal since they failed to clearly correlate these two levels of truth in the manner of Mahāyāna Buddhism. They remained at a theoretical level of comprehension, still relying upon intellectual arguments, rather than fully entering into religious experience.

d. Eighty-four Dharmas of Existence

The eighty-four dharmas, which the Jōjitsu regarded as temporary existents at the conventional level, were divided into five categories corresponding to the Kusha and Hossō systems of classification. The difference between the Jōjitsu and Kusha (*Abhidharmakośa*) classification is as follows:

I. Material (14 *dharmas*)

Besides the ten elements composed of the five sense organs and their objects, the Jōjitsu added the great elements of earth, water, fire and wind.

These the Kusha had regarded as attributes of the sense-objects and thus were not listed independently.

II. Master of the Mind (1 *dharma*)

Identical to the Kusha.

III. Attendant Mental Faculties (49 *dharmas*)

All subdivisions of the dharmas are identical to the Kusha listing with the exception that under the category of 'Irregular Functions' the following three dharmas are added:

1) Dislike
2) Pleasure of sleep
3) Sleep

IV. Disassociated Elements (17 *dharmas*)

The following additions are made to the Kusha listing:

1) Old age
2) Death
3) Dharmas of the average man
4) Unmanifested dharma

Also, 'Communionship' (Kusha #61) was absorbed into 'life' (Kusha #65).

V. Unconditioned Elements (3 *dharmas*)

Identical to Kusha.

Besides seeking to extinguish these eighty-four dharmas in order to attain *nirodha satya*, the *Satyasiddhi śāstra* enumerated three false notions of reality that had to be discarded.

e. Elimination of the Three Improper States of Mind

These three hindrances to Enlightenment consisted of the following:

1) Attachment to temporary designations
   The naïve realist's view that temporary designations denote real existents. To eliminate this error, the individual must be led to realize the impermanent nature of phenomena, which are a product of causal combinations of elements and thus empty (*śūnya*)

2) Attachment to the dharmas
Even the elements, which form the basis of temporary designations must be recognized as impermanent and hence unreal or empty of substance.

3) Attachment to the idea of emptiness itself
Although comprehension of the unreal nature of both designations and dharmas has been attained, there remains an awareness of the concept of emptiness itself which must also be eliminated in order to attain *nirodha satya* or Nirvana.

f. Twenty-seven stages of Spiritual Awareness

An important feature of the *Satyasiddhi śāstra* was the presentation of twenty-seven systematized stages of spiritual advancement. These were in effect, a development of the four steps to Arahanthood in Early Buddhism consisting of: 1) Entering the stream (Pa. *sotāpatti-magga*), 2) Once-returner (*sakadāgāmi-magga*), 3) Non-returner (*anāgāmi-magga*) and 4) Arahant (*arahatta-magga*). In subsequent evolution, the stages of spiritual progress were expanded and defined in greater detail. Those who practiced the teachings and had transcended beyond the comprehension of the Four Noble Truths were termed 'holy' (*ārya*), while those who had abandoned evil but not yet attained an understanding of the Four Noble Truths were considered to be 'wise' (*bhadra*). There are considerable differences in the classifications of the various schools but in the *Satyasiddhi śāstra*, the first two stages fell into the realm of 'wise' and the remaining twenty-five dealt with the 'holy' path:

1) To hear the teaching, have faith in it and practice it as instructed. 2) Without ever having heard the teaching, to be observing it and religious practices. 3) With true wisdom to become aware of the Four Noble Truths and at the same time to observe their emptiness.	Moving in the direction of the holy path

4) One who has already embarked upon the holy path.
5) Once returned—(in the process),[12] will not be reborn in the Realm of Desire.[13]

6) Once returned (completed)
7) Non-returner (in the process). Those who do not return to the Realm of Desire.
8–18) Non-returner (completed) composed of eleven varieties:
   a) One who initiates his efforts towards Enlightenment between the Realm of Desire and Realm of Form.
   b) One who is born in the Realm of Form and without spending much time there seeks Enlightenment.
   c) One who has spent considerable time devoted to spiritual practices and then seeks Enlightenment.
   d) One who without any special practice, after a long period of life begins to seek Enlightenment.
   e) One who reaches the Realm of Form and proceeds into the fourth stage of meditation and then seeks Enlightenment.
   f) One who reaches the highest heaven of the Realm of Non-form and seeks Enlightenment.
   g) One who reaches neither the Realm of Form nor Realm of Non-form but simply as a result of multiple births in the Realm of Desire seeks Enlightenment
   h) One who at this moment of life seeks Enlightenment without experiencing rebirth.
   i) One who seeks Enlightenment by following religious practices based upon his belief and understanding of the teaching.
   j) One who seeks Enlightenment by means of his own ability to comprehend the truth.
   k) One in the state of non-return, who accomplishes *nirodha samāpatti*[14] and seeks Enlightenment.

According to the *Satyasiddhi śāstra*, the foregoing eighteen stages belong to individuals who still have something remaining to be accomplished in order to attain Nirvana. This is overcome in the final nine arahant steps:

19) One who has the nature of losing his past attainments.
20) One who has the nature to protect and not lose his attainments.
21) One who fears losing his attainments and would prefer death rather than doing so.

22) One who has the nature of remaining at his level of attainment.
23) One who has the nature of advancing further.
24) One who has the nature of never losing his degree of attainment.
25) One who becomes emancipated from the hindrances of human ignorance (caused by clinging to self) by his own wisdom.
26) One who is released from the hindrance of entering *nirodha samāpatti* (and clinging to the experience).
27) One who has the nature not to lose the attributes (virtues and merits) of his degree of attainment.

After achieving this final step, arahanthood is attained.

One unusual feature of these twenty-seven stages that Mahāyānists notice is the fact that only one form of ignorance is overcome (clinging to self). Mahāyāna Buddhism recognizes two forms of ignorance, which correspond to two of the attachments the Jōjitsu sought to eliminate: the clinging to self and the attachment to the dharmas. Here, in the important stages of religious awareness, the Jōjitsu only mention emancipation from the hindrance of human ignorance (clinging to self) but do not discuss the release from clinging to the dharmas. Such an inconsistency is a further reason why critics believe this school did not reach the complete level of Mahāyāna thought, for their theory was not clearly correlated with practice. Even though this school cannot properly be classified as Mahāyāna, it did by its emphasis upon *nirodha satya* and the middle way of the two levels of truth, create a new perspective in Abhidharma thought and the fact that the sect has historically been alternately classified as both Hīnayāna and Mahāyāna implies that it served as a stepping stone to Mahāyāna.

3. RITSU SHŪ (Vinaya School), Precepts of the Buddhist Sangha

The name of this sect is derived from the third division of the Buddhist *Tripiṭaka* devoted to the Vinaya or moral regulations. According to Ritsu belief, the observance of moral practices is the first step in conditioning the individual whereby he will later be able to comprehend the sutra and Abhidharma teachings. The Ritsu sect has been the only sect of Japanese Buddhism to devote itself solely to this particular section of the canon. If we classify the other Nara sects according to their scriptural emphasis, they would be listed accordingly:

Sūtra piṭaka	Hossō, Kegon
Abhidharma piṭaka	Sanron, Kusha, Jōjitsu
Vinaya piṭaka	Ritsu

Although the other sects differed in their emphasis, each transmitted their own form of vinaya practices; the Ritsu however, was the only sect that placed these rules before meditation, devotions or philosophy as the means of attaining Enlightenment.

a. Historical Transmission

At the time of the historical Buddha's Enlightenment, the vinaya or rules and regulations for conduct, had not yet come into being but according to the *Mahāprajñāramitā śāstra*, only a few hundred years later five hundred varieties existed. This figure was probably hyperbolic but it does demonstrate one of the basic reasons why Early Buddhism splintered into sects, the disagreement over the interpretation of the *śīla* (precepts).

According to legend, the historical Buddha created the first precept in dealing with a newly ordained monk who returned to his home and resumed sexual relations with his wife.[15] After this, subsequent regulations developed as problems arose within the Buddhist community and the existing vinaya rules clearly state the circumstances surrounding their formulation. The precepts of conduct and behaviour set forth during the lifetime of the historical Buddha were not sufficient to meet the needs of the growing Buddhist communities of later periods scattered among diverse geographical areas. To fit these new situations fresh precepts had to be devised that coincided with the spirit and teachings of the historical Buddha; the result of this movement led to differences of interpretation and the rise of new sects. By the time Buddhism was introduced to China, four different types of vinaya were transmitted:

Name	Text
Dharmagupṭa	Vinaya of Four Categories (Jap. *Shibunritsu*)
Sarvāstivāda	Vinaya of Ten Recitations (*Jūjuritsu*)
Mahīśāsaka	Vinaya of Five Categories (*Goburitsu*)
Mahāsaṃghika	Mahāsaṃghika Vinaya (*Makasōgiritsu*)

Among these, the *Vinaya of Four Categories* was the only text to maintain a lasting popularity and consequently became the basis of the Chinese Lu (Jap. Ritsu) sect founded by Tao-hsüan (596–667), a pupil of Hsüan-tsang. It did not have a large following in China. The vinaya text of this school was divided into four sections (Jap. *shibun*):

I—Introduction—*Śīla* for monks (20 vol.)

II—Collection of regulations pertaining to receiving the *śīla* and preaching (15 vol).

III—Regulations pertaining to retreat, repentance, clothing, medications etc. (14 vol.)

IV—Regulations pertaining to housing and miscellaneous items (11 vol.)

When Buddhism initially arrived in Japan a very free situation existed without any clear definition of how one 'became a Buddhist', nor was there any formal practice of the vinaya regulations. Approximately thirty-seven years later during the reign of Emperor Sūshun when Soga no Umako wanted to create a temple of nuns, he asked a Paekche monk how the women and a monk candidate could properly receive the *śīla*.[16] The monk informed him that to hold the ceremony properly in a civilized country such as China, the presence of ten vinaya masters was required, in a less civilized country the number could be reduced to five. There were not a sufficient number of masters in Japan at that time to meet even the minimum number and Umako had to send his three candidates to Paekche.

The teaching of the various sects as they arrived in Japan was primarily philosophical and not related as yet to the practical matters of religion such as the behaviour and discipline of the clergy, nor the difficult issue of ordination. It was a problem that Buddhism faced whenever it sought to become established in a new nation; some way had to be devised to properly transmit the teachings and establish the institution. Although each of the sects had their own form of vinaya, the Ritsu was far more expert since vinaya was their sole concern. If Buddhism was to prosper in Japan, it was essential that qualified individuals be ordained possessing an understanding of the responsibilities of their office. Emperor Shōmu (724–748 A.D.) was keenly aware of this problem and sent the priests Eiei of the Gangōji and Fushō of the Daianji to China to study the means by which the proper vinaya could be brought to Japan.

One of the first startling realizations that Eiei and Fushō had when they arrived in China was the fact that those who had not properly received the vinaya on the ordination platform were not considered to be priests. Concerned regarding the condition of their Japanese brethren, they asked the vinaya master Tao-hsüan (702–60), to immediately leave for Japan and begin instruction in the vinaya, he arrived in 736.

After Eiei and Fushō had completed ten years of study in China, they requested one of the most famous Chinese vinaya masters, Chien-chen (Jap. Ganjin) to formally transmit the vinaya sect to Japan. Upon receiving their request, Chien-chen inquired among his disciples for volunteers willing to go to the new country but found they were extremely reluctant due to the hazards of the journey. Chien-chen then decided to personally make the voyage and upon announcing his decision, found that many of his disciples now wished to accompany him.[17]

Since the Chinese government at that period did not allow monks to travel abroad, particularly to propagate Buddhism, the trip had to be disguised as a pilgrimage to Mt. T'ien T'ai. Eiei and Fushō made the plans and included a number of Japanese monks such as Gembō, planning to return to Japan. One disgruntled monk however, whose fitness had been challenged, informed the local officials that the monks were planning to ally with the sea pirates who had been besieging the area. A government raid was conducted upon the monastery and the boat and supplies confiscated, while a number of monks were imprisoned.

After several months in prison, Eiei and Fushō were released but further attempts to reach Japan also ended in failure due to shipwreck and the attack of the sea pirates; Eiei became ill and died. Finally, after five unsuccessful attempts, on the 26th day of the 12th month in 753, Chien-chen (Ganjin) successfully reached Japan in the party of the returning official emissary but by now he was partially blind. In the 2nd month of 754, he was officially welcomed at the Tōdaiji temple and two months later the first *kaidan* was constructed. At that time Emperor Shōmu, his consort and daughter, accompanied by 440 lay members, received the *śīla* and 80 monks of other sects received the priestly ordination.

Unfortunately by the time Ganjin arrived, the Ritsuryō government had already formulated some definite ideas of its own concerning ideal priestly behaviour, which were supported by certain senior monks serving as government officials. It was natural for Ganjin to presume that after all the difficulties he had experienced in reaching Japan at the express request of the government, that he should be solely in charge of matters concerning ordination. In the eyes of the government on the other hand, Ganjin may have been a great vinaya master, but he was not knowledgeable regarding either the language or situation in Japan. A Japanese system of ordination had already been devised by now and Ganjin's presence was viewed primarily as a formality to fulfill orthodox Buddhist requirements. If a candidate for ordination received government sanction, no need was visualized for the type of training Ganjin considered to be necessary; thus from the start the relationship between Ganjin and the government was strained. In 758 Ganjin resigned as an official of the *Sōgō* (Bureau of Priests) and placed his disciple Hosshin in charge of official ordinations. The *Zoku Nihongi* tactfully gave the reason for Ganjin's retirement to be that he found political affairs too confusing for his advanced age (he was 71).

The first official *kaidan* (platform of ordination) was constructed at the Tōdaiji temple, which was representative of all Six Sects of Nara. Ganjin was permitted to build his own *kaidan* and centre of Buddhist studies at the Tōshōdaiji in 759. Eventually the government established three official *kaidan* of the nation with headquarters at the Tōdaiji and branches at the Yakushiji in Shimotsuke and Kanzeonji in Chikuzen. These became the most influential *kaidan* of the period.

b. Kaidan (Śīla Platform)

In the Early Buddhist community, the frequency of ritual gatherings such as ordination within the monastic community gradually became a hindrance to private religious practice, this was primarily true in the extremely large monasteries where ordinations were frequent. From the beginning, ten monks were considered necessary to conduct an ordination ceremony except in backward areas where five were deemed sufficient. In keeping with the concept of *Sanghakamma* or transactions of the community, it was not possible to allow a group of this size to privately convene within the precincts of the monastery proper. Either the entire community (*samagga*) had to meet in unison or the representatives conducting the ritual (*kamma*) had to retire to a smaller bounded area (*sīmā*) outside the monastery confines and create their own small sangha to carry out the intended purpose.

Initially in India, the *sīmā* was set up with stake or rock markers in an isolated area outside the monastery confines but eventually, as the monks were frequently attacked or robbed, the ordination area was moved to a specific location within the monastery itself. According to the *Shibunritsu*, the *sīmā* was to have its boundaries delineated by stakes, rocks or a mound and be dedicated with proper ritual. It also had to be set off from the sangha confines proper by a buffer zone, the width of which could not be straddled by an individual. Tao-hsüan (596–667) in his commentary on the text, stated that there was to be no limit on the size of the enclave except that since the area was also to be used for the confession of transgressions, it should be capable of holding twenty people.[18]

In China and Japan, the actual place of ordination took on a special significance and a platform was constructed consisting of three steps. The specific method of construction was devised by Tao-hsüan, who maintained that this form of *sīmā* (Jap. *kaidan*) have three steps symbolizing the three emptinesses: of self, dharmas and both.

In China and subsequently in Japan, it was believed that an individual could not become a full-fledged monk until he had stepped on the *kaidan*. The Ritsu sect acted as the interdenominational guardian of this honour during the Nara period and when the Tendai later sought to build their own *kaidan*, their action was viewed not only as a threat to the Ritsu sect but as a challenge to the entire established form of Nara Buddhism.

c. *Granting of the Śīla*

In the case of official entrance to the sangha as a monk (*bhikṣu*) or nun (*bhikṣuṇī*), official permission had to be granted by the entire sangha and a proper ceremony held. Granting the *śīla* to the laity however, who in the strictest sense were not members of the sangha, could be done by any properly ordained monk or nun. This ceremony was actually an acceptance into the religion and consisted of agreeing to the daily observance of restrictions regarding the following:

Five Śīla

1—Killing
2—Stealing
3—Sexual indulgence
4—Lying
5—Drinking

On special occasions or days of observance when the laity visited the temple, they kept additional restrictions for the period of twenty-four hours:

Eight Śīla

1–5—Equivalent to above but with strict observance of sexual abstinence
6—Refraining from the use of perfumes for the hair or body
7—Refraining from professional entertainment
8—Refraining from sitting or sleeping on elaborately decorated beds
9—Refraining from eating after the hour of noon

These were called the 'Eight Śīla' although they seemingly consisted of nine precepts. The ninth article represented the goal of the former eight, which created the proper conditions for purity of body as symbolized by the fast after noon, a regular practice of the monks and nuns.

According to Ritsu belief, the strict observance of the *śīla* ideally led to purification and Enlightenment but it is obvious that this depended upon the level of individual religious awareness. The devout layman was usually not sufficiently advanced to be interested in a goal as intangible as Enlightenment and thus for his endeavours he was promised a good future rebirth. This has led to the question whether the Ritsu taught two separate goals and if only the advanced religious were believed to possess the potentiality for Enlightenment? Ritsu scholars argue that the goal depended strictly upon the individual and that laymen had as much chance to attain Enlightenment through their practice of the five or eight *śīla* as religious, fulfilling the entire code of precepts.[19]

The first stage in religious life was that of the novice or disciple, a stage for both males and females. They were granted ten *śīla* and the ceremony could only be conducted by a qualified monk or nun. The basic condition was that the monk belong to the sangha a minimum of ten years (twelve in the case of nuns) and be qualified to have disciples. The monk or nun who granted the ten *śīla* would become the novice master during that stage of religious life. Technically the granting of the *śīla* was done at the discretion of the individual monk but since the novices did dwell among the sangha, official permission was required as well. This permission was merely a recognition of the novice's presence in the community, since at that stage the candidate was considered too immature to be examined. The master-disciple relationship was continued until such a time as the master decided the individual was ready to become a full fledged member of the sangha. The *śīla* received by the novices were as follows:

Ten Śīla

1–9—Equivalent to the 'Eight śīla' (and their goal)
10—Not touching gold, silver or any other form of wealth

Male disciples went directly from the stage of novice to become a full-fledged monk but for the females there was an intermediary stage, usually at the age of eighteen, for two years duration known as the *Sikṣamāṇā* (Jap. *Shikishamana*). For this stage, the following special *śīla* were granted:

Six Śīla

Refraining from:

1—Killing
2—Stealing
3—Coming in contact with a man below arm level
4—Telling small lies
5—Drinking intoxicants
6—Eating at improper times (after noon)

The permission of the sangha was required before entering this stage and its main intention was apparently to determine whether pregnancy existed or not.[20]

When a master determined a male disciple ready for entrance to the sangha, or that a female disciple had successfully completed her intermediary stage, the official ordination ceremony could be held. This required the approval of the entire sangha; however, in the case of the monks, since it was so difficult to assemble everyone together at the same time, the actual approval was left up to the ten masters conducting the ceremony. Traditionally, these participants in the ordination were known as the 'three masters and seven witnesses.'

Prior to officially entering the sangha, a candidate had to select a master under which to begin his religious life. This was similar to the master-disciple relationship existing while a novice and in fact, could be a continuation of it. This master (Skt. *Upādhyāya*), was one of the three masters conducting the ordination ceremony and it was his duty to be certain the candidate was equipped with three robes and an alms bowl.

The ceremony of ordination began with the announcement of this master's name. The candidate would then show veneration to all ten monks present by touching his forehead to each monk's foot. The second ordination master (Skt. *Karma kāraka*) acted as an official master of ceremonies. It was his duty to clarify whether the candidate's choice for a spiritual master was willing to accept or not, as well as to instruct the candidate on use of his robes and alms bowl, etc.

The third ordination master (Skt. *Raho nuśāsaka*), who was either chosen or volunteered from among the ten monks, acted as an official examiner. The candidate was removed from the group and in an isolated place questioned whether or not he was qualified to enter the sangha. Supposedly the isolation was to avoid embarrassment. According to the *Shibunritsu,* ten official questions were asked at this time:

1—his name
2—the name of his intended master
3—if the candidate has attained the required age of twenty
4—if he has his three robes and alms bowl
5—if he has parental approval
6—if he has debts
7—if he possesses slaves
8—if he belongs to the military
9—whether he is a male or not
10—if he has various diseases

These questions were actually technicalities since supposedly prior to being accepted for this ceremony the candidate had already resolved the following essential questions relating to his acceptance to the sangha:

1—if he has every committed a *pārājika* crime (which means if he has ever been a monk and expelled)
2—if he has ever raped a nun
3—if he has ever previously pretended to be a monk
4—whether he is still wavering between Buddhism and a non-Buddhist faith
5—whether or not he has been castrated
6—if he has murdered his father
7—if he has murdered his mother
8—if he has ever murdered an arhat
9—if he has ever been destructive to the sangha
10—if he has ever caused the Buddha body to bleed

} Five Cardinal Sins of Buddhism (6–10)

11—if he is non-human
12—if he is an animal

13—whether he has more than one sexual organ (this and #5 were apparently tests for abnormalities)

After the official examination was completed, the master-examiner reported to the masters and witnesses and the candidate was then allowed to request ordination. He announced his master and it was reaffirmed that he had no hindrances in qualifying as a monk. Official approval of the three masters and seven witnesses was requested three times, in which they indicated their agreement by silence. After this the master of ceremonies instructed the candidate on the proper use of clothing (ideally to consist of rags unless donated), food (which was not allowed after noon), housing (ideally under a tree) and medicines (most commonly the ammoniac cow's urine). Next the new monk was instructed regarding the four major crimes that incurred expulsion from the sangha. The rest of the precepts he was later taught by his master.

In the case of nuns, the restrictions were somewhat stricter, not only requiring that the future spiritual mistress have twelve years of experience, but also that her fitness be approved for each ceremony. The questions of the examiner were the same except that in the *Shibunritsu*, the question regarding military service was omitted for women.

After her official ordination by the nuns community, the female candidate was required on the same day to be ordained by ten masters of the monk's sangha. Theoretically the nuns were autonomous, but this was one area where they came under the monk's jurisdiction. The ordination before the monks was merely a ritual and it appears that the examination was omitted. After this, the new nun was instructed regarding clothing (in her case five robes were required, presumably the extra ones were designed to cover her shape), food, housing (females were not allowed to live outside the monastery) and medicine as well as the eight crimes for women that incurred the penalty of expulsion.

d. Complete Regulations for Ordination (*Skt. upasampadā*)

Vinaya precepts were divided into two different categories: 1) passive, consisting of prohibitive regulations aimed at preventing improper actions and 2) active precepts designed to abet the practice of a holy life.

The latter mainly dealt with topics pertaining to the conduct of ceremonies, retreats, special types of allowable clothing, medicines, etc. The passive precepts were more applicable to the life of the individual religious and they consisted of 250 articles relating to monks and 348 for nuns. Even these precepts were not purely negative since they were believed to act as a moral force within the individual. From this standpoint, each regulation was considered to be composed of four aspects:

1) *Śīla* teaching	(i.e. admonition you should not kill)
2) *Śīla* essence	(i.e. interior result or moral force in the life of an individual taking a vow against killing)
3) *Śīla* practice	(i.e. daily practice of non-killing)
4) *Śīla* appearance	(i.e. exterior result of practicing non-killing upon one's environment and the lives of others)

Naturally, the second of these aspects was the most important from the standpoint of leading an individual to Enlightenment. The very act of accepting the precepts or making the vow to obey them was considered to create changes within the individual that would ultimately increase his wisdom and understanding. In this manner, the *śīla* were regarded far more philosophically than mere rules or regulations to be observed. The cause and effect balance was considered crucial as well as distinguishing between the theoretical formulation of a precept and its observance in daily life.

The regulations for monks and nuns were divided into eight major categories. The following is a brief summary of their nature:

I. Cardinal offences incuring expulsion (*Skt. pārājika*) monks 4, nuns 8

According to the *Shibunritsu*, the gravity of these misdeeds creates a situation: 1) analogous to having one's head removed (hence it is impossible to function towards Enlightenment), 2) where all good is eliminated, 3) where the individual can no longer share practices in common with his brethren (hence is expelled). These consisted of four major offences for the monks:

1) Sexual indulgence
This is listed first in Hīnayāna vinaya, where self attachment was considered to be the major impediment towards Enlightenment. The Mahāyāna vinaya, with its emphasis on altruistic behaviour, placed killing as the most serious crime.
2) Stealing
The result of attachment to external objects in contrast to the foregoing, which represents attachment to inner desires.
3) Killing
Refers to the taking of human life either by suicide or the inducement to make others kill. Supposedly this regulation came into being when a monk of Vaiśālī, after listening to the historical Buddha's sermon on the impurities of the body, fell into a nihilistic mood and requested a non-Buddhist to take his life.
4) Lying
The crime that can be accomplished without exterior objects and is vocal, in contrast to the foregoing physical crimes.

In considering whether or not a transgression fell into one of these categories, the object of the crime, conditions under which it occurred and possible exceptional circumstances were all taken under careful consideration.

Besides the foregoing misdeeds, the nuns had four further proscriptions to observe:

5) Not to touch with the mind of desire, a male of similar attitude below the arms or above the knees.
6) Not to allow a male filled with desire to hold one's hand or perform seven other actions.[21]
7) Not to knowingly conceal another nun's misdeeds
8) Not, despite three warnings from fellow nuns, to follow a monk expelled from the sangha.

II. Offences requiring temporary suspension and repentance (*Skt. saṃghāvaśeṣa*) monks 13, nuns 17

Those who committed these misdeeds were required to perform expiation. Monks who freely admitted their transgressions had to spend six full days of repentance before a minimum of twenty sangha members; the nuns, half a month. If the sins were concealed for a period, then the offender was to be isolated for a time equivalent to the concealment as well. These offences were considered to be analogous to having one's head crushed; if repentance did not follow, the religious state would be lost. For the monks these consisted of the following transgressions:

1) Intentional masturbation
2) Touching the opposite sex with desire
3) Indecent conversation with the opposite sex
4) Attempting to make a laywoman infatuated in order to obtain donations
5) Being an intermediary between the union of a human male and female
6) Building a living quarters exceeding size limitations for one's own benefit without consulting the sangha
7) With the aid of a donor to build a living quarters exceeding size limitations without sangha approval
8) Freely accusing another religious of a cardinal offence without basis
9) Out of hatred to stretch the truth in such a way as to malign one's enemy
10) To desire to destroy the sangha and despite three warnings to refuse to desist.
11) To conspire with one accused of the foregoing offence and fail to heed three warnings
12) To injure the faith of the laity and despite three warnings to refuse to cease
13) For a stubborn monk to refuse to accept the wise counsel of the sangha despite three warnings

The nun's misdeeds consisted of the following:

1–3) Same as monks
4) To initiate a secular lawsuit on her own at a government bureau
5) To knowingly grant Buddhist *śīla* to an accused female criminal

6) To treat a monk who has merely studied the teachings as a master
7) Being alone in four places: crossing a river, entering a village, lodging or walking behind a monk
8) Receiving donations from a man possessing the mind of desire
9) Encouraging a man with desire to donate food and clothing
10)–13) Same as monks
14) With a mind of desire to live near a monk and refuse to move despite three warnings
15) One who has committed the foregoing offence and been instructed regarding its nature but still refuses to heed the warning
16) To threaten to give up the Three Treasures in anger over a minor incident and despite three warnings, to refuse to yield
17) Trying to revive a resolved quarrel within the community and refusing to cease meddling despite repeated warnings

III. Questionable Offences (*Skt. aniyata*) monks 2, nuns 0

These two articles apply in the situation where a monk has been in a compromising situation without the presence of a third party and although guilt cannot be proven, a degree of suspicion is entertained. The conditions depend upon whether the situation occurred in 1) a secluded place or 2) in the open. Based upon the report of a reliable witness, the offence can be judged by the sangha to fall into the categories I, II or V.

IV Offences requiring forfeiture and repentance (*Skt. naiḥsargikā prāya cittika*) monks 30, nuns 30

Regulations pertaining to the misuse of property. These offences could only be eliminated if the religious repented and brought the article in question to the sangha.

Examples of precepts for the monks are as follows:

To receive an extra robe and neglect to obtain permission for it for more than ten days
To receive a robe from an unrelated nun
To unnecessarily receive robes from unrelated laity
To have pure black or pure white wool bedding

Twelve of the nun's rules differed from the monks. Examples of precepts specifically created for them are as follows:

To ask a patron to supply a needed item and later change her mind and wish for something else instead
For the nun's sangha to use money donated for building construction for robes or other purposes
To dispose of items she dislikes, keeping those she favours

V. Offences requiring simple repentance (*Skt. śuddha prāya cittika*) monks 90, nuns 178

These precepts do not refer to any specific type of property and the religious who breaks them can expiate by confession and repentance. Typical examples of regulations for the monks are as follows:

Using deceptive words
Being double-tongued
Destroying plants, the storehouse of living creatures
Eating at improper times (after noon)
Drinking (considered to be the cause of other misdeeds)
Beating another monk out of anger
Without being sick, to attempt to obtain favourite food and drink
Going out to view a military camp without reason
Spending time at a military camp to watch the parades, weapons, etc.
To knowingly travel with a thief

Sixty-nine of the nun's precepts were identical to the monks. The following are examples of special precepts:

Shaving body hair
Indulgence in music or dance
Various homosexually inclined acts
Entering a secluded place with a male
Repeating words of a master that she does not understand

VI. Light Offences requiring simple confession (*Skt. pratideśanīya*) monks 4, nuns 8

These required confession to another religious in order to be absolved. They are all related in some manner or another to food. The monks precepts were as follows:

1) Upon entering a village to receive food from an unrelated nun even though not ill
2) Upon encountering a nun, while dining with a lay family, who improperly orders the hostess how to serve, and fail to reprimand her
3) Taking advantage of the laity to receive food
4) To request a lay member to traverse a dangerous road without warning in order to bring food

The nun's precepts were not to request the following eight special foods as donations: sesame, oil, honey, sugar, milk, curds, fish or meat.

VII. Minor etiquette offences (*Skt. śaikṣadharma*) monks 100, nuns 100

These were lesser miscellaneous offences that were easily committed. If they were intentional, expiation could be effected by repentance to a senior religious; if unintentional, simple self-reflection was adequate. The nun's regulations were quite similar to the monk's with slight variations. The following are typical examples of the nature of these precepts:

To wear one's religious robes improperly
To giggle or show teeth upon entering a house of the laity
To rush to receive donations

VIII. Rules for the prevention of sangha quarrels (*Skt. adhikarana śamatha*) monks 7, nuns 7

Judicial rules to calm arguments such as requiring the accused to be brought before the sangha before formal accusation. Some of the vinaya collections did not recognize these seven precepts as being applicable to women since they considered females to be naturally of a more passive nature. In that case, they reduced the total of nun's precepts to 341.

The principle philosophy behind these regulations was the belief that the control of exterior behaviour conditioned the mind, making it receptive to Buddhist teachings and capable of spiritual advancement. The vinaya plays a crucial role in Buddhism representing the tangible application of Buddhist doctrines to create and maintain a society (sangha) dedicated to the pursuit of Enlightenment. Although the interpretation of individual regulations for monks and nuns naturally differed in accordance with the social environment of a given society, the transmission of the vinaya represented the actual establishment of the Buddhist sangha, for without proper standards for ordination, the clergy could not properly exist. This is why the transmission of the Ritsu sect to Japan was an essential step in the development of Japanese Buddhism. The rules later were modified to suit Japanese needs and eventually, during the Heian period, other sects gained the right to conduct their own ordinations in keeping with their vinaya regulations, but the precedent and basis had been established by the Ritsu sect.

4. *SANRON SHŪ* (*Mādhyamika*), *Philosophy of Ultimate Reality*

The Sanron school was one of the most influential of the Six Sects and its philosophy dominated the early Nara period. It represents a variety of Indian Mādhyamika thought based specifically upon three texts (lit. *san ron*):

1) *Treatise on the Middle* (*Chin. Chung-lun*) Contains the verses of the *Mūlamadhyamaka kārikā* and commentary by Piṅgala.
2) *Treatise of One Hundred Verses* (*Po-lun*) Attributed to Āryadeva[22]
3) *Treatise of Twelve Categories* (*Shih-erh-men-lun*) Attributed to Nāgārjuna

The principle philosophy of these texts was the refutation of views believed to impede the attainment of Enlightenment and the revelation of the true meaning of Buddhism by means of the middle way of the two levels of truth. They attempted to refute all views establishing either the existence or non-existence of the dharmas, maintaining that conceptual ideas such as 'this is truth', 'this is good' or even 'this is Buddha' were false insofar as Absolute truth (*paramārtha satya*) transcended both speech and thought. The particular views they sought to disprove can be classified into four successive categories of attachment:

1) *False views of the non-Buddhists believing in the existence of the self and dharmas*
   Under this category they attacked the concept of *ātman* as well as the extremes of the materialists.

2) *False views of Abhidharma*
Primarily a refutation of the Sarvāstivādin notion of the eternal existence of the dharmas in the three worlds.
3) *False Jōjitsu concept of the emptiness of self and dharmas*
A refutation of the Jōjitsu attachment to the emptiness of self and dharmas.
4) *False views of Mahāyāna believers clinging to non-existence*
In the light of the Hīnayāna clinging to the concept of the existence of the dharmas, and in some instances clinging to the concept of the non-existence of the dharmas, Mahāyānists attempted to refute both categorical views but fell into the pitfall themselves of becoming attached to their own denial of Hīnayāna.[23]

The method of refutation was by the principle of the *tetralemma*, or by classifying all views into one of the following four categories:

1) Existence (it is A)
2) Non-existence (it is $\sim$A)
3) Both (it is A and $\sim$A)
4) Neither (it is neither A nor $\sim$A)

Next they proceeded to dialectically disprove these theses by *reductio ad absurdum* arguments. Their contention was that truth transcended all four categories and involved the surrender of all forms of conceptualization. It is questionable if we can properly term this approach a 'dialectic' in the strict Aristotelian definition, for in the first place, it employs the reversal of the law of the excluded middle rather than the law of contradiction, and more important, its aim is strictly soteriological rather than eristic. The Mādhyamikas consistently maintained the view that truth transcended reason.

Beginning from the time of Kumārajīva in the fourth century, some Chinese San-lun (Jap. Sanron) scholars became dissatisfied with treatises primarily designed to refute false views and desired a more affirmative basis for their school. As a result they added the *Mahāprajñāpāramitā Śāstra* (Jap. *Daichidoron*), attributed to Nāgārjuna, to the three treatises giving it equal status. This tradition alternately waxed and waned up until the sixth century when Chi-tsang firmly established the three treatise school. The four treatise sect did briefly surface in Japan during the Nara period and was known as the Shiron shū.

a. Historical Transmission

There is considerable confusion regarding the transmission of the Sanron sect commencing with the selection of a first patriarch. Some texts begin with the historical Buddha, while others prefer to commence with Mañjuśrī, followed by Aśvaghoṣa and Nāgārjuna.[24] Although no particular reasons are cited for the selection of patriarchs prior to Nāgārjuna, a logical connection can be made with the Mahāyāna concepts set forth by Aśvaghoṣa in his first century *Awakening of Faith*.

Although Nāgārjuna is regarded as the historical founder of the Mādhyamika school in India, it would be a mistake to consider the Sanron form of Mādhyamika representative of the entire scope of his philosophy; it merely reflects one aspect. Every school of Mahāyāna Buddhism is indebted to Nāgārjuna in some manner and most consider him as a patriarch.

Āryadeva, the immediate disciple of Nāgārjuna, continued the Mādhyamika tradition and is regarded next in the line of transmission. Following him there is some uncertainty and two different lines were established; one leading to Mādhyamika development in China, and the second to the famous sixth century Indian Nālanda scholars such as Bhāvaviveka. According to the most popular view, the Chinese line was transmitted from Āryadeva to Rāhulabhadra, then on to the commentator Piṅgala, the central Asian Sūryasoma and then to Kumārajīva (350–409). In China, Kumārajīva's disciples such as Seng-chao (370–414), Tao-sheng, Tao-jung, Seng-jui, Seng-tao and T'an-ying carried on the teachings. Tao-sheng and Seng-tao transmitted the tradition to southern China, while Seng-chao and Tao-jung worked in the north.

One of the most famous successors was the Korean Seng-lang (died ca. 615), who clarified the three treatise position. This line was carried on by his immediate disciple Seng-ch'üan, who became the master of the illustrious Fa-lang (507–581). The latter was so popular that he attracted a thousand students with twenty-five immediate disciples but his most famous follower was Chi-tsang (549–623), who is generally considered to be the founder of the Chinese San-lun school, since he systematized the sect's doctrine. After Chi-tsang's death, this version of San-lun eventually came to an end in China.

At about the same time, a new form of Mādhyamika thought was introduced by the Chinese pilgrim Hsüan-tsang and by Hsien-shou (643–712), a student of the Indian Divākara (who came to China in 676). The new trend reflected the parallel Nālanda developments of Mādhyamika scholars such a Bhāvaviveka (490–570) and the seventh century Jñānaprabha and Siṃha-raśmi. Both types of Mādhyamika were ultimately transmitted to Japan.

Although it is generally believed that Prince Shōtoku's Buddhist master Eji, was a Sanron scholar, the first official transmission of the sect is attributed to Ekan, a Korean pupil of Chi-tsang, who arrived in Japan in 625 and taught at the Gangōji. The second transmission is somewhat unclear. Some sources attribute it to the rather obscure Fukuryō (dates unknown), a naturalized Chinese disciple of Ekan, who was believed to have studied in T'ang China.[25] Fukuryō resided at the Daianji and appears to have had an illustrious career, becoming one of the Ten Masters of education. Most contemporary scholars bypass Fukuryō and credit the second transmission to his son[26] and disciple, Chizō, who established the sect at the Hōryūji. The third transmission is attributed to Chizō's disciple, Dōji, who went to China in 701 and studied there for nearly eighteen years. Upon his return he founded the Daianji school of Sanron. In this manner, during the Nara period the teachings of Sanron divided into various sub-sects dependent upon transmission, at the Gangōji, Daianji, Saidaiji, Hōryūji and ultimately at the Tōdaiji temple.

The so-called new Sanron, representing the sixth and seventh century Indian tradition, as opposed to that of Chi-tsang, also arrived in Japan. The Daianji records of 747 mention the existence of a Betsu Sanron in addition to the Sanron practiced at the Daianji and Hōryūji temples. This Betsu Sanron must have represented the new Sanron school. The Gangōji, which had the oldest Sanron tradition, apparently did not allow the new form to enter, while the Tōdaiji, the last temple to receive the sect, did not differentiate the existence of a Betsu Sanron, but enshrined a portrait of Bhāvaviveka; it can thus be theorized that the new Sanron dominated this temple.[27] By the Heian period, the Gangōji, Daianji, Saidaiji, and Hōryūji forms of Sanron had disappeared. The last to vanish was the Tōnan-in group of Sanron housed at the Tōdaiji that finally ended with the death of the priest Echin in 1169. After that the Sanron school, which had philosophically dominated the early Nara period, continued to exist merely in the form of academic study. We will now examine the main characteristics of Sanron doctrine.

b. *Nirvana as the 'Absolute'*

The problem of establishing a position regarding the existence and nature of an Absolute was present in Buddhism from the days of Śākyamuni. With a primary concern for the existential plight of man and the solution for human suffering, the historical Buddha rejected speculation concerning a transcendental Absolute as a total waste of time. It was more important for man to solve the urgent problems of the present rather than conjecture about the nature of the unknowable. The Buddha flatly rejected all concepts of an Absolute *entity* be it in the form of a creator god or all-inclusive Cosmic being. The only acceptable form of an Absolute, if indeed it can properly be called that, was Nirvana, the unconditioned cessation of becoming (*pratītya-samutpāda*), that transcended the notions of either being or non-being.

In Early Buddhism it was obvious that knowledge of the 'Absolute' Nirvana was impossible, since knowledge relates to particulars and thus is relative in nature. Nirvana entailed an intuitive experience that could only be expressed in relative terms in the form of a negation of what it was not. In their attempt to explain Nirvana, the Early Buddhists negated the existing world (as experienced by ignorant man) and this approach led, even during the lifetime of the historical Buddha, to charges of nihilism or 'escapism', although the utmost affirmation was present in the seemingly negative approach.

After the death of the historical Buddha, in an effort to demonstrate the impermanency of the self, the Sarvāstivādins set forth their thesis of the eternal existence of the dharmas in the three worlds. To their critics, it appeared that they had fallen into the error of regarding the dharmas as substantial realities. In contrast, schools such as the Satyasiddhi sought to counterbalance such an extreme by stressing the nominal reality of the dharmas even in the present, but their attempts appeared to be advocating a nihilistic theory of non-being. The Mādhyamika viewed both approaches as extremes and in an effort to establish a truly balanced middle way, set forth their own concept of Śūnyatā or 'Absolute' Emptiness. This represented in effect, a renewal of the Early Buddhist effort to explain Nirvana in terms of what it was not, but this explanation clearly emphasized Nirvana (=*Śūnyatā*) as an attitude of mind rather than a locus.

c. *Philosophy of Śūnya (Emptiness)*

Śūnya (Pa. *sunna*), was initially used to denote 'emptiness' or 'devoid of reality' in the sense that it denied the existence of any form of Absolute being (or substance), unchangeable and eternal. Every existent was viewed as a product of Interdependent Origination, subject to change and impermanence, hence in the Buddhist definition unreal. Nāgārjuna in particular emphasized *śūnya* as a synonym for Interdependent Origination (*pratītya-samutpāda*)

From the earliest stages, Nirvana was described as *śūnya* in that it was devoid of predicates; even those of existence, unity and self-sufficiency or their antonyms. In this respect it is somewhat dangerous to consider Nirvana as an Absolute, since the general connotation of that term implies an essence or ontological being. Nirvana is purely a subjective experience, being both ontologically and epistemologically empty (*śūnya*). It represents neither a locus nor a transcendental stage but merely the attitude wherein false discriminations and illusions of conceptualization are dropped. This is identical to the experience of *Śūnyatā* (Emptiness) or as Nāgārjuna describes it:

> There is *mokṣa* (release or liberation) from the destruction of karmaic defilements which are but conceptualizations. These arise from mere conceptual play (*prapañca*) which are in turn banished in *śūnyatā*. MK XVIII, 5[28]

Once again the equation of Nirvana and *Śūnyatā* represents an effort to describe the undescribable by negating the qualities it does not possess. Such an endeavour to avoid limiting the 'Absolute', and thus transform it into a relative absolute, was the basis of the Mādhyamika refutation of all views, concepts and ideas. Their denial went so far as to reject even the denial itself *ad infinitum*, maintaining at the same time that nothing existed beyond this process. In effect, the supreme or 'Absolute' truth (*paramārtha satya*) represented the constant negation of the limitations imposed by human reasoning.

d. Two Levels of Truth and the Four Stages of Explanation

The concept of two levels of truth (Absolute and Conventional) is of vital importance in Mādhyamika and all further Mahāyāna schools of thought. As Nāgārjuna stated "those who do not know the distinction between the two truths cannot understand the profound nature of the Buddha's teaching."[29]

Paramārtha satya, the level of truth that entails the complete cessation of the function of reasoning, was regarded as the supreme experience, wherein reality and its intuitive comprehension become identical. This does not mean however, that the Absolute truth is totally distinct from conventional knowledge or truth (*saṃvṛti satya*) as affirmed by common sense. As Nāgārjuna emphatically stated:

> Without relying on events of common practice (i.e. relative truths), the absolute truth cannot be expressed. Without approaching the truth, nirvana cannot be attained.
>
> MK XXIV, 10[30]

Conventional truths are merely the manner by which the real appears to its percipients viewed through their false thought projections and empirical determinations. Literally, it is a covered (*saṃvṛti*) truth, clouded by the categorizing and conceptualizing functions of the human mind. The two levels of truth merely represent two different mental views of the same reality.

The Absolute truth, or view of reality without distortion, consists of a single uniform and undifferentiated experience. In contrast, conventional truths are composed of multitudes of differing degrees of reality, dependent upon the mental attitude of the viewer. Even all Buddhist teachings ultimately fall into the level of conventional truth since they are in effect, merely means of attaining the non-rational, unteachable, unknowable. But these varying degrees of conventional truths are the basis for the realization of Absolute truth. This is why the concept of *upāya* (adapted teachings), by which any appropriate means could be utilized to lead an individual to Enlightenment became a cornerstone even during Early Buddhism.

Just as the historical Buddha utilized the Indian deities and promise of rebirth in *deva* heavens as an inducement for non-Buddhists and laity to practice virtue, so Nāgārjuna utilized his dialectic to tax human reasoning to its limits, facing its shipwreck and ultimate abandonment. This was merely a more sophisticated *upāya*. The aim of the dialectic was not to prove anything by logic except the absurdity of believing logic to be capable of revealing ultimate reality. The constant denial at once removed and embraced all extremes by establishing a middle, which in turn had to be discarded as soon as it too became a determining agent. This process of continual negation is known as the four stages explaining the two levels of truth and consists of the following:

1) For non-Buddhists who maintain the belief in being as opposed to non-being, their view is to be regarded as a conventional truth as opposed to 'Absolute' truth.
2) When the former theory of being and non-being are opposed by the concepts of neither being nor non-being, the former are regarded as conventional truth and the latter as 'Absolute' truth.
3) When the four opposed theories above are set forth in contrast to further denials, those theories become conventional truths and the denials can be regarded as 'Absolute' truth.
4) When the denials set forth above become conventional truth, their further denial will represent 'Absolute' truth.

Thus the *upāya* of denial progressed *ad infinitum*. As soon as a theory is grasped as an 'Absolute' truth, it has in effect become relative and once again must be denied in the on going effort to seek the limitless undefinable 'Absolute'. This represented the middle way or constant progress towards an 'Absolute' Absolute.

In this ongoing search however, the 'Absolute' was never regarded as totally transcendent from the present world. It momentarily transcends the graspable or knowable, but still is present although unseen. Man resides in the midst of the 'Absolute', yet is unable to comprehend it because of the false illusions created by his own limiting mind. This is why the Mādhyamikas constantly stressed that '*nirvāṇa* is *saṃsāra* and *saṃsāra* is *nirvāṇa*.' In the same manner when they spoke of the method to attain Enlightenment, they had to admit that from the aspect of 'Absolute' truth, such a thing did not exist. All existents in their natural as-it-is state are actually Enlightened even though they may be unaware of the fact. In essence all are Buddhas, be they mentally residing in hell or Enlightenment, the only difference is found within the illusions of their own mind. Just as the drugged man can sit in the comfort of his own living room and imagine he is burning in searing flames or floating upon a euphoric cloud, so the unenlightened and Enlightened share the same locus. The difference is subjective not ontological; thus at this level the question of how to attain Enlightenment is futile.

Still, at a conventional level the difference between the mental states of Enlightenment and ignorance has to be recognized. Here it can be seen that the essence of Enlightenment is merely the shattering of the delusions of ignorance. Depending upon the capacity of the individual, this breakthrough may be accomplished early or after a long trying period, but when it does occur, it is instantaneous. The ignorant dream suddenly crumbles into bits and the individual realizes that the world of Enlightenment is indeed the same phenomenal world in which he has always lived, but never actually seen.

e. Theory of the Eightfold Negation

The Sanron school regarded the theory of the two levels of truth as a proverbial finger pointing to the moon. It offered a means of shocking the mind into a realization of its own delusion. By constant denial the pretensions of speculative reasoning were exposed, forcing a mental ship-wreck; the analytical antecedent of the Zen *kōan*. The eightfold negation acted as a similar *upāya*. In the Sanron version, as initially formulated in Chinese, the negation appears as follows:

No birth, no extinction
No annihilation, no permanence
No identity, no diversity
No coming, no departure

In effect, these eight negations totally deny all the qualities of becoming. Each denial attacks the belief in any form of self-subsistent entity that can come into existence, endure, be compared to others or disappear. But at the same time an affirmation is also implied. The proposition that there is neither birth nor extinction can indicate the complete affirmation of the present moment, cutting loose the hindering ties of viewing life as a series of chronological beginnings and ends. Even logically, the inversion of the law of the excluded middle has a positive aspect. The proposition that there is no identity and no diversity can imply that the world is both one and many at the same time, or that the one is equivalent to the many, incapable of existing independently.

Many different interpretations can be made of this eightfold negation, which Nāgārjuna regarded as the core of his teaching, but the most significant are those relating to the problems of human life and religious practice. The following represents a popular interpretation:[31]

1) No birth, no extinction
The denial of the birth of the ignorant man as an entity into the Three Worlds of existence. In other words, the negation of the notion that the Three Worlds of suffering are separate from Nirvana.
2) No annihilation, no permanence
The rejection of the belief that after death there is either annihilation or a further existence (such as a heaven).
3) No identity, no diversity
The rejection of the notion of the universe as either composed of one original body (such as a Cosmic consciousness) or of many elements (atoms as permanent entities).

4) No coming, no departure
Denying the concept of Nirvana as a departure from this world or the idea that a Buddha might 'come' to this land from Nirvana.

These eight denials were viewed as the only means of characterizing reality, since nothing positive could be said. The four stages of the two levels of truth represented a vertical attempt to approach reality, this approach was horizontal. The ultimate aim of both was to point out the all-inclusive middle path leading to the "Absolute'.

f. Four Methods of Interpreting the Dharmas

The Abhidharma schools had classified the elements of existence into categories of varying numbers. In contrast, the Sanron offered a very simple classification that attempted to penetrate each existent from a multitude of angles in order to present an overall view, not merely of the existent but also of its interdependent relationships with its container world. The following is their system of classification:

1) *Interpretation by name only*
Accepting the designating label assigned by conventional language such as 'flower', 'petal', 'colour'.
2) *Interpretation based upon direct and indirect causes*
Explaining the essence of an existent by the other existents responsible for its present state. i.e., the flower is viewed in relation to the tree or bush upon which it grows, soil, sunshine, rain, etc.
3) *Interpretation by viewing the ultimate spirit of the middle way in each and every dharma*
Since the preceding method of merely isolating the dependent relationships of the flower does not reveal its true essence, by this method the flower is viewed as embodying the totality of existence. Clearly this is an antecedent of the Kegon and Zen notions that the universe can be embodied in a single rock, which is not merely a participant but complete in itself to the subjective mind viewing it. Such a realization is considered equivalent to Enlightenment.

4) *Using all other dharmas without restriction or limitation to interpret a single dharma*
The previous three interpretations were considered to reveal the middle way of existence, enabling the truth to be perceived in each and every dharma. But beyond this lies the ability to perceive not only 'Absolute' truth or the totality of existence within each existent, but to see as well, the particular attributes of other existents. In other words, cognizing truth in the flower represents the intuition of Enlightenment but beyond this is the further ability to once again return to the discriminative multitude of dharmas or the conventional world and perceive in the flower the brilliance of the heavens, warmth of the sun, rich smell of the earth.

The affirmative nature of this approach is extremely significant. The Sanron, in keeping with the Mādhyamika viewpoint, are not willing to cease with the experience of Enlightenment, but insist that the application of Enlightenment be made to the conventional world; this was an essential feature of Nāgārjuna's philosophy that often is overlooked due to the attraction of his dialectical arguments.[32] The emphasis upon the practical application of Enlightenment became an essential feature of Mahāyāna Buddhism, symbolically expressed by the bodhisattva.

g. Classification of Sutras

It has been traditional in the various schools of Buddhism, to establish a classification of sutras ranked according to their superiority in explaining the doctrine of that particular sect. For the Sanron, who believed all sutras were merely adapted teachings (*upāya*), receiving their value in accordance with the ability of the reader, such a classification had little merit. They did however, divide the scriptures into two major *Piṭakas*, reflecting the attitude expressed with in them. These consisted of Śrāvaka (representing Hīnayāna works) and bodhisattva (Mahāyāna) teachings. Chi-tsang, who was a scholar of the *Lotus Sutra*, further divided the sutras into three *Dharma cakra* (wheel of Dharma):

1) The root (fundamental *Dharma-cakra*)
Consisting of sutras preached for the bodhisattva alone shortly

after the Enlightenment of the Buddha. i.e. the *Avataṃsaka sūtra.*

2) The branches
Consisting of all Hīnayāna and Mahāyāna texts ranging between the *Avatataṃsaka* and *Lotus* sutras. These were designed for those with inferior ability.

3) The trunk
Teachings which lead all branches back in a single ultimate vehicle to the root. i.e. the *Lotus sutra.* This teaching was set forth for those who had already been conditioned by the teachings of the branches.

This classification was an effort to demonstrate that the various teachings of Buddhism do not lead to different goals, but ultimately all are embraced within the one vehicle of the historical Buddha's teaching, in essence the realization of inner Enlightenment. This was first taught in the form of the *Avataṃsaka,* but since these teachings were not understood, the varieties of branches were created. The classification reflects the spirit of the *Lotus Sutra.*

The Sanron sect played an extremely important role in the history of Japanese Buddhism since it crystallized the essence of Nāgārjuna's philosophy. This thought, in conjunction with Yogācāra, had formed the basis of Mahāyāna Buddhism and it was natural that it play a significant role in Japan and become, in conjunction with the Hossō school, a major foundation in the development of Japanese Buddhism. The Sanron presentation of the constant denial of conceptualized reality also served as a reminder to succeeding Buddhist sects not to fall into the error of becoming unduly attached to their own doctrine and thereby losing the spirit of Buddhism.

5. *HOSSŌ SHŪ* (*Vijñānavāda, Yogācāra*), *The Role of Consciousness*

The object of this sect, as its Japanese title, Hossō (lit. dharma characteristics)[33] implies, was to investigate and clarify the essential nature and phenomenal manifestation of all existents. Academically, the philosophy of this school is most popularly known as Yuishiki (Skt. Vijñaptimātratā), which emphasizes its view of consciousness (*vijñāna*), as the basis of the appearance of the phenomenal world.

The Vijñānavāda sect was initially founded in India during approximately the fourth century A.D., by the quasi-historical Maitreya and the brothers Asaṅga and Vasubandhu. Traditionally it is believed that this Vasubandhu was the same as the author of the *Abhidharmakośa*, basis of the Japanese Kusha school.[34] Kusha doctrines do have considerable similarity to Hossō, in particular the analysis of the dharmas comprising existence; no doubt this was why the Kusha subsequently became an appendage of the Hossō sect.

Other Indian patriarchs of the Vijñānavāda school are considered to be Dharmapāla (born mid-6th-century) and Śīlabhadra (529–645). The famous Chinese pilgrim Hsüan-tsang studied under Śīlabhadra at Nālanda university and brought the teachings to China, becoming the first patriarch there of what became known as the Fa-hsiang school.[35] Subsequent Chinese patriarchs were K'uei-chi (632–82), the chief disciple of Hsüan-tsang, who systematized the doctrine of the sect and is considered to be the Chinese founder. He was succeeded by his disciple Hui-chao (649–714) and Chih-chou (dates unknown).

The sect was transmitted to Japan on four different occasions: first by Dōshō, who studied under Hsüan-tsang, secondly by Chitsū and Chitatsu, who also studied under Hsüan-tsang and his pupil K'uei-chi, thirdly by a Korean priest, known in Japan as Chihō, a disciple of Chih-chou, and lastly by Gembō, who also studied under Chih-chou.

a. *Principal Texts and Critical Classification*

The most important text in this school is the *Jōyuishikiron* (*Vijñapti-mātratā-siddhi*), which is composed of ten commentaries made upon Vasubandhu's *Triṃśikā kārikā* or *Triṃśikā* (Thirty verses). Within these commentaries quotations are made from six sutras and eleven commentaries, and these are frequently considered to form the basis of the sect's doctrine. The six sutras consist of the following:

1) *Daihōkō butsu kegongyō* (Buddhāvataṃsaka nāma mahāvaipulya sūtra)
2) *Gejin mikkyō* (Saṃdhinirmocana sūtra)
3) *Daijō nyūryōgakyō* (Laṅkāvatāra sūtra)

4) *Daijō mitsugonkyō* (Ghana-vyūha sūtra)
5) *Nyorai shutsugen kudokushōgonkyō* (non-extant)
6) *Abidatsumakyō* (non-extant)

Among these, the *Gejin mikkyō* is most closely identified with Hossō doctrine. A number of Abhidharma treatises were also used, the most important being the *Yugaron* (*Yogācāra bhūmi śāstra*) by Asaṅga.

In its critical classification of the scriptures, the Hossō school divided the *tripiṭaka* into three philosophical periods consisting of the following:

1) *Teaching of Existence*
For the purpose of destroying the attachment to the concept of the self, these teachings set forth the existence of the dharmas or elements of existence. i.e. Hīnayāna sutras.
2) *Teaching of Emptiness*
Because of the tendency to cling to the belief in the existence of the dharmas, these sutras set forth the doctrine of Emptiness. i.e. various Prajñāpāramitā sutras.
3) *Middle Way Teaching*
The most profound teaching that avoids attachment to either the belief in existence or the nihilistic danger of clinging to non-existence. Mahāyāna sutras such as the *Kegongyō*, *Gejin Mikkyō*, *Konkōmyōkyō*, *Hokekyō* and *Nehangyō*.

b. Emphasis upon Consciousness

The chief concern of the Vijñānavādins was the soteriological aspect of human consciousness, which they believed to be the key to Enlightenment. In this respect they were continuing the tradition of Early Buddhism, as expressed in the *Dhammapada:*

> Mind foreruns all, is the foundation of all, is the origin of all. If one speaks or acts with and evil mind, suffering follows him as the wheel follows the ox hoof.
>
> Verse I

The Early Buddhists had viewed Enlightenment as an attitude of mind in which human attachments, particularly to the notion of a permanent self, were surrendered. To accomplish such a goal, the Abhidharma schools subsequently presented their analysis of the dharmas to prove the 'self' to be merely a collection of elements, but in the eyes of the Mādhyamika, they had merely substituted a new *desideratum*. Yet despite their own efforts of constant denial, with the lapse of several centuries, opponents believed that the Mādhyamikas themselves had fallen into the same solecism by making the middle way of Emptiness an object of attachment.

The Vijñānavādins also viewed other shortcomings in Mādhyamika philosophy besides the danger of becoming attached to the concept of Emptiness. For instance, the Mādhyamikas maintained that Enlightenment resulted from the transcendence of dualistic thought, but neglected to investigate the psychological process of how this might happen within the individual. The Vijñānavādins thus made the discovery of the nature of the subjective experience of Enlightenment their goal.

From the time of the historical Buddha, the major concern of Buddhism was individual subjectivity and very little interest was exhibited in the nature of the so-called exterior 'objective' world except insofar, as it served as a container for man and related to his conduct as a source of attachment and clinging. Theories regarding the origin of the world fell into the realm of useless and even harmful metaphysical speculation, since involvement with such considerations were believed a waste of precious time that could be devoted to attaining Enlightenment. In the *Abhidharmakośa*, when the seventy-five elements of existence were presented, the analysis offered a description of the components of man and his psychological states. Although the Abhidharma demonstrated more interest than other Buddhist schools in the nature of the exterior world, relating it to their psycho-cosmic Three World theory, their interest was primarily soteriological.

The one-hundred dharmas of existence of the Hossō sect are very clearly related to the *Abhidharmakośa* classification with one distinctive difference in order. The *Kośa*, in line with its effort to prove the non-existence of a self, began with material elements (*rūpa*); the Hossō classification on the other hand, commences with the mind and its eight varieties of consciousness. These consisted of the five fundamental consciousnesses: eye, ear, nose, tongue and tactile, as well as a sixth consciousness that dealt with the mental functions of cognition, and was believed to rise in co-ordination with the five sense consciousness, although it could also act independently such as during the state of dreaming or meditation. The seventh consciousness was considered to function as a centralizing unit or 'notion of ego.' The former six consciousnesses were regarded as dependent upon this centralizing unit, or superficial subconscious, which at the same time, always rose in conjunction with the eighth deep subconscious, designated as the 'store consciousness.'

c. *The Ālaya Vijñāna (Store Consciousness)*

According to Vijñānavādin thought, this consciousness is the basis of the false subject-object dichotomy existing within the mind of the ignorant man and the creation of his empirical world. This does not mean the Vijñānavādins were solopsists or believed that the *Ālaya vijñāna* actually created an 'objective' world in the manner of a Cosmic Consciousness, for they continually asserted that the *Ālaya vijñāna* itself was interdependent. What they did mean was that the world as ignorant individuals comprehend it is merely a fabrication of their own subjective consciousness. They explained this contention by a unique epistemological view briefly summarized as follows:

The individual is aware of the exterior world only when his consciousness is functioning. Objects exist for him as he perceives them or in retrospect remembers them, otherwise they have no significance; to assume meaning, an object must become a content of consciousness. In this respect it can be said that one function of consciousness consists in appearing as an object. This does not mean that the consciousness itself creates the object, for it is an interdependent organ, but it does 'create' it in the manner that the individual ultimately perceives it. The seven lower consciousnesses, function in unison with the Store Consciousness to receive and transmit sensa from the exterior world and in the process distort the data so completely that they are in effect 'creating' a new object. On occasion we realize that our consciousness has deceived us into accepting sensory illusions, such as a stage prop as a three-dimensional reality or mistaking a shadowy tree for a prowler. But actually all our impressions of the exterior world are delusions; the result of past and present ego-emotional attachments that arise from the Store Consciousness and in turn taint the other seven consciousnesses.

The second function of consciousness is its role as the perceiving subjectivity. At the same time that consciousness appears as the object, it also acts as the subjectivity viewing that object and herein lies the basis of dualistic thought. The ignorant man believes the objects he perceives are true existents in the exterior world, but in reality what he sees are merely the phantoms conjured up by his own Store Consciousness. As Vasubandhu stated: "there arises consciousness in the form of the outer world, sentient beings, self and understanding, but none of these have any reality; since they do not exist, consciousness does not exist".[36] Just as the apparently veridical entities posited by consciousness are totally unreal, so the consciousness which stands as an ostensible entity in opposition to them, and in fact is even affirmed in its existence by them, is equally illusory.

In this particular variety of epistemological subjectivism, the *Ālaya vijñāna* was regarded as the basis of all phenomenal existence perceived by ignorant man in the form of the relationship between subjectivity and objectivity. This consciousness was believed to contain the 'seeds' (*bīja*) or direct causes for the manifestation of phenomenal existents and the seeds in turn received their tendency or propensity (*vāsanā*)[37] to arise as a result of their interdependent relationship with the other seven consciousnesses. For example, a child gradually acquires the habit of separating a four-legged furry creature with a wagging tail from the other objects in his environment and designate it 'dog'. Certain impressions are deposited within the mind regarding the nature and appearance of 'dog' that are integrally related to past and present experience. i.e. an encounter with a dog might always be associated with warmth, soft furriness and love until such a time that an unpleasant experience qualifies or changes that comprehension. Thus it is possible for two individuals encountering the same dog to receive drastically different sensual impressions arising from their stored impressions; one might pleasantly experience meeting an affectionate friend, while the other senses a fearful ill-smelling and dangerous enemy or even the object of an allergy. The dog does not change its nature but in each instance it is viewed in the light of past associations. These impressions are further influenced by the present situation; whether the dog belongs to a friend or stranger, the environment of the meeting place, previous events in the day, as well as future anticipations. It is therefore possible for the same person on two different occasions to view the identical dog in an entirely different manner. On a day after a quarrel with an employer, pressed by financial worries, lack of sleep and dire forebodings, even the most engaging puppy can be viewed with disgust. The reaction would not be merely emotional for the senses would also be affected, and the puppy could appear to be gray, unkempt or even sickly. Every other object in the environment would be tainted in a similar manner.

Each individual's comprehension of the so-called objective world is actually a product created from past associations and present conditions and thus can be said to be imagined. This does not mean that the object itself does not exist but merely that the unenlightened are incapable of perceiving it as-it-is or in its true nature. An artist can squeeze the same colour red from a tube onto his palette and paint a bright carnation on one canvas and bloody carnage on another. But to the viewer's eye, the red of the carnation, the red of the blood and the red still splashed on the palette may easily appear to be three different shades, since each has been manifested by the *Ālaya vijñāna* in a different manner according to its associations. For ignorant man this creates an egocentric predicament, the solution to which can only be found in Enlightenment.

The 'seeds' (*bīja*) of the *Ālaya vijñāna* were considered by the Vijñānavādins to possess six characteristics:[38]

1) *They are created momentarily.*
   This means that they cannot be regarded as eternal existences.
2) *When the seed functions, ist manifestation and function are simultaneously interdependent.*
   Once it cognizes an object, it establishes an interdependent relationship.

3) *The seeds are consistent in each species or category.*
In other words, a cognized object cannot erratically change into something else.
4) *The seeds have definite characteristics as good, evil or neutral.*
These are not confused in their relation to the individual and his progress towards Enlightenment.
5) *The seed cannot manifest or function without numerous causes.*
For example, the perception of a pencil is dependent upon eyesight, proper lighting and so on, not merely the seed alone.
6) *Material and psychological aspects draw separate results.*
Each seed draws its own result.

Occasionally the misunderstanding has arisen that the *Ālaya vijñāna* acts as an independent consciousness, functioning voluntarily as a source of creation (*antarvyāpāra puruṣa*), or 'Absolute Mind'. This is clearly a mistaken interpretation that probably results from the Vijñānavādin emphasis upon the uniqueness of this consciousness rather than its relationship with the exterior world.[39] A considerable number of sectarian arguments also erupted in China concerning whether the *Ālaya vijñāna* was to be regarded as a pure or defiled consciousness.[40] These disputes seem to be largely based upon different conceptions of the nature of the *Ālaya vijñāna* before and after its conversion.

It is obvious from the foregoing description of the *Ālaya vijñāna* of the ignorant man, that this is a defiled phenomenal consciousness producing defiled manifestations.[41] Enlightenment entails the complete 'reversion of the *Ālaya vijñāna*' (*ālaya paravṛtti*), which drastically changes its nature in Vijñānavāda philosophy. After Enlightenment, it was assigned a new name, 'Mirror-wisdom' (*ādarśa-jñāna*) since subsequent to its conversion, the *Ālaya vijñāna* functions exactly like a mirror, no longer falsely presupposing the objects it cognizes, but simply casting true reflections of the exterior world. In this respect, the attainment of 'Mirror-wisdom' signifies that the defiled *Ālaya vijñāna* has ceased to exist and that this eighth consciousness has now become purified. In turn this conversion forms the basis for the transformation of the other seven consciousnesses in the following manner:

1–5—Five Sense Consciousness→Action Wisdom (*kṛtyānuṣṭhāna-jñāna*)
Now work to benefit others rather than serving the individual ego.
6—Mental Functions→Observation Wisdom (*pratyavekṣaṇā-jñāna*)
Capable of gathering and coordinating the data from the senses without distortion and utilizing this knowledge for the good of others (i.e. to lead them to Enlightenment)
7—Notion of Ego→Equality Wisdom (*samatā-jñāna*)
Whereby self and others are comprehended as interdependent oneness.

Each of these consciousnesses in their transformations become so purified that in effect, they are transformed into supernatural powers.

d. One Hundred Dharmas of Existence

In order to analyze the psychological means whereby Enlightenment could be attained, the Hossō sect categorized the millions of elements of existence into one hundred varieties:

I. Mind (citta dharma)

1) Eye 2) Ear 3) Nose 4) Tongue 5) Tactile	Five Fundamental Consciousnesses

6) Mental functions of cognition (*mano-vijñāna*)
7) Notion of Ego or consciousness that acts as a centralizing unit (*kliṣṭamana*)
8) *Ālaya vijñāna*
composed of three functions:
  a) Active—Embraces or acts as the basis of the preceding seven consciousnesses
  b) Passive—The seven consciousnesses embraced within the *Ālaya* also act as seeds to condition this consciousness
  c) Attachment—the interaction with the seventh consciousness

II. Attendant Mental Faculties (caitasika dharma)

A. Universal (sarvatraga)

These five dharmas arise with every other mental function and can be classified as good, evil or neutral depending upon their conduciveness to Enlightenment

9) Attention (*manaskāra*)
10) Contact (*sparśa*)
11) Sensation (*vedanā*)
12) Conception (*saṃjñā*)
13) Volition (*cetanā*)

B. Limited (viniyata)

These functions are capable of responding in a good, evil or neutral fashion, but do not necessarily arise in unison with all aspects of Category I (Mind); hence are termed 'limited'. They arise only in certain circumstances in conjunction with the mind. i.e. desire is triggered by its object.

14) Desire (*chanda*)
15) Judgement (*adhimokṣa*)
16) Memory (*smṛti*)
17) Concentration (*samādhi*)
18) Knowledge (*prajñā*)

C. Good (kuśala)

Aspects of mind related to goodness (attainment of Enlightenment)

19) Faith (*śraddhā*)
20) Endeavour (*vīrya*)
21) Shame (*hrī*)
22) Modesty (*apatrāpya*)
23) Non-covetousness (*alobha*)
24) Non-malevolence (*adveṣa*)
25) Absence of ignorance (*amoha*)
26) Flexibility of mind (*prasrabdhi*)
27) Diligence (*apramāda*)
28) Equanimity (*upekṣā*)
29) Non-violence (*ahiṃsā*)

D. *Evil (kleśa)*

Hindrances to the attainment of Enlightenment

30) Greed (*rāga*)
31) Instinctive resistance (*pratigha*)
32) Ignorance (*mūḍha* or *moha*)
33) Pride (*māna*)
34) Doubt (*vicikitsā*)
35) Five false views (*dṛṣṭi*)
    a. Considering self exists and belongs to 'me'.
    b. Extreme views—i.e. self is eternal, infinite, non-eternal.
    c. Views which reject the law of cause and effect.
    d. Clinging to false views as being true.
    e. Improper discipline (monastic practices).

E. *Lesser Evils (upakleśa)*

These rise in association with the major hindrances.

36) Anger (*krodha*) which arises from #31
37) Enmity (*upanāha*)
38) Rationalization of conduct (*mrakṣa*)
39) Worry (*pradāsa*) Suffering from remembrance of past anger and hatred or from unpleasant present situations.
40) Parsimony (*mātsarya*)
41) Jealousy (*īrṣyā*)
42) Deceit (*māyā*), to create an illusion.
43) Fraudulance (*śāṭhya*)
44) To cause injury (*vihiṃsā*)
45) Arrogance (*mada*) pride of possession.
46) Shamelessness (*āhrīkya*) lack of self-reflection.
47) Lack of modesty (*anapatrāpya*)
48) Restlessness (*auddhatya*)
49) Depression (*styāna*)
50) Disbelief (*āśraddhya*)
51) Indolence (*kausīdya*)
52) Negligence (*pramāda*)
53) Forgetfulness (*muṣitasmṛtitā*)
54) Distraction (*vikṣepa*)
55) Non-discernment (*asamprajanya*)

F. *Irregular Functions* (*aniyata*)

In contrast to previous categories, which had one definite function, this category is determined by time and place.

56) Regret (*kaukṛtya*)
57) Drowsiness (*middha*) torpor
58) Reflection (*vitarka*) conjecture
59) Careful investigation (*vicāra*)

III. *Form Elements* (*rūpa dharma*)

The five organs and their objects plus dharmas that can become the object of consciousness.

60) Eye (*cakṣus*)
61) Ear (*śrotra*)
62) Nose (*ghrāṇa*)
63) Tongue (*jihvā*)
64) Body (*kāya*)
65) Form (*rūpa*)
66) Sound (*śabda*)
67) Smell (*gandha*)
68) Taste (*rasa*)
69) Touch (*spraṣṭavya*)
70) Elements as objects of consciousness (*dharmā-yatanikāni*)
    a. The smallest atoms composing the substantial elements of existence.
    b. The smallest atoms composing the insubstantial forms such as space, light, darkness, colour, sound, smell, etc.
    c. An imperceptible form possessing the power or efficacy to prevent the commission of an evil act, such as received at ordination.
    d. Reflection of the ten dharmas (organs and their objects) upon the human mind as illusion.
    e. Forms such as sound, taste, or smell, produced in superior meditation.

IV. *Disassociated dharma* (*citta viprayukta saṃskāra*)

Neither material nor psychological.

71) Acquisition (*prāpti*)
72) Life (*jīvitendriya*)

73) Shared qualities (*nikāya-sabhāga*) common qualities among a species.
74) Nature of common ignorant man (*pṛthagjanatva*)
75) Thoughtless trance (*āsaṃjñi samāpatti*)
76) Annihilation trance (*nirodha-samāppati*)
77) Result of thoughtless and annihilation trances (*āsaṃjñika*)
78) Name (*nāma-kāya*)
79) Phrase (*pada-kāya*)
80) Character or letter (*vyañjana-kāya*)
81) Birth (*jāti*)
82) Old age (*jarā*)
83) Subsistence (*sthiti*)
84) Impermanence (*anityatā*)
85) Becoming (*pravṛtti*)
86) Distinction of causes and effects (*pratiniyama*)
87) Harmony (*yoga*)
88) Speed (*java*)
89) Order (*anukrama*)
90) Direction (*deśa*)
91) Time (*kāla*)
92) Number (*saṃkhyā*)
93) Gathering of direct and indirect causes essential for the totality of conditioned dharmas (*sāmagrī*)
94) Non-existence of direct and indirect causes essential for the totality of conditioned dharmas (*asāmagrī*)

V. Unconditioned Elements (*asaṃskṛta-dharma*)

95) Space (*ākāśa*)
96) Extinction through intellectual power (*pratisaṃkhyā-nirodha*)
97) Extinction due to lack of a productive cause (*apratisaṃkhyā*)
98) Extinction through the emotionless state of the Fourth Stage of *Rupadhātu* meditation (*aniñjya*)
99) Extinction of sensation and conception (*saṃjñā*)
100) As-it-isness (*tathatā*)

In this manner the worlds of ignorance and Enlightenment overlap in the range of the dharmas which commence with the rise of consciousness in the ignorant man and terminate with the highest expression of Enlightenment (*tathatā*).

d. Doctrine of the "Three Natures" of Human Existence

The one hundred dharmas were analyzed from a vertical aspect in the Hossō doctrine of the 'three natures' of man's existence. According to this theory, each dharma assumes a specific category of being assigned to it by the creative and observant consciousness. These 'natures' or characteristics are as follows:

1. *Illusory discriminative nature* (*parikalpita-lakṣaṇa*)

The false assumption made by ignorant man that phenomenal appearances represent true reality, when actually they are manifestations of the individual's own mind. The belief that this illusion represents veridical phenomena is the cause of attachment. This stage of being can be described as false existence and represents the naïve affirmation of existents and self as independent permanent entities.

2. *Dependent nature* (*paratantra-lakṣaṇa*)

The recognition that phenomena exist only as the result of a combination of causes and conditions, hence are dependent. This stage of understanding can be described as the recognition of temporary or conventional existence subject to change and impermanence.

3. *Fully accomplished or true nature* (*pariniṣpanna-lakṣaṇa*)

Recognition of the true reality of all phenomena as interdependent. This is true existence as the comprehension of as-it-isness, or the existence of phenomena in an indeterminite, interdependent manner.

These three views of existence are explained symbolically by the popular allegory of the rope. Supposedly, on a dark night an ignorant man mistakes a coil of rope for a snake and becomes frightened. An Enlightened One happens to pass by and persuades the agitated man that he is mistaken, his imagined snake is merely a rope; the illusion of snake is void (*śūnya*). He still clings however, to the belief in the existence of the rope as a reality. Next he proceeds to realize that the rope is composed of hemp and created into its present condition by means of various direct and indirect causes, and its appearance as rope is merely a temporary illusion that will eventually cease to exist; the phenomenon of rope can be termed neither an 'existence' nor a 'non-existence'. The same can be said of the nature of the hemp which composes the rope. The appearance of the snake, the rope and the hemp are all dependent upon the attitude of the viewer and symbolize the 'three natures' of existence.

In the foregoing allegory, the confused eyes of the ignorant man symbolize the 'illusory discriminative nature' (*parikalpita*), and the fears created by his illusions represent birth and death, or the sufferings of human existence. These arise from the false notion of self, which can only be dispelled by recognizing its emptiness (interdependence, impermanence and insubstantiality). The recognition of the rope as rope symbolizes the appearance of existents that are products of interrelated conditions such as people, animals, tables and chairs, etc. The awareness of the empty nature of the rope represents the comprehension of the emptiness of all existents (being dependent, changeable and temporary). This is termed the awareness of the 'dependent nature' (*paratantra*) But it still is important to recognize the fact that the coiled rope actually does resemble a snake, just as the self does have a temporary existence in the conventional world. Finally, the hemp forming the essence of the rope, represents the 'true nature of ultimate reality' (*parinişpanna*) or the essential unity resulting from the interdependence of all phenomena.[42]

The concept of the 'three natures' of existence serves not only as an approach to Enlightenment but also can be regarded as the means by which an Enlightened One can return to act and communicate within the realm of daily life. This was viewed as an essential feature of perfect Enlightenment in the Hossō school.

e. The Three Vehicles and Enlightenment

In Japan, the Hossō sect has frequently been termed quasi-Mahāyānistic by its critics particularly since it classified the inherent potentiality for individuals to attain Enlightenment into five categories:

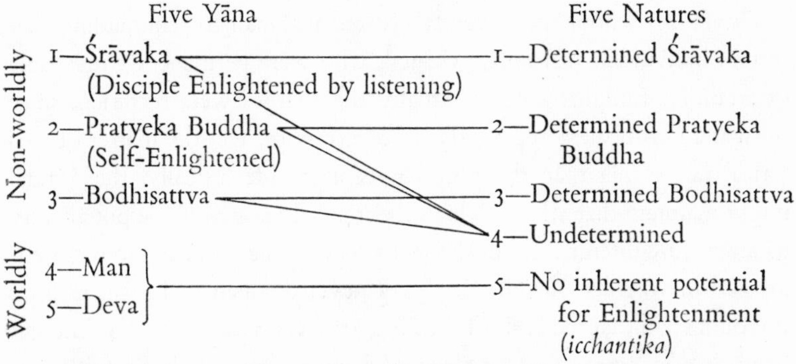

Individuals belonging to the first three categories were believed to possess the determined fundamental quality or seed (*bija*) to become Enlightened in one of the three *yāna* (vehicles or courses), while those in the undetermined category possess the nature to attain Enlightenment, but as yet their course is unclear. For example, an individual possessing *bija* of both a Śrāvaka and Bodhisattva, is capable by the cultivation of virtue, of becoming a Bodhisattva, the most perfect form of Enlightenment. On the other hand, some may possess only the seeds of Śrāvaka and Pratyeka Buddha, in which case, the latter would be the more desirable goal. Individuals in the worldly categories of man and *deva* were considered to totally lack an inherent potentiality for Enlightenment and thus be incapable of rising beyond the position of man or *deva* within the Three Worlds of suffering.

The concept that Enlightenment could be a determined inherent potentiality has long been a controversial topic among the Buddhist sects. The Sarvāstivādins refused to recognize such a potentiality and maintained that Enlightenment was an acquired quality, while later Mahāyāna schools such as the Tendai and Kegon, idealistically emphasized the existence of an inherent Buddha nature in all sentient beings. Within the Yogācāra itself the subject was disputed, since some scholars maintained

Enlightenment was totally inherent, while others insisted it was acquired. The Japanese Hossō based their position upon the views of Dharmapāla, who considered it both as an inherent and acquired quality.

The Hossō school was severely critized in Japan for contending that certain individuals (*icchantika*) existed, who were permanently incapable of attaining Enlightenment. Actually the charges were sectarian, since what the Hossō were apparently concerned with, was the matter of empirical fact rather than theoretical possibility. Idealistically, the Tendai might maintain that all individuals theoretically possessed the potentiality to attain Enlightenment, but the fact was that the majority were so engrossed in worldly pursuits that they never attained it. In this respect, it would seem that the basis of the Hossō view was not radically different from that later proposed by Shinran, founder of the Jōdo Shinshū sect, who was profoundly concerned with the plight of the worldly majority of men effectually incapable of attaining Enlightenment by traditional means. Hossō critics, and probably a few Hossō elitists, interpreted the *icchantika* concept as the deliberate exclusion of a certain class of individuals from the possibility of Enlightenment. But actually, what the Hossō were attempting was a classification of fact in the traditional Abhidharma style, which always presents the danger of limitation. It is hardly fair to designate the school as quasi-Mahāyānistic for this effort, particularly in view of their belief in the Four Varieties of Nirvana, which specifically emphasizes, in typical Mahāyāna spirit, the saving role of the completely Enlightened One.

Four Varieties of Nirvana

1—Original self-nature Enlightenment
A quality possessed by all sentient beings, the universal truth in all existents.

2—Nirvana with a physical body
Enlightenment based upon the complete elimination of the hindrances of ignorance.

3—Nirvana without a physical body

(2 and 3: For Śrāvaka and Pratyeka Buddhas)

This is not like the Hīnayāna concept of *Mahāparinirvāṇa*, since it actually still does entail a human body, but a body that has been greatly transformed for the eighth consciousness (*Ālaya vijñāna*) has reverted into Mirror-wisdom.

4—Non-residing Nirvana The Enlightened One does not reside in Nirvana since his wisdom and compassion demand that he become involved in aiding others. At this stage all eight consciousnesses have become transformed into the four wisdoms.	Attained only by a Tathāgata

Another Mahāyāna criticism of the Hossō was their refusal to accept the *ekayāna* (one-vehicle) doctrine set forth in the *Lotus* and *Nirvana* sutras. According to this doctrine, the Buddha set forth a single teaching by which all can attain Enlightenment, the path of the Bodhisattva. The other courses of Śrāvaka and Pratyeka Buddha were merely offered as *upāya* (adapted teachings) to lead individuals into the Bodhisattva way.

It is obvious from their classification of the four varieties of Nirvana that the Hossō recognized the Bodhisattva way as the superior form of Enlightenment. They considered both the Śrāvakas and Pratyeka Buddhas as inferior realizations, since the first sought Enlightenment solely for their own benefit, and the latter neglected to impart the fruits of their realization to others. But in view of the Hossō theory of determination, they refused to consider the Śrāvaka and Pratyeka Buddha courses solely as *upāya*. Instead they termed the *ekayāna* as taught in the *Lotus* and *Nirvana* sutras to be an *upāya* for those who possessed an undetermined potential. Four types of individuals fit into this category:

1) Those possessing, seeds to become either a Bodhisattva or Śrāvaka;
2) Bodhisattva or Pratyeka Buddha;
3) Śrāvaka or Pratyeka Buddha;
4) Śrāvaka, Pratyeka Buddha or Bodhisattva.

These could all benefit by the *upāya* of *ekayāna* in order to attain a higher state through the cultivation of virtue. On the other hand, the Hossō maintained the *Lotus* and *Nirvana* sutras were not composed for the benefit of the worldly (*icchantika*). In this respect, they claimed only the

Gejin Mikkyō, with its doctrine of five categories, could be understood as the true all-encompassing teaching of the Buddha. It is obvious that later charges against the Hossō for lacking the Mahāyāna spirit were sectarian. At the same time the debates over *ekayāna* ultimately forced both sides into untenable extremes confusing fact with potentiality.

The uniqueness of Hossō thought lies in its attempt to explain the plight of man in terms of the analysis of the human mind, and by demonstrating how the condition of ignorance can be transformed into Enlightenment within the mind. In this respect, its approach slightly differed from the Sanron but both philosophies clearly emphasize that in essence, *saṃsāra* and *nirvāṇa* occur within the same locus. Hossō philosophy became dominant during the latter half of the Nara period and its study has continuously played a significant role in Japanese Buddhist history.

6. KEGON SHŪ (*Avataṃsaka*), *The Philosophy of Totality*

This school is based upon the *Daihōkōbutsu Kegongyō* (*Buddhāvataṃsaka-mahāvaipulya-sūtra*), popularly known as the *Kegongyō*. A product of contributions made by a number of unknown Indian authors over several generations, this sutra was completed by the third century A.D.[43] It has always been regarded as one of the most profound and perfect elucidations of Mahāyāna thought.

In the theological development of Buddhism, this sutra is placed as the preaching of the Buddha under the bodhi tree on the second seventh-day following his Enlightenment. Of course, this does not refer to an actual historical time or place, but rather to the position the sutra holds in the traditional Mahāyāna system of classifying the events in the life of the Buddha in relation to the development of teachings. The second seventh-day symbolizes the first preaching of the essence of the Buddha's Enlightenment, which was incomprehensible to ordinary men and subsequently followed by Hīnayāna teachings designed to condition the minds of the audience.

The *Kegongyō* has been described as a grand play in three acts with the Buddha Mahāvairocana as protagonist assisted by his faithful attendants Mañjuśrī and Samantabhadra.[44] As an effort to capture the essence of Enlightenment, the sutra is dramatic, creative and at times almost unapproachable.

Three important translations were made in China that influenced the development of the Chinese Hua-yen (Kegon) school:

1) By Buddhabhadra (418–420 A.D.) 60 fascicles
The old version of the sutra depicting eight assemblies or gathering of disciples at seven different places (three earthly and four *deva* heavens). It is often called the sutra of 'seven places and eight assemblies.'
2) By Śikṣānanda (695) 80 fascicles
The new version which contains five chapters the former translation lacks. This account has nine assemblies.
3) By Prajñā (698) 40 fascicles
A translation of the chapter of the sutra entitled "Entering the *Dharmadhātu*", which describes the journey of the youth Sudhana in his quest for Enlightenment. In this tale, Sudhana is advised by the bodhisattva Mañjuśrī (symbolizing wisdom) to seek various masters for instruction, and subsequently visits 53 persons from different walks of life until finally he encounters the bodhisattva Samantabhadra (symbolizing compassion), who assists him in the realization of the *Dharmadhātu* (Enlightenment). This text is known as the *Gaṇḍavyūha*).

The title of the sutra has a long tradition of complex interpretations. Literally *Avataṃsaka* means 'flower-wreath'. No particular flower is designated, as in the case of the *Lotus sutra*, and the secondary implications of 'flower' as 'decoration' are equally emphasized. The seven Chinese characters forming the title each have been given ten interpretations in keeping with the constant repetition of the number ten in Kegon philosophy, symbol of infinity. By assigning ten definitions to each character, the implication is made that each has infinite interpretations embracing the totality of the dharmas.

a. Historical Transmission

The nominal founder of the Hua-yen sect in China was Fa-shun (557–

640), who was also known by his priestly name of Tu-shun. Although there are many unsolved problems regarding his actual role in the Hua-yen school and relationship with the former Ti-lun sect,[45] which apparently was absorbed into the Hua-yen at this period, it appears that he was a man of Hua-yen practice, if not a great philosopher.

The second Chinese patriarch was Chih-yen (602–68), who wrote a number of important commentaries on the *Avataṃsaka sūtra*. He had considerable influence upon his illustrious disciple Fa-tsang (643–712), who believed that his own work merely expanded the view of his master. Fa-tsang was responsible for systematizing Hua-yen philosophy and is considered to be the actual founder of the sect; an alternate name for the school in China was Hsien-shou, the posthumous name of this patriarch.

Fa-tsang was extremely eclectic in his thought and derived strong influence from the Yogācāra concept of *Ālaya vijñāna*, as well as Aśvaghoṣa's *Awakening of Faith*. He sought to establish a middle way, uniting what he considered to be the non-existence (*Śūnyatā*) teachings of Nāgārjuna and the Yogācāra concept of existence in the form of the *Ālaya vijñāna*. These two views he believed were symbolically represented in the *Avataṃsaka sūtra* by the bodhisattva attendants: Mañjuśrī, symbol of wisdom, (*prajñā*) and non-existence, and Samantabhadra, representing the function of compassion in the phenomenal world or existence.[46]

In line with his views, Fa-tsang established five Indian patriarchs of the sect, commencing with the mythical Samantabhadra and Mañjuśrī, followed by Nāgārjuna, Vasubandhu and Aśvaghoṣa respectively. Although Aśvaghoṣa historically antedated Nāgārjuna and Vasubandhu, Fa-tsang considered that his views were theologically closer to Hua-yen concepts. Fa-tsang's writings were mainly based upon the old version of the *Avataṃsaka sūtra*, although the Śikṣānanda translation did appear near the end of his lifetime.

After Fa-tsang, the orthodox historical transmission of the Hua-yen skips one generation since his direct disciple, Hui-yuan (673–742), opposed certain of his master's views and subsequently was not considered as his proper successor.[47] This seemed to be more of a personal conflict among contemporaries than heresy. Fa-tsang's 'indirect heir' was Ch'eng-kuan (738–839), who did not attempt to go beyond the founder's interpretations although he based his writings on the new version of the *Avataṃsaka sūtra*. Ch'eng-kuan was extremely interested in Ch'an (Zen) philosophy, which had become very popular during the Sui and T'ang dynasties. The Chinese preferred its simplicity and practicality over the more abstruse philosophies of the other schools, and Ch'eng-kuan sought to unify the two teachings. He was succeeded by Tsung-mi (780–841), a former Ch'an scholar, who went even further in emphasizing Ch'an simplicity and practicality. After this fifth patriarch, Hua-yen philosophy developed no further in China. It is not accidental however, that the official list of patriarchs composed of five Indian scholars and five Chinese, reached the symbolic number of ten, so crucial in Hua-yen philosophy.

Hua-yen teachings spread to Korea during the lifetime of the third patriarch, Fa-tsang. At the time when he was still studying under Chih-yen, a monk from Silla, I-hsiang, (625–702) was a fellow disciple. Upon returning to Korea (Silla) I-hsiang founded the Hua-yen sect in that country and it is reported that later, when Fa-tsang completed his commentary on the *Avataṃsaka*, he sent it to his friend, I-hsiang and requested his views.[48] Another student from Silla, Shen-hsiang (?–742) later came to China and received instruction from Fa-tsang. Upon completion, instead of returning to Korea, he went to Japan and arrived during the early Nara period.

Prior to the arrival of Shen-hsiang, scriptures related to Hua-yen had already been brought to Japan by the Vinaya master Tao-hsüan in 736 but had not been studied. When Shen-hsiang arrived, the influential Japanese priest Ryōben, or Rōben (689–773), sought to hear his lectures and in 740 persuaded Emperor Shōmu to invite Shen-hsiang to deliver an Imperial lecture on the *Kegongyō*. This lecture stirred considerable interest among the aristocracy and captured the imagination of the Emperor. Three years later under Emperor Shōmu's edict, the Great Buddha Mahāvairocana of the Tōdaiji temple was cast, subsequently known as the Great Buddha of Nara. The *Kegongyō* was described in an Imperial edict of the day as being a principal sutra of the nation, marking the official beginning of the Kegon sect in Japan, with Ryōben carrying on the work of Shen-hsiang.

Fa-tsang had founded the Hua-yen sect at the time when China was searching for a new form of stability and order in the form of the T'ang dynasty. During the reign of Emperor Shōmu, Japan was in a similar situation and at its apogee in borrowing T'ang institutions. The new school appeared to meet the same needs in Japan as it had in China. The Emperor was so inspired by its totalistic symbolism that he sought to identify himself with the Great Buddha Mahāvairocana, the centre of the universe, as symbolic of the centre of the Japanese nation. But this is a topic that will be discussed in detail later under Nara politics and the foundation of the *kokubunji* (provincial temple system).

The Tōdaiji temple housing the Great Buddha was destroyed by two civil wars; first in 1180 during the Genji-Heike battles and reconstructed by Chōgen (1121–1206) and secondly, in 1567 during the Muromachi period, not to be rebuilt until the Tokugawa period by Kōkei (1648-1703). It was again threatened during the early Meiji period by the *Haibutsu kishaku* anti-Buddhist movement but managed to survive. In the same manner, the Kegon sect has maintained a nominal existence up until the present day with its basis at the Tōdaiji temple.

b. Doctrine of the Interdependent Origination of the Dharmadhātu

With its emphasis upon the existential predicament of man, Early Buddhism avoided metaphysical speculation regarding the nature of the exterior world but the historical Buddha did accept the contemporary Indian world view of the existence of a number of heavens and hells; these he primarily used for didactic purposes. The Abhidharma schools in their analysis of the psychological aspects of Enlightenment and subjects of attachment, were largely responsible for the creation of what somewhat incongrously might be termed an 'empirical metaphysics'. In other words, they dealt with the metaphysical that could be discovered upon the path of inner experience. This was correlated to a symbolic and modified Hindu world view to create the psycho-cosmic system known as the Three Worlds (*Kāma*, *Rūpa* and *Arūpa dhātu*), a detailed classification of psychological states ranging from the lowest existence of the Realm of Desire (*Kāma dhātu*) to the highest stages of meditation just short of Enlightenment (*Arūpa dhātu*). Certain zealots in the Abhidharma tradition departed from the mainstream of Buddhist thought and attempted to establish actual physical locations for the heavens and hells, as well as other tangible features.[49] The Mahāyānists rejected these but they did not discard the basic empirical metaphysical system. In fact they embellished upon the concept by analyzing the subjective nature of Enlightenment and subsequently creating myriads of Buddhas and Buddha lands beyond the Three Worlds, symbolizing the experiential attributes of Enlightenment and the complete transcendence of the artificial conventional boundaries of time and space.

From its inception, the Buddhist psycho-cosmic system had two levels of interpretation that ultimately were experientially identifiable. The first level related to *bhakti* or devotional Buddhism. The heavens and hells of the Realm of Desire (*Kāma dhātu*) were used as *upāya* in Early Buddhism to induce the laity to practice virtue by offering tangible rewards and punishments. At the same time, the mythical denizens of these realms, the Indian *deva*, served devotional purposes, designed to ultimately lead to mental purification. At the second level, the heavens and hells and higher worlds were strictly correlated with mental conditions and stages of meditation.

Even in Early Buddhism, it was possible for devotional practices relating to the Three Worlds to lead to a higher experiential mental state. For example, according to the *upāya* of the three *kathā* (graduated forms of discourse), the lay practice of giving and discipline would lead to birth in a happy heaven.[50] The logic behind this teaching was that once the layman began to seriously practice virtue, he would reach a state of mental purification wherein he would no longer seek the worldly goal of rebirth in a heaven, and strive for higher religious awareness.

Mahāyāna Buddhism was far more laity oriented than Early Buddhism and the Buddhas, bodhisattvas and Buddha lands were used even more extensively than the heavens and hells of the Three World system for their soteriological roles had increased. An apex was finally reached in Tantrism, where it was believed that the higher states of meditation and even Enlightenment could be attained by means of specific devotional practices to certain Buddhas, bodhisattvas and Indian *deva*. Such mysticism is already evident in the Kegon concept of the *Dharmadhātu*.

The term *Dharmadhātu* (lit. Realm of the dharmas), was used philosophically to denote the subjective essence of Enlightenment, Absolute truth and the all-embracing totality of the infinite universes (realms of experience) revealed within Enlightenment. Devotionally, the *Dharmadhātu* was equivalent to the *Dharmakāya*, symbolized in Kegon thought as the great Buddha Mahāvairocana, who manifests the infinite universe but yet is inherent within each and every existent. Certain problems do arise when the subjective nature of this concept is overlooked, since it then would appear to offer a speculative metaphysical world view very contrary to the teachings of the historical Buddha. But without a subjective experiential approach, Kegon thought is logically inconceivable, since it violates the basic principles of reasoning.

Experientially in Kegon philosophy, the entire universe is embraced within a single thought. But if we analyze that universe or its comprehension in accordance with the 'individual' religious awareness, we will find that four different views exist corresponding to the four stages of spiritual realization:

1) *Dharmadhātu of Phenomena* (*Ji hokkai*)

The conventional view of the universe as observed from the common sense standpoint. It contains all the phenomena of the empirical world, each with their individual characteristics and limitations. Existents are accepted without question as real independent entities. Such a view is analogous to observing waves upon the ocean, each appears to be distinct and independent.

2) *Dharmadhātu of Principle or Universal Truth* (*Ri hokkai*)

The undifferentiated world that underlies and sustains phenomena. This is the realm that can be fully grasped only by intuition, the realm of *śūnyatā*. It can be compared to observing the water itself, being oblivious to the waves on the surface.

3) *Dharmadhātu of the Unity of Phenomena and Universal Truth* (*Riji muge hokkai*)

View in which truth and phenomena are completely interpenetrated and united. In other words, they become identical, and to see one is in effect to visualize the other, a feat that only an Enlightened One is capable of accomplishing. It is possible at this level of religious realization to see the Buddha-nature present in all existents, no matter how lowly. It can be compared to recognizing the identity and interdependence of the waves and water.

4) *Dharmadhātu of the Unity of Phenomenon and Phenomenon* (*Jiji muge hokkai*)

View of the world in which all existents, while still preserving their individual identity, mutually interrelate and interpenetrate each other to form the whole. Just as the waves are manifestations of the same water and function in harmony without loss of identity, so the dharmas, which are all manifestations of the Absolute interrelate in harmony.

The first three of these stages were common among schools of Mahāyāna Buddhism but the last stage represents the unique Kegon contribution, and is the basis for their claim of being the most profound or 'complete' teaching. These stages of awareness also correspond to the Kegon classification of the teachings into five divisions.

c. Critical Classification of the Teaching in Five Divisions

Following the tradition of Mahāyāna schools, the Kegon sect established a critical classification of the development of Buddhist thought. Their view naturally reflects sectarian bias and was designed primarily for the purpose of comprehending the role of Kegon philosophy in the development of Buddhism. The classification of five divisions was originated by Ta-shun in his *Wu-chiao chih-kuan* and completed and systematized by Fa-tsang. It can be summarized as follows:

1) *Hīnayāna teachings* (*shōjōkyō*), known as *guhō* (ignorant of the dharma of Emptiness) *shōjōkyō*[51]

The historical Buddha first taught the *Avataṃsaka sūtra* immediately following his Enlightenment but only the bodhisattvas were capable of comprehending him, thus he divided the great teaching into what appeared to be 'three vehicles' in order to appeal to individuals in accordance with their capacity for understanding. This variety of teaching is considered to be the shallowest, analogous to the situation where a guide pretends that the final destination is a midway resting place in order to encourage his weak party; once the oasis has been safely reached, they are prepared to hear the more advanced teachings.

The purpose of this preliminary doctrine was to eliminate the false views of non-Buddhists regarding the nature of the 'self' and to clarify the theory of cause and effect. Nirvana at this level was regarded as total extinction. Supposedly the schools in this group split into twenty sects because they failed to progress to the Kegon final level of truth.

2) *Early Mahāyāna teachings* (*Daijōshikyō*)

Teaching that realizes the emptiness of both self and dharmas, classifies the characteristics of the dharmas in detail, and explains Enlightenment in terms of the eight consciousnesses and two levels of truth. They fail however, to set forth the Interdependent Origination of the *tathatā* and the identity of phenomena (*ji*) and principle (*ri*). They also maintain classifications such as the five categories in which, while some groups are denied perfect Enlightenment, others are completely denied all potential of Enlightenment.

The types of thought placed in this classification are: the Sanron concept of Emptiness (*kū*) and the Hossō view of existence (*u*).

3) *Final Mahāyāna teachings* (*Daijōshūkyō*)

Teaching the identity of the worlds of phenomena and principle (*jiri-muge*) and the Interdependent Origination of the *tathatā*. This supposedly represents the limit of Mahāyāna philosophy, but beyond it remain the doctrine of the mutual identity of phenomena (*jiji muge*) and the teaching of sudden Enlightenment that does not rely upon language.

4) *Sudden teaching* (*Tongyō*)

This classification has two definitions:

a) Reaching the truth directly without use of language.
b) Reaching Enlightenment without establishing gradual stages

of perfection. i.e. one thought can instantaneously lead to Enlightenment.

All teachings prior to this Zen type of attitude are classified as 'gradual.' However, it was believed that this approach could lead to an extreme elimination of phenomena in which the practitioner would lose sight of the wonder of viewing the dharmas in their individuality and complexity, it therefore was still considered to be shallow.

4) *Complete teaching* (*Engyō*)

Teaching of the interdependence of the *Dharmadhātu*. All the dharmas have separate appearances but these interact and rise together; thus when one dharma arises all do simultaneously and when one is destroyed, all are destroyed. Each individual dharma is subjectively viewed as equivalent to the totality of the universe.

Such a concept was found in the Sanron classification of the dharmas and the Hossō view of the rise of the *bīja* in the subjective *Ālaya vijñāna*, but the Kegon placed their distinct emphasis upon the mutual identity of phenomena (*jiji muge*). They believed for instance, that if a rock was equivalent to the totality of the universe (*tathatā*) and a rooftile likewise, then the rock and the rooftile must be experientially identical despite their completely different appearances.

Emphasis was also placed upon the manifold interpenetrating relationships within phenomena. If a single rock was equivalent to the totality of the universe, then in that relationship, the rock would be principle and the totality its attribute. A nearby blade of grass would become the principle in its own relationship with the totality, yet the rock and blade of grass, as mutually embraced, would be mirrored within each other in a principle-attribute relationship *ad infinitum*.

c. *Ten Profound Interdependent Relationships*

In order to further explain the concept of the mutual identity and interpenetration of phenomena, ten varieties of relationships were presented:[52]

1) *Interdependent simultaneous correspondence* (*dōji gusoku sōōmon*)

All existents come into being simultaneously without distinction of chronological order, thus one speck of dust contains and is identical to the totality of dharmas. (relationship in time)

2) *Interchangeable freedom of spatial aspects of dharmas* (*kōkyō jizai mugemon*)

Broad and narrow, large and small, are apparently contradicting and contrasting qualities, yet they complement and embrace each other, for one cannot exist without the other. (spatial relationship)

3) *Functional harmony between the non-identical one and many* (*ichita sōyō fudōmon*)

Although the one and many are interdependent, they cannot be confused. Just as the rays of light from a thousand lamps overlap and penetrate each other yet remain separate, the one, based on universal truth, embraces the many but at the same time, fulfills its function as the one. (functional relationship)

4) *Mutual interdependence of dharmas* (*shohōsōsoku jizaimon*)

In contrast to the previous example, a single lamp presupposes the existence of many lamps; without such a presupposition, the single lamp cannot exist. The one is thus interdependent with the many. The same relationship exists between the ray of light issuing forth from the lamp and the lamp itself, one cannot be separated from the other; both are interdependent. (essential interdependence)

5) *Complementary simultaneous manifestation and invisibility* (*Onmitsu kenryō gujōmon*)

If we look at a single dharma in the phenomenal world, we are able to perceive it but not the totality of dharmas, which it embraces. It is just like gazing at a waxing moon, a sliver is apparent but the rest is in darkness. (manifestation and invisible aspects)

6) *Mutual interchangeability without the loss of individual identity for even the smallest dharma* (*misai sōyō anryūmon*)

The glass bottle can embrace hundreds of poppy seeds, yet if we observe it closely, each poppy seed is distinct. In the same manner, the gigantic universe contains all the small planets and stars without a single one losing its own identity. (individuality of dharmas)

7) *Aspect symbolized by the realm of Indra's net (Indaramō kyōgaimon)*

According to legend, the great god Indra, had a net woven with jewels tied into a mesh; in the brilliance of the light, each of these jewels reflected each other infinitely. (infinite inter-reflection of dharmas)

8) *Aspect of dharmas to make man realize the universal truth (takuji kempōshōgemon)*

Every existent in the phenomenal world has a potentiality to lead man to Enlightenment, since there is not a single dharma which does not embrace the infinite truth of all. According to Kegon thought, each mountain, river, tree or blade of grass can be the gateway to the realization of Enlightenment.

(potentiality of Enlightenment through a single dharma)

9) *Differentiation of the ten time periods (jisse kakuhō ijōmon)*

Past, present and future were each considered to have three further subdivisions, creating nine time periods; each of these were ultimately embraced within a single moment, making a total of ten periods. These periods in the conventional sense appear to be chronologically separated but in essence are mutually interdependent and interchangeable. All existents of the past, present and future are together within each moment, while still maintaining their chronological order.

(interrelationship of past, present and future)

10) *Harmonious unity between principle and attributes (shuhan enmyō gutokumon)*

Each phenomenon embraces the totality of existence, yet in that relationship the individual phenomenon is the principal, with the totality as its attribute. This role is interchangeable with the principal of one relationship becoming an attribute or part of the totality in another relationship; each dharma possesses the quality of being both principal and attribute. (interchangeability of principal and attribute relationship)

e. *Six Characteristics of the Dharmas (Rokuenyū)*

In order to further clarify the doctrine of the Ten Interdependent Relationships, this theory was set forth approaching the situation from a slightly different aspect; the interrelationship between individual dharmas and the whole in terms of essence, appearance and function, stressing the interdependence of apparently diverse qualities. Each dharma was believed to possess six characteristics: universality, particularity, similarity, diversity, formation and differentiation.

To give an example, these antitheses can be viewed in relation to the existence of a house in the following manner:

1) *Universality* (*sōsō*) The house embraces the combination of beams, roof, walls, floor, etc.
2) *Particularity* (*bessō*) Each beam, plank and roof tile composing the house is separate and individual. Without these individual components acting in harmony there could be no house.

} *Essence*

3) *Similarity* (*dōsō*) When we consider the above two antitheses, we must conclude that in this instance universality and particularity both serve the same purpose, to form the appearance of a house.
4) *Diversity* (*isō*) Despite the overall appearance of house, each of the components differ from each other in individual appearance. The beams forming the floor are each unique and lie in a horizontal row in contrast to the vertical wall beams. Each rooftile has not only a different spatial position but slightly differs in texture and finish.

} *Appearance*

5) *Formation* (*jōsō*) The function of all the components is the formation or completion of the house.
6) *Differentiation* (*esō*) Despite this single purpose, each component maintains its identity by playing an individual role in the overall design. i.e., each rooftile covers its own portion of roof, the beams each have their own individual area to support, etc.

} *Function*

These antithetical characteristics, immanent within each dharma, exemplify the Kegon conception of interpenetration and mutual identity. Each component of any pair of antitheses is demonstrated as totally dependent upon the others for its significance and existence. Without the 'particular' components of an individual house the 'universal' house could not exist (and vice versa), thus the 'universal' is established by the 'particular', or in Kegon terms, the universal is 'mutually identical' to the particular.

The foregoing views relate to the philosophical comprehension of mutual identity and interpenetration of the dharmas, the Kegon also placed emphasis upon the religious realization of the *Dharmadhātu* by the cultivation and practice of virtue.

f. Ten Stages of the Bodhisattva's Enlightenment

The essence of this practice towards Enlightenment is revealed in the chapter of the *Avataṃsaka* known and circulated independently as the *Daśabhūmika sūtra*. It offers one of the most systematic treatments in Mahāyāna Buddhism of the stages (*bhūmi*) leading to Enlightenment[53] and is closely correlated with the ten *pāramitās*, since each stage requires the special cultivation of a particular *pāramitā*. To date, scholars have not been able to agree upon a uniformal interpretation of these stages.[54] The following presents a brief summary of their nature:

1) *Joyful* (*pramuditā*)

Having overcome dualistic thought and attained holiness, the bodhisattva at this stage joyfully assists other sentient beings and practices the first *pāramitā* known as giving (*dāna*).

2) *Purity* (*vimalā*)

Becoming free from the mind that creates the pollution of ignorance and transgression of discipline, the bodhisattva of this stage practices all the *paramita* with special attention to the perfection of discipline (*śīla*).

3) *Illumination* (*prabhākara*)

Obtaining the deepest insight into all things by his meditation, the bodhisattva at this stage particularly cultivates the virtue of patience (*kṣānti*)

4) *Radiance* (*arciṣmatī*)

Emancipated from the conceptualized thought of the previous three stages, the burning flame of realization consumes ignorance, and the bodhisattva particularly cultivates the practice of diligence (*vīrya*).

5) *Nearly Invincible* (*sudurjayā*)

Comprehending all aspects of the truth, conventional and Absolute, the bodhisattva becomes nearly invincible and cultivates the *pāramitā* of meditation (*dhyāna*).

6) *Direct Presence* (*abhimukhī*)

Being able to observe the echo, dream-like nature of phenomena, the bodhisattva surrenders all forms of clinging and arrives at complete wisdom (*prajñāpāramitā*), or the comprehension that 'the Three Worlds are illusionary, merely the creation of one's own mind.' He practices the virtue of wisdom (*prajñā*).

The foregoing six stages complete the upward journey with the arrival at the wisdom (*prajñā*) of Enlightenment. But the process of Enlightenment cannot be completed until this wisdom is applied to the conventional world, hence the next four stages signify the application of Enlightenment to human society by means of compassion. These are the most significant stages of the bodhisattva's career.

7) *Far-reaching* (*dūraṃgama*)

Having completed his transcendence from the conventional world and attained the freedom to enter into wisdom, the bodhisattva overcomes the temptation to reside in serenity and now returns to the worldly activities of salvation and cultivates the *pāramitā* of *upāya* (applying adapted teachings to benefit others).

8) *Immovable* (*acalā*)

Constantly sustained by transcendental wisdom, the bodhisattva spontaneously engages in the work of salvation without conscious effort, and he constantly transfers his merit to others by means of his vows (*praṇidhāna*).

9) *Meritorious Wisdom* (*sādhumatī*)

Able to comprehend by his wisdom, all that lies within the hearts of men, the bodhisattva is able to attain the complete expression of his compassion by preaching, and in this regard he cultivates the virtue of the power (*bala*) of overcoming all hindrances.

10) *Dharma-cloud* (*dharma-meghā*)

Entering into Buddhahood, the bodhisattva attains complete freedom to benefit sentient beings and covers the dharma world just as a massive cloud, able to penetrate its every aspect. He cultivates the *pāramitā* of complete knowledge (*jñāna*).

In contrast to stage 6, which emphasizes the 'wisdom of Absolute negation' (*prajñā*) in the form of the perfection of Enlightenment, this final stage represents the 'wisdom of Absolute affirmation' or the perfection of the bodhisattva's ability to work in the conventional world; this completes the cycle of Enlightenment.

The Kegon sect made extensive cultural and philosophical contributions to Japanese history. Emperor Shōmu was inspired by its grand view of totality to apply its philosophy to national politics and create the *kokubunji* system and symbolically unite these provincial temples under the Great Buddha of Nara. Kegon thought, which represented one of the most profound forms of Mahāyāna philosophy, also exerted considerable influence upon later Buddhist developments, in particular the Zen sect.

B. Other Traditions Existing Within Nara Buddhism

The prevailing current of Buddhism during the Nara period was represented by the Six Sects, but besides these, a number of minor trends were already in embryo that eventually developed into the mainstream of Heian and Kamakura Buddhism. In this respect, the Japanese Buddhism of later periods did not represent new innovations, but rather a process of re-molding and the gradual evolution of thought.

1. Tendai of the Nara Period

In the remaining fragments of the *Hokkeshū-fuhō-engi*, composed by Saichō, founder of the Tendai sect, Prince Shōtoku is listed as the first promulgator of Tendai thought in Japan. This of course represented an attempt to provide the newly established Tendai sect with an advantage over the existing schools by linking it with a great cultural hero, antedating the sectarian movement in Japan. But the reason given to substantiate this claim was the fact that Shōtoku Taishi was believed to be the legendary *keshin* (incarnation) of Nangaku Zenji (Hui-szu) the second patriarch of the Chinese T'ien T'ai sect. Saichō was not the originator of the legend, for by his time it was already popularly known and accepted. It appears to have been first disseminated by one of Ganjin's disciples during the Nara period.[55] Besides this popular legend, the Tendai sect found a natural affinity with Prince Shōtoku on the basis of his alleged commentary on their principal text, the *Hokekyō* (*Lotus sutra*).

Although Shōtoku Taishi's affiliation with the Tendai sect appears to have been contrived, it is clear that Tendai doctrines arrived in Japan with the transmitters of the Ritsu sect. Tao-hsüan (Dōsen) arrived in Japan in 736, and his disciple Gyōhyō (722–797) of the Daianji temple became the master of Saichō. Although Tao-hsüan is principally known for his transmission of vinaya and Hua-yen texts, he had studied both T'ien T'ai and Ch'an Buddhism while in China, and it is most likely that the major works of Chih-I, enumerated in a sutra list dated 750 and presently contained in the *Shōsōin monjo*, were brought to Japan by Tao-hsüan.

Ganjin brought the three major works of Chih-I; the *Hsüan-i*, *Wen-chü* and *Chih-kuan*, to Nara in 754 along with many commentaries. He also imbued his disciples with an interest in T'ien T'ai and many of them, such as Hosshin, who succeeded Ganjin in charge of official ordination, had studied the teachings in China and subsequently lectured on them in Japan.

Another monk of the Nara period instrumental in transmitting early Tendai thought to Japan was Gyōga (729–803) of the Kōfukuji. Gyōga went to China in 753 for the purpose of studying Fa-hsiang (Hossō) thought and spent seven years there devoted to both Fa-hsiang and T'ien T'ai philosophy. When he returned to Japan he brought back a great number of T'ien T'ai sutras and commentaries.

The teachings transmitted by these early monks, in particular by Tao-hsüan and Ganjin, ultimately provided the source for Saichō's introduction to Tendai. And when we consider that Saichō only spent a total of nine and a half months in China, we have to presume that his trip was primarily intended as token in order to establish proper transmission and collect necessary texts. His initial knowledge of Tendai, gained prior to his journey, must have formed the basis for his establishment of the Tendai sect during the Heian period.

2. The Origin of Tantric Buddhism in Japan

The Tantric tradition in Japan prior to its systematization by Kūkai, founder of the Shingon sect, is known as *Kozō mitsu* (Ancient Impure Tantrism). One of the earliest examples of this form of teaching appears to have occurred in the year 577 when Paikche sent a 'magical priest' (*jugonji*) to Japan. From this time on, such priests are commonly recorded as enjoying popularity.

The immediate antecedents of the Shingon sect in Japan were the Sanron priest Dōji (674–744), who studied Tantrism in China and brought back a number of texts with him, and his disciple Zengi (728–812), the instructor of Gonzō (757–827), believed to have been the early master of Kūkai.

Tantric oriented Buddhism actually was a by-product of the official bureaucratic emphasis upon the attainment of superior abilities to benefit the nation by means of profound study. Ostensibly, the philosophies of the Six Nara Sects formed the content of scholastic study; however, this learning was of little avail in meeting the immediate desires and needs of both the aristocracy and government. Priests were expected to have theurgic powers and in their search to obtain them, they naturally turned to esoteric means. This movement particularly gained momentum after the beginning of the Tempyō era (729). Tantric rites were coupled with Shugendō, the ascetical movement founded by the half-legendary En no Gyōja during the late seventh century, that was a syncretism of Taoism, Confucianism, native shamanism and Buddhist Tantrism. A mountain practice center was established at the Hisosanji in Yoshino, where distinguished priests of various sects gathered and called themselves the *Jinen chishū* (Sect of Natural Wisdom). Gomyō (749–834), a prominent leader of the Hossō sect, divided each month between mountain practice and study at his temple. This combination of Tantric and Shugendō practice became quite widespread by the end of the Nara period.

Another impetus towards the growth of Tantric Buddhism evolved from the practice of chanting sutras for the protection of the nation. The *Gokokusambukyō* (Three Sutras for the Protection of the State), consisting of the *Hokekyō* (*Lotus Sutra*), *Ninnōhannyakyō* (*Prajñāpāramitā sūtra* on Benevolent Kings Protecting Their Countries) and *Konkōmyōsaishōōkyō* (Sutra of the Golden Light) all were texts closely associated with Tantric rites. It was thus a very logical step for this form of Buddhism, which had already begun to capture the interest of religious and aristocracy alike by the end of the Nara period, to become the main current of the next era.

3. The Seeds of Zen

The famous Hossō patriarch Dōshō, is known to have studied Ch'an (Zen) teachings while in China. Upon his return to Japan, he established a Zen-in centre in the southeastern corner of the Gangōji temple. There he kept the Zen scriptures that he brought back from China and a number of his disciples interested in meditation used the centre as a place of study. This original sub-temple was later moved to the capital at Nara where it became known as the Heijō-ukyō zen-in.

Tao-hsüan (Dōsen), the vinaya master, also brought Zen teachings to Japan and transmitted them to Gyōhō, the master of Saichō. This probably influenced Saichō to later incorporated Zen meditation within the Tendai sect. But the time was not yet ripe for the development of Zen during the Nara period in Japan. This form of Buddhism was far too individualistic at a time when the government deemed the primary purpose of the new religion was to abet national goals. The ingredients were present, they merely awaited the proper historical moment for development.

4. The Temporary Existence of the Shutara (Sutra) Sect.

Considerable debate has evolved regarding the basis and origin of this sect, which apparently was a Japanese innovation. Many older scholars believe it was based upon the *Nehangyō* (*Nirvana sutra*),[56] or else was a subdivision of one of the Six Sects of Nara such as the Hossō,

Kegon or Jōjitsu. Serious problems arise however, with any of these explanations. Modern scholars generally consider that the Shutara sect was based upon the *Daihannyakyō* (*Mahāprajñāpāramitā sūtras*); their views are based upon the fact that the name Shutara (Chin. *Hsiu-to-lo*) was first used by Chi-tsang in reference to the *Daihannyakyō*.[57]

During the Nara period, three temples hosted the Shutara sect: the Daianji, Kōfukuji and Tōdaiji. At both the Daianji and Kōfukuji, there were two Shutara schools (the Daishutara and Jōshutara). These versions apparently represented the chanting divisions dividing the more than 600 volumes of the *Daihannyakyō*. The Tōdaiji housed only the Daishutara school and there is no indication that temples of older tradition such as the Gangōji or Hōryūji ever had any form of this school. Judging from the size of the Shutara school in the three temples hosting it, the Daianji appears to have been the place where it originated and the Sanron scholar Dōji, who began the *Daihannya-e* (Meetings for the *Mahāprajñāpāramitā sūtras*), is considered to have been the founder.[58] This sect did not survive into later periods.

5. Early Pure Land Thought

It is apparent that Pure Land devotion was present in Japan as early as the Asuka period. The first known reference to the *Daimuryōjukyō* (*Larger Sukhāvatī-vyūha sūtra*) appears in the writings attributed to Prince Shōtoku. Reportedly, the Prince also believed in the Tuṣita heaven of Miroku (Maitreya), which was confused with Amida's Pure Land at this early date. The clearest example of such a mixture is found in the *Tenjukoku* (Land of Heavenly Longevity) *mandara* created in the Prince's memory.

It was quite common for Sanron, Kegon and Hossō priests to study Pure Land sutras, and use them and the concept of Amida as objects of meditation during the early Nara period. In 640, shortly after his return from China, the Sanron priest Eon lectured on the *Daimuryōjukyō* and related works at a *sai-e* (vegetarian repast) held at the Kudaradaiji. Chikō and Reikō of the same sect shared his devotion, and Chikō is known to have created a *Jōdo* (Pure Land) *mandara*.

Although the Pure Land sutras formed popular subjects of meditation and study, it does not appear that the chanting of the name of Amida as advocated by Shan-tao (613–781), who systematized Pure Land thought in China, was practiced in Japan at this early date. The writings of Shan-tao were known during the Nara period however, for a Pure Land depiction of this era contained at the Taimadera presents a painting in the Chinese style of the *Kanmuryōjukyō* (*Meditation sutra*) with Shan tao's commentary. We can only presume that the chanting of the name of Amida was not practiced, because at this date there was still no widespread belief in Amida for the purpose of personal salvation.

Inscriptions such as that found on the Amida triad of the Yamato Shirinji temple dated 659, request happiness for the living and peace for the dead, but neglect to mention any desire for the living to attain birth in Amida's Pure Land. The devotion to Amida appears at this period to have primarily been designed to promote prosperity in the present life and peace for the dead. Exceptions to this general tendency are found in the Mannyōshū poet Yamanoue Okura (660–772)[59] and Lady Tachibana, the mother of Empress Kōmyō (701–760). Empress Kōmyō was also closely connected with Pure Land faith, and on the seventh day after her death, an Imperial edict was issued throughout the country to make paintings of the Pure Land and copy related sutras in every province of the land. The following year, in 761, Fujiwara Nakamaro built a temple in her memory within the confines of the Kōfukuji (the Fujiwara family's main temple), enshrining an image of Kannon and placing a tapestry of Amida's Pure Land upon the wall.

The Pure Land faith could not develop in Japan however, until such a time as it could become generally recognized as a means of individual salvation, rather than a method of putting the dead to rest. It also had to await the proper historical moment when dissatisfaction with the existing world would demand a higher affirmation.

From the many references during the Nara period to Tendai, esoteric Buddhism, Zen and Pure Land,[60] it is obvious that the rise of these sects during the Heian and Kamakura period did not represent the sudden introduction of new thought that attracted public attention overnight. Each tradition had a long history of gradual development in Japan, an incubation period during which they awaited the dynamic leadership and proper social conditions to catapult them into the mainstream of Japanese Buddhism.

C. Political Aspects of Nara Buddhism

1. Ritsuryō Government and Buddhism

Under the Ritsuryō system of government, a pyramid was formed with the Emperor and aristocracy at the head of a vast network of bureaucracy. With the Emperor as titular head of state, his political and religious roles were of prime importance. Thus when the Taihō Ritsuryō code was promulgated in 701, veneration of the Sun Goddess Amaterasu Ō Mikami at the Ise Shrine was decreed. This represented the first time the ancestral deity of the Yamato clan was legally recognized and officially enshrined at Ise under the newly centralized government. There was no question in the minds of the Ritsuryō leaders that the indigenous faith, so closely associated with the Imperial role, was superior to the newly imported foreign religion; still Buddhism could not be ignored and a place had to be devised for it within the system.

The Ritsuryō policy towards Buddhism remained consistent throughout the Nara period and despite the various revisions of the code, the *Sōniryō* (Rules and Regulations for Monks and Nuns) underwent very slight change. It was a curious policy from its inception, for normally under the system, '*ritsu*' referred to penal codes and '*ryō*' to administrative laws. Yet the *Sōniryō* was practically a penal code, containing not only prohibitions but also methods of punishment for transgressions and of its twenty-seven articles, eighteen dealt specifically with the subject of punishment. It is obvious that from the start the established government leaders were concerned about the temporal power of the Buddhist institutions and the progressive faction they represented. The situation was entirely different from the Shintō shrines, which were institutionally weak and disorganized; their *Jingiryō* contained no prohibitions nor punishments and dealt mainly with matters of ritual and festivals. The Ritsuryō leaders did not consider the Shintō shrines to be subject to common law. In this particular aspect, the Japanese departed from their adherence to T'ang Chinese precedents, for the Chinese did not deal so severely with Buddhism, and continually vascillated over the decision of whether or not to accept it as a native religion. They also wavered in firmly deciding to set forth the superiority of common law over monastic law; the Japanese entertained no such doubts, at least not in regard to Buddhism.

One would imagine that the *Sōniryō* as rules and regulations for monks and nuns, might contain articles pertaining to entrance to the priesthood, ordinations and such, but instead they were entirely confined to dealing with the behaviour of those who had already entered the religious life. In particular, they attempted to limit religious activity outside of recognized temples and institutions. For example, an edict issued in 718, was clearly aimed at proscribing the missionary activities of the priest Gyōgi, who during this period was considered to be one of the chief threats to the bureaucratic system.

The government also saw fit to interfere in the lives of individual priests or nuns if it was deemed for the national interest. For instance, in the year 703, the priest Ryūkan was ordered to return to the lay state during the reign of Emperor Mommu because he was extremely talented and had knowledge of the calendar; he was thus too useful to be allowed to devote himself to the religious life. In the government view, a priest was simply a religious individual appointed by the authorities to work for the prosperity and protection of the nation, spiritual goals were completely ignored.

Despite such strict measures and limitations, it is apparent that the government had difficulty from the start in exercising complete control over Buddhism. In 624 Empress Suiko set up the first form of *Sōgōsei* (Bureau of Priests) and this governing body was expanded and incorporated into the *Sōniryō*. The main type of duties these monks engaged in were: the removal of the names of religious who returned to the laity, recording deaths, arbitrating lawsuits, and granting permission to individual religious to change residence, such as to leave the temple for a hermitage. Under the Ritsuryō system, the priests on this bureau were, at least nominally, appointed by the Buddhist sangha itself and this meant they were not actually government officials and could not be treated as such. The government officially had to recognize them as the legitimate representatives of the Buddhist community. The jurisdiction of this bureau was limited to the capital area, in the provinces the governors or other officials assumed the *Sōgō* duties in cooperation with smaller governing bodies bodies belonging to the various temples. But even though the powers of the *Sōgō* were circumscribed; the very existence of the bureau represented a future potentiality for Buddhist autonomy and created a small wedge in the rigid government control.

On the whole, government control was not resented by the clergy, and many priests of the day were quite satisfied in serving as minor bureaucrats at one of the great official temples. In fact, this was one method whereby members of the lower classes could advance socially. The four great official bureaucratic temples that had been foremost in government influence prior to the establishment of the capital at Nara (Asukadera, Daianji, Kawaradera and Yakushiji) continued to exert their authority during the beginning of the Nara period until the building of the Tōdaiji, which became the centre of bureaucratic Buddhism for the remainder of the era.

One of the first challenges to government authority over religious affairs was the arrival of Ganjin. Although he did not overtly defy government control over ordination, his very presence raised the serious question of whether the government could properly decide who was fit to enter the religious life. This problem was not finally resolved until the Heian period when Saichō received permission to build his own Mahayana *kaidan*.

In the view of the government, control over entrance into the sangha was exceedingly important. Whenever monks or nuns decided to enter the order, their individual names were removed from the civil registration and they were granted tax exempt status. The Ritsuryō leaders did not want to repeat the mistake the Chinese had made by allowing such a large portion of the population to enter the religious life that the tax rolls were depleted, with resulting economic chaos.

Ordinations were also considered of particular advantage to the nation. At times of calamities or upon the death of an Emperor, mass ordinations would be held to restore prosperity. For instance, Saichō's master Gyōhyō, was one of more than 700 ordained in the year 741, and Kūkai's alleged master Gonzō, belonged to a group of 1,000 ordained in the fall of 770, each of whom had the character *gon* in his name. Naturally, the government was extremely sensitive regarding the matter of illegal ordinations or what was termed 'privately ordained priests' (*shidosō*), and those who ordained them. The majority of Nara Buddhism fell into the official bureaucratic mold, and the average priest of the day was either content to quietly pursue his studies or else minister to the needs of the aristocracy and government by participating in lavish rituals for the benefit and protection of the nation. Still, there were a few idealists present even during this period who believed the function of religion was to benefit and serve the people in their daily lives. The most outstanding example of such a priest was the controversial Gyōgi, friend of the masses and menace in the eyes of the Ritsuryō government.

2. Gyōgi Bosatsu, a Man of the People

Born in 668, Gyōgi entered the religious life at the age of fifteen, first entering the Asukadera and then the Yakushiji, where he received the *śīla* nine years later and became a disciple of Dōshō and other leading Hossō scholars. In 704, when his mother became ill, he returned to his home and transformed it into a temple. Later he took his mother to a small hermitage on Mt. Ikomayama where they lived up until her death. After that he began to preach and travel in the countryside attracting hundreds and even thousands of followers. Many legends evolved during this period regarding Gyōgi's divine powers and miraculous deeds. It is obvious that he must have had a compelling personality since he was always treated with awesome respect.

During his travels, Gyōgi was credited with building 49 temples (34 for monks, 15 for nuns), as well as countless other projects designed to ease the life of the countryside masses, such as boat landings, bridges, dams, irrigation systems, wells, hostels (imitating the Indian style) and so on. Sincerely interested in the welfare of the people, Gyōgi travelled about at the time when Ritsuryō taxation was most heavily exploiting the populace. His message of spiritual freedom made him welcomed as a saviour and his number of followers probably was not exaggerated. In any event, the Ritsuryō government quickly decided that he was a menace to their authority. The first edict was issued against him in 718, followed regularly by others. As late as 730, after he had already begun to win government acceptance, the *Zoku Nihongi* was still describing Gyōgi as an individual who gathered thousands of people on the outskirts of the capital and spoke words of illusion.

Before the Yōrō period (717–723) was over however, Gyōgi had managed to attact the interest of the aristocracy and his situation began to gradually change. He was invited by Empress Genshō to lecture in 721, and permitted to officially ordain two followers. Emperor Shōmu in particular, developed great respect for Gyōgi and the once outlawed priest rose to become an important figure at the capital during his reign, even playing a significant role in the building of the Great Buddha at the Tōdaiji. Gyōgi's new acceptance, grudgingly granted by the government, possibly reflected the Ritsuryō recognition that it was wiser to have him working within the system.

When Gyōgi died in 748, he was buried at the Ikomayama temple and left behind more than 3,000 disciples. He was the first individual in Japan to be posthumously granted the title of *bosatsu* (bodhisattva) by the Emperor.

Due to the efforts of a few men like Gyōgi, Nara Buddhism managed to exhibit some signs of vitality and stir from its moribund bureaucratic-scholastic condition. It is unfortunate that there were not more priests of such calibre. Yet, the few that there were served an important role by planting the seeds of faith among the common people that could be harvested generations later.

3. Emperor Shōmu and the Kokubunji System

As a means of extending its provincial control, the Ritsuryō government decided to imitate the Chinese *Ta-yün* system of national temples. These had been instigated by Empress Wu Chao in honour of the *Great Cloud Sutra* (Chin. *Ta-yün ching*) at the end of the seventh century in the capitals and prefectures of China in an attempt to legitimatize her succession to the throne. They quickly became the most prestigious bureaucratic temples. The system was most likely proposed in Japan by the priest Gembō, who returned from China in 735.

When a smallpox epidemic threatened Japan in 737, an edict was issued that every province should make an image of Shaka Nyorai (Śākyamuni) and copy the *Daihannyakyō*. This measure apparently did not terminate the epidemic. Then in 741 (13th year of Tempyō), Emperor Shōmu decreed that each province in Japan was to build a seven-storied pagoda and make ten copies of the *Konkōmyō-saishōōkyō* and *Hokekyō* to be enshrined in the pagodas. Also, each province was to establish one official temple of twenty priests to be entitled the *Konkōmyō-shitennō-gokoku no tera* (Temple for the Protection of the Nation by the Four *Deva* Kings of the *Konkōmyōkyō*) and as well, a temple for ten nuns to be called, the *Hokke-metsuzai no tera* (Temple of the Elimination of Sins by the *Lotus Sutra*). Popularly these were known as the *kokubun sōji* and *niji* respectively.

This official establishment of the *kokubunji* system in 741 did not necessitate a massive construction project. As early as the reign of Emperor Temmu (673–686), edicts had been promulgated to have sutras chanted throughout the provinces for the protection of the nation and as a result of such decrees, temples, images and other necessary ritual objects were already present in the provinces. According to the *Zoku Nihongi* (5th month, 15th day), in 716 an edict had been set forth calling for investigation of provincial temples in disrepair, the combination of deserted temples and the correction of the improper use of countryside temples by the local laity. With the subsequent establishment of the *kokubunji* system, these already existing temples were converted into the national temple system.

Just as Empress Wu initiated the Chinese *Ta-yün* system as a justification for a female usurption of the throne, Emperor Shōmu also visualized the *kokubunji* system as a means of strengthening Imperial hegemony. Impressed by the Kegon lecture of Shen-hsiang in 740, the Emperor on his way to visit Naniwa stopped at a Chishikiji temple to venerate an image of Mahāvairocana Buddha, the symbolic expression of Kegon totality. Supposedly it was at that time when he decided to build a grand Birushana (Mahāvairocana) Buddha image as the centre of the *kokubunji* system. His idealized plan relating Imperial hegemony to this Buddha was derived from the *Bommōkyō* sutra, an important Mahāyāna vinaya text of the day, in which the Great Buddha reportedly states:

> I am called Roshana and live in the ocean of the lotus world, surrounded by one thousand petals, each petal being a world, making one thousand worlds. I incarnate myself into one thousand Shaka, one to each of the thousand worlds. Further, on each petal, there are ten billion Mt. Sumerus, ten billion suns and moons, ten billion worlds of four directions . . . ten million bodhisattva Shakas are sitting under ten billion bodhi trees, each of them preaching the *Bommōkyō*, which you asked be taught. The remaining nine hundred and ninety-nine Shaka each manifest ten billion Shaka in the same way. The Buddhas on the one thousand petals are my manifestations and the ten billion Shaka are the manifestations of these thousand Shaka. I am their origin and I am called Roshana.[61]

Emperor Shōmu dreamt of applying such a hierarchical system to Japan with Mahāvairocana as the symbol of national unity; subsequently at the dedication ceremony, he took the religious name of Roshana.

Actually Emperor Shōmu's motivation in building the Great Buddha of Nara as the symbolic centre of the *kokubunji* system is not as idealistic as some writers would have us believe. He primarily visualized the project as a means of reuniting a nation that had become exceedingly restless under the harsh Ritsuryō system. Peasants chafing under heavy taxation were attempting revolts, the priest Gyōgi was the leader of a popular religious movement outside the Ritsuryō sphere, the Fujiwara family was exerting pressure on the throne, and the year 740 coincided with Fujiwara Hirotsugu's rebellion. A plan had to be devised to bring the dissatisfied elements back into the government fold and Shōmu believed the massive project of building the Great Buddha of Nara could be the solution. He was also considering moving the capital to Naniwa, which would not be the first time the Emperor temporarily changed his residence during what tends to be simplistically labeled the 'Nara period'; in all, it was a time of general unrest.

It is difficult in retrospect to assess Shōmu's exact intentions, but most likely they were half political and half a result of true devotion. After all, in 749, just after the casting of the Great Buddha was completed and gold was discovered for the first time in the province of Mutsu as a sign of the Buddha's benediction, Emperor Shōmu became the first Japanese Emperor to declare himself a servant of the Three Treasures (*sambō no yakko*) This represented a very serious move for the titular head of the indigenous faith.

In 743, an Imperial edict was issued to cast the image of Mahāvairocana at Shigaraki near Lake Biwa and the following year the frame was erected; however, in 745, the Emperor decided to maintain his Nara residence, and as a result the initial construction site was abandoned. A new area was selected in the eastern corner of Heijōkyō (Nara) on the site of a temple known as the Konshōji. There the casting began in 747 and was made eight times before it was completed in 749. During this period the temple name was changed to the Konkōmyōji, and finally to the Tōdaiji. In 757, before the gold leaf was finished, a grand dedication ceremony was held with the monk Bodhisena as master of ceremonies and the Empress and full court in participation. The finished statue, seated in lotus posture was fifty-three and a half feet tall and weighed 452 tons.

According to legend, Emperor Shōmu sent the priest Gyōgi to the Ise shrine to receive approval of the Sun Goddess prior to construction, and it is sometimes popularly believed that this event marked the beginning of the *honji-suijaku* (True nature-manifestation) theory, with an identification between the Sun Goddess and Mahāvairocana, the Great Sun Buddha. Actually, this legend appears in works of much later date such as the 14th century *Genkō Shakusho*, after the *honji-suijaku* theory had already been established. There is no evidence at this early date to support such an identification and the *Zoku Nihongi* is strangely silent. However, some attempts were made to reconcile the construction of the Great Buddha with native gods, and it is quite possible a mission may have been sent to the Ise shrine. We do know according to the *Zoku Nihongi* that in the twelfth month of the same year, the Shintō deity Hachiman journeyed from his Usa shrine in the form of a priestess to venerate the Great Buddha. At that time Hachiman became the official protector of the temple and throughout the provinces, *kokubun*-Hachiman shrines were constructed to serve as guardians of the *kokubunji*.

After its final completion in 757, the first year after Emperor Shōmu's death, the Tōdaiji assumed the position of the foremost of the official temples and the Six Nara Sects were systematically arranged within its confines. The completion of the *kokubunji* system and Tōdaiji temple heralded a change in the condition of Buddhism; it had finally achieved the status of a national religion. As a result of this new position, it was also to achieve new economic strength.

At their inception, each *kokubunji* temple had been granted ten *chō* (ca. 24.5 acres) of rice lands. This was regularly increased by further government grants as well as by the encouragement to rich local landowners to donate land as a means of gaining influence with provincial authorities. After the 743 legalization of the development of new lands (*konden*) with special tax-exempt privileges, aristocratic provincial families acquired large landholdings and soon many temples joined their ranks developing their own lands. The Tōdaiji temple eventually reached the stage where it housed 4,000 families as cultivators of its lands, as well as one hundred slaves. The time was at hand, as a result of the Ritsuryō's own ambitious plans, that Buddhist economic and social influence outgrew the system.

4. Rise of Institutional Corruption

The acquisition of wealth and power inevitably brought corruption to the Buddhist institutions. One of the first priests to yield to the temptations of success was Gembō, who had been the fourth transmitter of the Hossō doctrine to Japan.

Gembō was an outstandingly talented individual and it is difficult to assess his true character since he was so greatly maligned by jealous contemporaries. In 716, he went to China and while there his abilities were recognized by the T'ang Emperor, who bestowed upon him the purple robe, symbol of the highest rank for a priest. Once he returned to Japan in 735, with Kibi no Mabi, the well-known scholar, he quickly made an alliance with Tachibana no Moroe, the Minister of the Right. By such influence, Gembō was appointed to the Kōfukuji and received a gift of land from Emperor Shōmu. In 737 he was appointed *sōjō* on the Bureau of Priests and also received the purple robe for the first time in the history of Japan from the Emperor.

At this time a rather unusual incident occurred that has subsequently created considerable confusion among later historians and significantly increased Gembō's notoriety. It seems that the dowager Empress Fujiwara Miyako had been suffering from severe depression for some time and refused all visitors, including the Emperor, her son. According to the *Zoku Nihongi*, after a meeting with Gembō, the Empress was cured and the nation rejoiced, while Gembō was richly rewarded. Since the account is somewhat contradictory and ambiguous in classical Japanese, some historians mistakenly believed that Gembō had seduced Empress Kōmyō, the wife of Shōmu, while others thought that this was the wife of Fujiwara Hirotsugu, Gembō's later enemy.[62] In this particular situation Gembō appears to have been blameless. The wealth he received caused jealousy and resentment as well as serving as a temptation to his virtue; for the *Zoku Nihongi* subsequently reports that benefitting from such great rewards, Gembō ceased acting like a priest.

For some time, Fujiwara Hirotsugu had resented Gembo's favoured position and disagreed with his policies. In 740, when Hirotsugu sent a petition to the Emperor criticizing the problems existing in government, he blamed the national calamities on the activities of Gembō and and Kibi no Mabi. This was probably inspired by their well known worldly life-styles. When Hirotsugu's petition went unheeded, he began a revolt that ended a month later with his death.

It is not clear why Gembō was eventually exiled to Kyūshū in 745, no doubt his unpriestly behaviour and involvement in court intrigues were factors. He died there the following year under mysterious circumstances on the dedication day of the Kanzeonji temple, which ironically had been built in honour of the victory over Hirotsugu. According to legend, just as he was about to enter the temple, something in the air grabbed his body and split his head open. This was popularly believed to have been Hirotsugu's ghost and the story seemed to have developed as a moral tale, depicting the final reward for unvirtuous priests.[63] Most likely Gembō actually was assassinated by one of his many enemies. Although the degree of Gembō's corruption remains equivocal, we do not have to entertain any doubts regarding his contemporary Dōkyō, the most notorious priest of the Nara period.

Dōkyō was a distant relation in the line of Emperor Tenchi and affiliated with the Hossō sect. At an early age he became interested in Tantrism and retired to Mt. Katsuragi to master esoteric rites, such as the secret Nyoirin Kannon practices and astrological ceremonies. He was first brought to court in 752 upon the request of Empress Kōken and received an appointment at the Tōdaiji, where he became a *kambyō zenji* (healing master). As early as 754 he was justifying a government appointment by advising the Empress that since she was ordained, she should surround herself with ministers who were also ordained.

Empress Kōken was an exceedingly devout Buddhist and retired from the throne in 758, in favour of the young Emperor Junnin, a grandson of Temmu. Actually she continued to exercise her control from the background, a common practice in Japan, in accompaniment with the trusted Fujiwara Nakamaro (also known as Oshikatsu). Then in 761, the Empress became ill at her Ōmi palace and Dōkyō arrived to minister to her, curing her illness by means of astrological rites. After this, their relationship changed and Dōkyō had free access to her private apartments. The Empress was a lonely, unmarried forty-five year old woman obsessed with religion. It was a simple matter for an unscrupulously ambitious priest to manipulate her and Dōkyō's meteoric rise to power began from that date.[64] In 763 he was appointed *Shōsōzu* on the Bureau of Priests and the following year the Empress deposed the young Emperor, announcing that in future he would handle only ceremonial affairs. Her action immediately aroused the jealousy of Oshikatsu, who was enjoying manipulation of the throne himself, and he began a rebellion. By 765 Oshikatsu was defeated and slain, the young Emperor exiled to Awaji and Kōken reassumed the throne under the new title of Empress Shōtoku. The same year Dōkyō advanced in rank from *Daijin zenji* (Minister priest) to *Dajō daijin zenji* (Chancellor), a title previously reserved for members of the Imperial family. Finally in 766, Dōkyō was appointed *Hō-ō* (Dharma master), which was probably derived from Prince Shōtoku's alternative title of *Jōgū-Hō-ō*. For Dōkyō and the Empress, this new designation symbolized that he had achieved the same status Prince Shōtoku has enjoyed under Empress Suiko, he now determined government policy.[65]

Dōkyō proceeded to staff the *Sōgō* (Bureau of Priests) with his own loyal disciples and appointed them to other official posts as well. But despite his virtual domination of the government for seven years, few changes were actually made in the bureaucratic system. The Ritsuryō continued to function, albeit in a slightly modified fashion since the roles of Emperor and aristocracy were usurped by Dōkyō and his *Sōgō*. Certain fiscal problems did arise at this time as a result of irresponsible goverment spending on temple building, repair and temple donations, as well as increases in ordination, which removed large segments of productive population from the tax register. It was a unique historical situation; the Ritsuryō government placed ultimate power completely in the hands of the ruler, but it had no provisions for an infatuated Empress. With the death of Oshikatsu, a delight to his many enemies in that age of intrigue, no one was left to restrain her. To prevent such a situation from ever reoccurring in Japanese history, future generations were, with few exceptions, to bar females access to the throne.

The weakness of Nara Buddhism and attitude of the aristocracy were contributing factors to Dōkyō's rise. He willingly performed the miracles expected of him. In 766 for instance, he supposedly found the relics of the Buddha in a Bishamon (Vaiśrāvaṇa) image and the Empress held a celebration. Two years later the *Zoku Nihongi* was to declare the whole thing a fraud.[66] The same account also accused Dōkyō, who was beginning to cultivate staunch political opponents, and his followers of practicing left-handed teachings, a restrained comment upon his riotous life.

As Dōkyō's group became more worldly, other groups of dedicated Buddhist religious, in an effort to escape such secularization, left for the mountains with or without government permission. The climax eventually arrived when Dōkyō attempted to succeed to the throne. By the first month of 767, Dōkyō was already acting like an Emperor and issuing a New Year's edict, and in the fifth month he had a dream that the Shintō god Hachiman at Usa promised the nation would enjoy peace if he were to be made Emperor. The Empress cautiously decided to send the venerable Wake no Kiyomaro to Usa to confer with the deity Hachiman and confirm this dream. Despite pressure from Dōkyō, the reply Kiyomaro brought back was that only a member of the Imperial family descended from the gods was eligible to become Emperor; a subject could not usurp this role. Dōkyō was furious and succeeded in having Kiyomaro exiled and his sister, a nun, returned to the lay state and banished, but Dōkyō's own days of control were at an end. In 770 Empress Shōtoku died and Dōkyō's rising star waned overnight. By 772 he was to die in exile and be buried with common rites. The man who could perform miracles and sought to become Emperor, discovered at last the fragile nature of worldly power.

Dōkyō's role can be attributed to many factors such as the instability of the government, the aristocracy and the Empress, but above all, it represented another manifestation of shamanism, the aspect of the indigenous faith that in the early days allowed the Imperial family to achieve its religious leadership over the other clans and eventually unite the nation. Although paying exterior homage to Buddhism, the aristocracy had not abandoned their old ways nor their belief in theurgy. Dōkyō fulfilled their expectations for he was skilled in the shamanistic arts, having studied on Mt. Katsuragi, which just a half century earlier had been the home of En no Gyōja, the famous shamanistic founder of Shugendō. We can only wonder what might have happened if Dōkyō had been a member of the Imperial family and actually eligible to succeed to the throne?

After the death of Empress Shōtoku and banishment of Dōkyō, Emperor Kōnin succeeded to the throne and began to make some drastic changes. He was faced with an unstable government, campaigns against the Ezo (Ainu) and the immediate need to correct the economy and conditions of institutional Buddhism. In 770, he immediately reappointed the priests to the *Sōgō* that Dōkyō had earlier replaced with his own followers. Kōnin also allowed religious the freedom to take up residence in mountain and forest hermitages. This form of spiritual life was now recognized as a necessary asset to combat the worldliness of the capital priests. Those who already had been illegally living in hermitages were pardoned and welcomed back to the capital where their idealism was sorely needed. Strict government supervision was placed over the Nara temples and their now vast land holdings. The Imperial attitude is best symbolized in an edict issued in the first month of 780, upon the occasion of a Buddhist pagoda being struck by lightning. Formerly when such calamities occurred, the Emperor would cite his own inadequacies to blame, but in this incident, although he admitted he might have been negligent, he placed the major blame upon the improper conduct of the religious.

As a result of the reforms initiated by Emperor Kōnin, the Hossō sect rallied from their initially weak position to dominate scholastic studies at the end of the Nara period, toppling the Sanron. In this respect, the reforms were somewhat successful but the Emperor was not able to further them.

By the third month of 780, the Emperor's entire efforts became centred on quelling the Ezo rebellion in the northern province of Mutsu, and he no longer had time to direct further Buddhist policies. Finally in uncertainty and despair over the deteriorating frontier situation, Kōnin, who was already an old man, abdicated and shortly thereafter died. He was succeeded by Emperor Kammu, who once again directed his energies towards the solution of domestic problems.

One of the first crucial decisions Kammu made after coming to the throne in 781, was to move the capital; that seemed to be the easiest solution. Numerous attempts had been made to move the capital during the Nara period but none were permanent. Kammu decided to transfer the capital to Nagaoka, in neighboring Yamashiro province, believing such a move would benefit ending the Ezo rebellions by lifting the impurity that had settled over the nation. By 785 the palace was completed at Nagaoka and other buildings well along in progress, when Fujiwara Tanetsugu, in charge of construction, was assassinated by the Emperor's younger brother Prince Sawara, who had ambitions on the throne. This was a serious blow to Kammu. Also in 789 the army suffered disastrous losses in the Ezo campaign at Taga castle. It seemed that Nagaoka was not an auspicious site for the new capital after all. By 794, after ten years of mishaps and one of the most politically trying periods during Kammu's reign, he decided the capital at Nagaoka would be abandoned. Upon the advice of Wake no Kiyomaro, who was now restored to Imperial favour, Heiankyō (Kyōto) was selected as the site of what would hopefully prove to be an auspicious capital.

Kammu, up until the move to Kyōto had continued the reform policy towards Buddhism that Emperor Kōnin had originated. Shortly after the transfer, when the new capital did prove to be favourable and Sakanoue Tamuramaro successfully crushed the Ezo rebellions, Kammu was able to turn towards domestic policies and commenced one of the strictest systems of control over Buddhist institutions in Japanese history.

D. Buddhist Interreaction with the Indigenous Faith—Shinbutsu Shūgō

Once Buddhism gained official government support, a natural movement occurred to unite the new religion with the indigenous faith; this is generally known in its early stages as *shinbutsu shūgō* (unification of gods and Buddhas). The government encouraged such a process by supporting the construction of *jingūji* (shrine-temples). Not much is known regarding this gesture but the first mention of such a combination is found in 698, during the reign of Emperor Mommu, when according to the chronicles, the Taki-daijingūji was moved;[67] this implies that their origin was of even earlier date.

Besides the government, numerous other factions supported the development of *shinbutsu shūgō*. Shintō priests viewed it as a means of sharing the lucrative government benefits bestowed upon Buddhism, idealistic Buddhists recognized it as a way to approach the masses and the common people accepted it as a natural phenomena.

One of the first philosophical developments in this movement was a change in the concept of *kami*. With the construction of *jingūji* and the practice of sutra chanting for the indigenous gods (the early histories relate thirty-eight such incidents), it was commonly accepted that the native deities had embraced Buddhism and decided to protect the Dharma. This was an important step for Buddhism.

The assimilation of autochthonous deities as guardians of the faith has always been an important process in Buddhist evolution. During the lifetime of the historical Buddha, the Indian *deva* were accepted as guardians and also didactically utilized as a means of instructing the laity. In this respect they served as a stage of mental conditioning for the reception of further teachings. Superficially it might appear that their role was extremely minor but this was not the case.

The goal of Buddhism has always been Enlightenment, an intuitive experience that transcends discriminative reasoning. As such it cannot be considered an attainment to be acquired by intellectualism. And as long as the goal is achieved, it is not possible to classify one means superior to another, for the process is entirely a subjective matter, depending upon the individual. From the start, the paths of faith and learning have always shared equal importance in Buddhism, although the transmission and clarification of the doctrine by scholars has tended to emphasize and strengthen the intellectual approach. This has even misled some into the false notion that Buddhism is purely an intellectual endeavour, a rational philosophy rather than a religion. From such a standpoint, belief in assimilated deities or even the Mahāyāna Buddhas and bodhisattvas may seem degenerate. What is disregarded is the fact that the attainment of the intuitive goal of Nirvana can just as easily be accomplished by *bhakti* or religious devotion as it can be by philosophical study. In fact, the obvious deities of form can more easily be recognized and ultimately set aside than subtle attachments to abstract gods of thought. The methods of faith versus study do not represent 'lower' or 'higher' paths but merely two different approaches, dependent upon individual needs, to the same goal of Enlightenment. The assimilation of the indigenous *kami* into Japanese Buddhism was not merely an historical accident but an important and essential development in the evolution of Japanese Buddhism.

During the Nara period, the native *kami* began to assume two different attitudes towards Buddhism; the role of guardians to the Dharma, whereby they maintained their independence as gods, and secondly, the role of suffering sentient beings seeking to escape their present condition and attain Enlightenment. Some scholars maintain that the guardian role was politically inspired, while the development of the concept of *kami* as suffering creatures in search of Enlightenment, was a natural process derived from the changing view of the indigenous gods under Buddhist influence, from abstract to humanistic beings.[68] This is an interesting theory, but it is difficult to historically substantiate. Many native gods such as Izanami and Izanagi, the Sun Goddess and her brother Susano-o, and Ōkuninushi no Kami were anthropomorphic from their origination. On the other hand, there is no question that Buddhist influence did increase this tendency. The commencement of iconographic representation of deities unquestionably served to humanize their nature, and there also appears to have been an increase in the practice of granting deceased heroes the status of *kami* at this time. The safest assumption is that the conception of the *kami* as guardians and as suffering sentient beings were both natural developments.

To consider this, we first have to question who was responsible for the propagation of *shinbutsu shūgō* among the common people? As we have seen, the Ritsuryō government carefully restricted the legal activities of Buddhist priests and although regional aristocrats might benefit the *kokubunji* and other Buddhist institutions in the provinces, no real attempt was ever made by the Nara Sects to convert the masses. The main sources of the common man's knowledge of Buddhism during the Nara period were the wandering priests or holy men, who worked outside the sphere of official sanction and more often than not, were extremely eclectic in the various teachings and beliefs that they had acquired. The complex process of uniting the *kami* with Buddhism must have evolved from the local conception of the role of each *kami*, as well as the degree of Buddhist influence present. The inconsistencies present even in the final systematization of the *honji-suijaku* (True Nature-manifestation) theory of the Heian and later periods demonstrate strong regional influences. It is natural to imagine that at this time, the great and powerful *kami* might become the guardians of the local temples, while the lesser *kami*, as they grew more humanized, should be treated as unenlightened gods and instructed in the teachings.

The recorded incidents of both *kami* as guardians and as suffering beings appear to be quite contrived. The most blatant example is the role of Hachiman as guardian of the Tōdaiji, but reports indicate similar calculation. For instance, the *Nippon Reiiki* relates the long story of the priest Eshō of the Daianji temple, who during the era of Hōki (770–80) witnessed the appearance of the Taga Ō Kami in the form of a white monkey requesting to hear the *Lotus Sutra*.[69] The moral of this tale ostensibly is that those who prevent others from Buddhist practice will suffer future retribution such as rebirth as a monkey *kami*. But a number of undercurrents are also presented such as: encouragement to the laity to donate, the right of priests to expect donations in exchange for sutra chanting, the improper use of Shintō shrine lands as the personal property of the Shintō priests, and finally, the punishment that befalls even Buddhist priests who fail to heed the request of a Shintō god (in this case, the white monkey destroys their temple). In brief, the Buddhist author merely used the alleged incident as a means of popularizing his own views. A similar happening was the appearance in 715 of the god Kehi of Echizen province to Fujiwara Muchimaro, requesting a temple be built in order that he might receive the Buddhist teachings and overcome the karma that caused him to remain merely as a god.[70] The priest Mangan, who roamed throughout the countryside preaching and carving images, had a comparable experience in 763 at the Tadojingūji, when the deity of that shrine announced its desire to take refuge in the Three Treasures.[71]

Incidents such as the foregoing suspiciously appear to conceal underlying motivations but sufficient such occurrences are recorded to demonstrate that they had become common practice and reflected the mood of the society. Political inspiration alone would not have been adequate to create such ingrained folk beliefs that surfaced during the Heian period and have survived up to modern times.

The first step in the Buddhist assimilation of the native gods was to treat them as either guardians of the faith or as suffering sentient beings in search of Enlightenment. Later, as the Buddhist institutions began to make a conscious effort to disseminate their teachings among the masses, the movement gained momentum and the *kami* were to be raised to an even higher status with the development of the *honji-suijaku* theory.

E. Lasting Influences of Nara Buddhism

From the standpoint of historical development, it is possible to regard the Nara period as merely representing the transfer of Buddhist institutions to Japanese soil. By the end of the era, the Six Nara Sects remained alien implants apparently exerting imperceptible influence upon Japanese thought. The vast majority of the populace were scarcely aware of the new religion and even the capital aristocracy, who had been most exposed to its teachings, still failed to recognize it as more than a superior form of magic. It is even questionable how many of the thousands of religious ordained by the Ritsuryō government actually understood the basic teachings of the faith to which they had supposedly dedicated their lives. In this respect, despite the creation of massive temples and innumerable images, Nara Buddhism does not appear to have successfully made an imprint upon Japanese society. But if we examine the situation closer, we will find that the kaleidoscope presents another view:

1. Scholastic Foundation

In the first place, although the Six Nara Sects did not convert the masses, nor in fact even the aristocracy to a proper understanding of Buddhism, they did provide the ground-work for the future Buddhist developments that transformed the entire nation. Like a mammoth time capsule, Nara Buddhism introduced to Japan over a thousand years of Buddhist thought and the major elements of future Japanese Buddhism. It was impossible to assimilate such a vast amount of knowledge immediately but with the ingredients present, they could be placed to simmer in the cauldron until they had acquired a flavour to suit Japanese taste. It is not accidental that Nāgārjuna became a patriarch of every new sect of Buddhism introduced during the Heian and Kamakura periods; the study of Nara scholars had provided the foundation stone. They initiated not merely the stimulus to pursue further learning, but completed the basic studies as well, the groundwork for future thinkers. In this respect it is virtually impossible to compare Kamakura Japanese Buddhism with developments in other lands without realizing the inestimable role of the Nara sects in conditioning Japanese thought. For instance, in making a superficial comparison with Early Buddhism, Pure Land thought might appear to offer a drastic monotheistic divergence, but viewed as a development based upon the philosophies of Nāgārjuna and Vasubandhu, Pure Land thought can be comprehended as an evolution *within* the Buddhist tradition. In this respect, the Nara foundation stone is of inestimable significance.

2. Social Impacts

As a vehicle of higher civilization, the influence of Nara Buddhism upon Japanese society is so great that it defies description. All facets of Chinese culture and learning that arrived in Japan during this period were either directly or indirectly related to Buddhism. Prince Shōtoku initiated the practice of sending *kenzuishi* (Sui embassies) to China in

607 and throughout the Nara period missions (*kentōshi* after 618) were continually sent bringing back knowledge that ultimately affected every area of Japanese society.

The origin of the Japanese educational system began in Buddhist temples at institutes such as the Gakumonji of the Hōryūji and with endeavours by famous educators such as Kibi no Mabi (692–775) and Iso no Kami Yakatsugu, who in 780 converted his home into the Ashukuji with a private study centre.

Ganjin is commonly believed to have introduced the art of Chinese medicine to Japan and temples such as the Shitennōji established early *seyaku-in* or dispensaries for medicinal herbs, as well as hospitals and asylums. Dōshō of the Hossō sect and his famous disciple Gyōgi, were the first to disseminate knowledge of civil engineering among the populace by constructing bridges and dams, irrigation systems, wells and highways besides various transportational improvements. Gyōgi is even credited with developing the Arima hotspring and establishing an herb dispensary there. Even farm improvements were stimulated under the tutelage of such travelling Buddhist priests, as well as on the vast temple holdings.

In accompaniment with new improvements for living, came new methods of dealing with death. When Dōshō died in 700, he was the first to be cremated in Japan at his own request. In 703 Empress Jitō was cremated, followed by Emperor Mommu in 707 and the practice became commonly accepted during the Nara period. It well suited Shintō concepts of purification and also served the practical purpose of preserving scarce agricultural lands. Buddhist funeral rites gradually developed under indigenous influence and evolved into the cults of Jizō bosatsu (Kṣitigarbha) and Emma (Yama), popular during the Heian period, as well as stimulating Pure Land thought. But even more important were the gradual changes in social attitudes.

3. Attitudes Towards Life

There is no question that although Buddhist philosophy was not comprehended by the aristocracy and masses during the Nara period, certain basic Buddhist attitudes towards life were assimilated that left indelible marks upon succeeding generations. One such view was the nascent comprehension of the transitory and illusory nature of human life. The last words of Prince Shōtoku were echoed again in two hymns on impermanence found written on the back of a *koto* at the Kawaradera and subsequently included in the *Mannyōshū:*

> Despising the oceans of birth and death,
> I yearn for a highland free from tides.
>
> 3849
>
> In the world many dwell in transitory abodes
> without knowledge of the land beyond.
>
> 3850

Even the renowned courtier and hedonist Ōtomo Tabito (died 731), famous for his poems on wine-drinking and the enjoyment of life, could pause in the year 728 to reflect: "The more I comprehend the emptiness of this world, the sadder I become" (*Mannyōshū* 793). Such views of impermanence represented a drastic change in Japanese thought. Some might believe that Buddhist influence is most clearly represented by the specific mention of the name of a Buddha or bodhisattva, but too often thoughtless references, which appear so abundantly in later literature, display negligible influence. The transformation here reflects a more mature and realistic view of life than the odes of previous days. Buddhism had begun to cast a quiet shadow upon the light, often frivolous love poetry, bringing with it a touch of the bittersweet flavour that permeates Heian literature. It cannot properly be described as pessimistic since the underlying emotion evokes a catharisis; once human impermanence is accepted as a reality, then more appreciation can be directed towards the existing moment. In a certain sense, the attitude reaffirms the indigenous appreciation and sensitivity towards nature. For the human being who had truly accepted the inevitability of his own death as well as the impermanence of his surroundings, becomes free at last to wholly enjoy the present murmur of water in the stream, the sound of birds or the peaceful sunset.

The closeness to nature inspired by the mingling of Buddhism with the indigenous faith went hand in hand with the Buddhist attitude towards the taking of life. The abandonment of hunting for pleasure and meat eating along with the skillful development of vegetarian cooking, became Japanese characteristics. And even in the crowded insensitive atmosphere of a modern industrial society, an inhumanity against a palace swan in Tōkyō or a deer in Nara still is capable of arousing national outrage.

In summary, the Nara period was an important stage of Japanese Buddhism. The imported seed was planted that eventually would ripen and mature into a unique native fruit during succeeding generations. The grandiose temples fell into stagnant corruption and the era ended upon the note of reform, but the Buddhist institutions had learned from their initial mistakes and the need for independence from the government was painfully obvious, although not easily achieved. The reforms had restored some vitality, at least in the Hossō sect, and basic preparations had already been made for the evolution of Heian Mikkyō (esoteric) Buddhism; in short the stage was set.

CHAPTER IV

HEIAN BUDDHISM (794–1185), DEVELOPMENT OF A NEW DIMENSION

By the emergence of the Heian period, the evolution of Japanese Buddhism had arrived at a near standstill. True, there had been a brief flurry of academic activity during the late Nara which continued into the early Heian, but it was not enough to offset the general stagnation that had set in at the close of the Tempyō era. The renewed scholastic activity, primarily found in the Hossō sect, was merely a response to the Kōnin and Kammu reforms and renewed popularity of the Hossō sect in China; it was not a creative spark and destined to soon die out. This does not mean that the Six Nara Sects were not the possessors of a solid core of Buddhist philosophy vitally important for the basis of future growth, but they lacked dynamic and innovative leadership. The ability to respond to government pressure is quite different from the faculty to boldly initiate new directions. Success in the latter requires a certain genius and either a very keen sense of timing or luck to tap the right circumstances. If we compare the two men who ultimately succeeded in establishing new Heian directions, we might say that for Saichō, it was a case of idealistic good fortune, while for Kūkai, a careful timing of the appropriate historical moment.

A. TENDAI SHŪ, The Teaching of the Lotus

1. Saichō, the Founder

Saichō was born in 767 in the province of Ōmi of the Mitsuobi family, believed to have been originally immigrants from China. His father was so devoted to Buddhism that the family home was converted into a temple, and by the time Saichō was twelve, he entered the *kokubunji* monastery of Ōmi, becoming a disciple of Gyōhyō. He received his first ordination at the age of fourteen and in 785, at nineteen received complete ordination as a monk at the Tōdaiji *kaidan.* Up to this point, his life appears to have been quite normal but approximately three months after his ordination, he went to live in a small hermitage on Mt. Hiei.

A great deal of speculation has been made regarding Saichō's reasons for this unusual action. Politically it was a very unsettled period and the Nara sects had not fully recovered from Dōkyō's influence. The Kōnin and Kammu reforms were in effect, and Emperor Kammu had just moved the capital to Nagaoka and embarked upon his ten year period of disasters. Perhaps Saichō was influenced by the general political instability or disillusioned by the formalism and corruption of the Six Sects. It is also quite probable that as a native of nearby Ōmi province, he was already acquainted with Mt. Hiei.

Little is known of the early history of Mt. Hiei, but from its mention in the biography of Fujiwara Muchimaro written by Enkei, and in a poem by Yōshun contained in the *Kaifūsō* compiled in 851, it appears that there once had been a temple on the mountain that already was deserted by the Heian period. It is very likely that Saichō was familiar with the site.

After spending some time in a small hut on the mountain, in 788 Saichō established the Hieizanji temple and carved an image of Yakushi, the healing Buddha, as the central image. Sometime during this period, Saichō began to study Tendai scriptures. As a devoutly religious idealist, he was undoubtedly impressed by Tendai practice as a welcome change from the somewhat sterile theology of the Six Sects. Each of the schools theoretically offered practical application of their philosophy, but the mood of the Nara sects was scholastic rather than devotional. The major practices were magical rites to improve the memory or expand the mind for study, and on occasion to impress the credulous aristocracy. These were not the type of daily devotional exercises contained in the writings of Chih-I, the founder of Chinese T'ien T'ai.

Saichō's isolation in his hermitage on Mt. Hiei did not prevent him from making important court contacts. By this period the more idealistic monks living in such hermitages were viewed more favourably than their worldly counterparts in the cities. A *Naigubusō* (Imperial court priest) named Jukyō upon meeting Saichō, was impressed by his sincerity, and was subsequently influential in having Saichō appointed one of the ten court *Naigubusō* in 797.

In 802, Wake no Hiroyo, son of the famous Kiyomaro, the confidante of Emperor Kammu instrumental in the transfer of the capital, was requested by Emperor Kammu to arrange a Lotus Sutra Meeting at the Takaosanji (present Jingoji temple). More than ten leading priests from Nara were invited with Saichō the main speaker. As a result of this meeting, Saichō attracted the attention of the Emperor and was promised the opportunity to visit T'ang China in order to transmit T'ien T'ai teachings to Japan.

Accordingly, in the seventh month of the year 804, Saichō left the port of Matsuura in Hizen province aboard one of the four *kentōshi* ships that sailed for China. His contemporary Kūkai was aboard the first ship that arrived in Fukien province the tenth day of the eighth month. Saichō's second ship was slightly later, arriving at Ningpo on the first day of the ninth month; the other two ships failed to arrive. Kūkai immediately went to the capital Ch'ang-an, while Saichō proceeded to Mt. T'ien T'ai. The fact that he failed to visit Ch'ang-an while in China, later became a challenge leveled against Saichō by his enemies, to pose as 'a monk who sought the Dharma in China.'

At the time of Saichō's arrival, the T'ien T'ai sect had just completed an important revival under Chan-jan (711–82), the sixth patriarch of the school. Saichō studied briefly under two of Chan-jan's leading disciples: Tao-sui and Hsing-man. He also received instruction in meditation from Hsiu-jan. Just prior to his return to Japan, while awaiting a ship to embark, Saichō met Shun-hsia, Tantric master of the Lung-hsing temple and disciple of Śubhākarasiṃha, and was initiated into esoterism; a fortuitous incident that drastically changed the future direction of Japanese Tendai.

Finally, after nine and a half months in China, Saichō returned to

Japan having successfully gained spiritual sanction for the transmission of the T'ien T'ai school. He brought 450 volumes and 230 sections of Buddhist scriptures with him.

The Tendai sect that Saichō ultimately established in Japan was not an exact copy of Chinese T'ien T'ai; there were a substantial number of differences that increased with successive generations. To begin with, even prior to embarking for China, Saichō had studied Tendai doctrines and been influenced by the version of Tendai set forth by Ganjin and his disciples of the Ritsu sect. He had also been interested in Zen (Ch'an) meditation, acquired from Ganjin's disciples. These studies he continued while in China, adding to them, what became most indicative of the future direction of Japanese Tendai, a fascination with Tantrism (*Mikkyō*). Saichō's subsequent transmission has popularly been termed *Enmitsuzenkai*, referring to Lotus teaching, Mikkyō, Zen and Ritsu (or vinaya). These, in accompaniment with the Pure Land *nembutsu*, were to effect considerable differences in the direction of Japanese Tendai practice.

Another distinct difference between Saichō's version of Tendai and its Chinese parent, was in the realm of nationalism. Chinese T'ien T'ai tended to be universalist and quite apolitical in nature, but in Japan in keeping with the Nara heritage, the Tendai sect played an important role devoted to the protection of the nation. Although it did not have the rigid government restrictions the Six Nara Sects had been forced to endure, the Tendai clearly felt compelled to respond to a national obligation. In his *Kenkairon* (Treatise on Māhāyāna *śīla*), Saichō repeatedly wrote, 'for the sake of the nation chant the sutra, for the sake of the nation, lecture and expound the sutra.' He was also the first to use the stirring nationalistic phrase '*Dainipponkoku*' (Great Country of Japan). The ideal was to preserve and protect the nation and make it into a Buddhaland. Closely associated with this nationalism was an obvious respect for the indigenous deities. When we combine these characteristics with Saichō's belief in the ultimate ability of the *Lotus Sutra* to open the path to salvation during the impending *Mappō* (Degeneration of the

Dharma) period, it is easy to see the basis of the future Nichiren sect's inspiration.

Saichō also initiated certain institutional changes in his version of Tendai. Hitherto in China, the T'ien T'ai sect had been wholly an order of monks, but Saichō visualized a *bosatsu* (*bodhisattva*) sangha embracing both laity and monks; the emphasis of course, remained on the latter. Furthermore, he established two study areas on Mt. Hiei: one related to the thorough teachings of the *Lotus Sutra*, and the second, of equal importance, devoted to Tantric studies. Before entering either area for study, a monk had to receive the Mahāyāna *śīla* and make a vow not to leave the mountain for twelve years. This somewhat harsh regulation was to ensure that Tendai monks avoid the pitfalls of going out into the world without first having obtained adequate spiritual maturity. Initially it enabled Tendai to escape some of the problems of disunity their Shingon contemporaries experienced.

T'ien T'ai in China, which was already permeated with Hua-yen (Kegon) influence, had developed a very other-worldly atmosphere, quite divorced from the practical realities of Chinese society. This attitude was undoubtedly influenced by the concept of 'one equivalent to the many', shared by both schools. The Hua-yen idealistically emphasized Absolute Truth, while T'ien T'ai viewed the synthesis of the many into Ultimate Oneness, but both approaches inspired contemplation rather than social criticism. This aspect was not transmitted to Japanese Tendai. The keynote for Saichō was a spirit of reform, fighting the corruption of the Nara Sects and for the revolutionary establishment of a Mahāyāna *kaidan*. The reasons for this difference were related to the personality of the founder, Japanese social conditions, and the fact that Japan received the Buddhist scriptures in practically complete form. They had an overall view of the philosophical developments and could afford to be eclectic both in doctrine and attitudes.

Other minor Japanese Tendai innovations were in the style of chanting (*shōmyō*) and special pilgrimages in the mountain peaks (*kaihōgyō*), which inevitably led to an affinity with the Shugendō movement. Thus the

Tendai that Saichō transmitted had distinct differences that increased with the passing of time.

In the year 805, when Saichō returned to Japan, Emperor Kammu was critically ill and Saichō was invited to the palace. He held a *keka* (Rite of Repentance) and gained Imperial favour. As a result, the following New Year, the Tendai sect was officially granted its first two *nembun-dosha* (annual priests).[1] This in essence, signified the foundation of the sect in Japan. However, it began upon a rather ominous note-as a reward for service to the Emperor, a servitude to the government was implied as well as the taint of court worldliness.

By the third month of the year 805, Emperor Kammu died and Saichō lost his powerful patron and protector. Kammu was briefly succeeded by Emperor Heizei and in 809 Emperor Saga came to the throne. Eventually, Saichō was once again to find an Imperial patron in the latter, although his relations with court never again became as close as they had been during the days of Kammu.

During the ensuing years Saichō did establish a relationship with his contemporary Kūkai, founder of the Shingon sect. Beginning in 809, when Kūkai arrived at the Takaosanji in the vicinity of the capital, Saichō wrote requesting to borrow some of the rare esoteric texts Kūkai had brought to Japan. At the time Saichō was forty-two and already an established religious leader, while Kūkai, seven years his junior, was still relatively unknown. Saichō's request must have been exceedingly important to Kūkai, since it represented one of the first signs of recognition from the established religious community. The relationship that ensued developed upon mutual need and dissolved when that exigency no longer existed, since the personalities and ideals of the subjects were so disparate. Saichō was extremely idealistic, sensitive and introspective. Humble, as his first epistle to the inconnu Kūkai demonstrates, he was at the same time, adamant in his belief that the corruption of the Nara sects should be reformed. Kūkai, on the other hand, was supremely confident, ambitious, and skilled in the art of compromise. His philosophy, reflecting Shingon universalism, was to embrace all views and attitudes in the belief that ultimately his own concepts would triumph. To Saichō, such willingness to compromise and work with the corrupt Nara Sects undoubtedly appeared insincere and hypocritical. But to Kūkai, Saichō's attempt to introduce Tendai, a sect that in China had antedated Nara Kegon philosophy, must have appeared reactionary and Kūkai adamently refused to accept Saichō's contention that Tendai philosophy and Shingon esoterism were identical. Tendai in China was in a state of decline, while esoteric philosophy represented the newest approach of the day. Kūkai was unwilling to compromise his views in this area.

The difference between Saichō and Kūkai represented a vast personal as well as ideological chasm. But this rather strange relationship did weather a turbulent eight years before it completely dissolved. The beginning of the end occurred on the 23rd day of the 11th month of the year 813, when Kūkai harshly refused Saichō's request to borrow the *Rishushakukyō*,[2] a rare esoteric text, stating that esoteric texts were to be passed on from Master to disciple rather than merely studied theoretically. His refusal demonstrated his intention of ending the relationship, for by this time, with the patronage of Emperor Saga and the religious recognition he had already gained, Kūkai had no further need to pretend friendship. But the relationship did draw on until the rather strange affair of Taihan in 816.

Taihan originally was a monk of the Gangōji temple in Nara, who decided to enter the Tendai sect after meeting Saichō. In subsequent years he became Saichō's most intimate disciple, although he did not display any particular brilliance. In the beginning of the year 810, when Saichō was suffering from ill health, he turned his affairs over to Taihan and early in 812, named Taihan as his successor. This move apparently upset the relationship since it aroused the jealousy of other monks and perhaps damaged some of the close friendships Taihan had already made on Mt. Hiei. As a result, during the sixth month of that year, unable to cope with the situation of Saichō's complete trust and the turbulent other undercurrents, Taihan abruptly quit Hiei leaving a message for Saichō to the effect that he could no longer tolerate his own corruption and sought a period of self-reflection. The astonished Saichō immediately wrote to Taihan imploring his return but to no avail. From the correspondence, it is obvious that Saichō was unaware of any wrongdoing on the part of Taihan and could not understand his motives for leaving Mt. Hiei, which has lead to the general theory that Taihan's departure was caused by jealousy among the monks of his relationship with Saichō.[3] It is not clear, but it is quite possible that the desire to see Taihan once more was an underlying motive in Saichō's request to receive the esoteric *abhiṣeka* from Kūkai at the Takaosanji during the fall of 812. At that time Saichō asked Taihan to attend the ordination and the event marked their first reunion. Early the following year Saichō entrusted Taihan, along with his disciple Enchō, to Kūkai for study. He also wrote to Kūkai's disciples at the Takaosanji requesting that a shrine built for Saichō on the mountain be turned over to Taihan, and that Saichō planned to occasionally visit him there. However all of Saichō's concern and entreaties regarding Taihan were ultimately rejected.

In the last letter Saichō sent to Taihan during the year 816, he wrote as a sorrowful old man of fifty, who found the loss of his favourite disciple one of the most regrettable incidents in his life. He appealed once more in the letter for Taihan to return, reminding him of their *innen* (*karma*), as well as of the fact that the teachings of the Lotus and Shingon were ultimately identical, imploring him to return and work with him to propagate the faith. The reply to this letter was drafted by Kūkai in Taihan's name, announcing not only Taihan's refusal to return to Mt. Hiei but also challenging Saichō's contention that the teachings of the Lotus and Shingon could be regarded as the same. The letter permanently sundered the relationship between Saichō and Kūkai.

The entire incident of Taihan is a strange event in the lives of both religious leaders. Perhaps it does demonstrate the human side of the idealistic Saichō, but at the same time it exhibits a baffling aspect of Kūkai. The man who could so easily compromise in other areas displayed so little patience with Saichō, to whom one would imagine he should have felt some degree of gratitude. It had been Saichō's interest that brought Kūkai respectability in religious circles at a time when he was still unknown. In particular, Saichō's reception of the *Vajra* and

Garbhakośa abhiṣeka's in 812 followed by numerous religious and court luminaries, immeasurably assisted Kūkai's rise to fame. Immediately after this, when Saichō requested to receive the higher ordination as a master of esoterism, Kūkai abruptly informed him that he would require three years of study, whereas Kūkai himself had mastered the material in China in a matter of months. The following year marked Kūkai's refusal to lend Saichō the *Rishushakukyō*, which in effect precluded any further borrowing of texts Kūkai had brought back to Japan. Then finally, we must question why Kūkai intervened in such an unusual manner in the personal relationship between Saichō and Taihan? These are all unanswerable questions. Taihan became Kūkai's disciple but never attained any form of eminence in the Shingon sect. His loss was painful only to Saichō, who the same year, at the age of fifty, decided to leave the capital and Mt. Hiei for the Kantō area.

Saichō's loss ultimately became a source of future strength. When he left the capital, he visited Prince Shōtoku's shrine at the Shitennōji in Naniwa and resolved to carry on the struggle for Tendai independence. In Kantō his activities centered around such temples as the Mitonoji and and Onodera, both under control of Ganjin's leading disciples, who were sympathetic to his cause. He completed the *Ehyō Tendaishū* (Basics of Tendai) which attracted the attention of Tokuichi, a brilliant Hossō scholar of Aizu prefecture. Tokuichi subsequently wrote a work challenging it and the debate began. The hitherto humble Saichō tenaciously sprung to Tendai defence and in 817 wrote the *Shōgon jitsukyō* (Mirrored Reflection of the Provisional and True). The principle argument in this debate was over the merits of the Tendai soteriological concept of *ekayāna* (one vehicle) versus the Hossō *triyāna* (Śrāvaka, Pratyeka Buddha and Bodhisattva careers). This was an important moment in Saichō's life because he finally came to realize the hidden strength contained within his idealistic refusal to compromise, and gained the confidence to press forward his goal of total Tendai autonomy with the establishment of a Mahāyāna *kaidan*.

In the fifth month of the year 818, Saichō boldly announced his intention to abandon the Hīnayāna *śīla* he had received at the age of nineteen at the Tōdaiji, and requested Imperial permission for an independent Mahāyāna *kaidan* based upon the *Bommōkyō sūtra.*[4]

From modern retrospect, the idea of establishing a Mahāyāna *kaidan* does not particularly appear to be revolutionary, but in Saichō's day it was, for it represented a direct challenge to the older established sects of Nara Buddhism as well as a challenge of the government's power to intervene in religious affairs by controlling ordinations. Theologically, the establishment of a Mahāyāna *kaidan* was not a significant matter. Saichō chose to base his *kaidan* upon the precepts of the *Bommōkyō* and the Nara sects argued that this *śīla* was designed for the laity and thus inferior for monks. Institutionally, their pride was injured by the direct challenge to their supremacy and the effort to do something so drastically different by a sect that had barely come into existence, and certainly had not yet proven itself. But from the standpoint of institutional development, the question of who had the power to ordain and grant the *śīla* was of paramount importance; Saichō was in effect requesting the liberation of the Buddhist order from Ritsuryō control.

The Tendai sect had received its legal recognition in New Year 806 with the granting of two official *nembundosha*, but Saichō believed that the school could never be truly independent until it had the right to control the ordination of its priests. In fact, in his *Kenkairon*, (Treatise on Mahāyāna *śīla*), he even went so far as to urge the elimination of all government control over the Buddhist order, to be replaced by self-government.

Undoubtedly there were also practical considerations motivating Saichō in his desire to establish a *kaidan*. The Tendai sect had lost a large number of aspiring priests during the period of their brief sojourn in Nara for final ordination. According to the Tendai records of ordained priests between 807 and 818, twenty-four priests were ordained in Nara from Mt. Hiei, of these only ten returned to Tendai, two dropped out for natural causes, but twelve went to the Hossō school in Nara.[5] Immature religious were very apt to be swayed by the worldliness and sophistication of the Nara Sects, who promised more glamorous immediate careers than the isolation of twelve years on Hieizan. It was difficult enough to attract worthy disciples, there was no point in needlessly exposing them to the temptations of the old capital before they were spiritually prepared.

Upon receiving Saichō's petition, the court consulted the Nara *Sōgō* whether the Tendai sect should be permitted to build a *kaidan* and they bitterly opposed the idea. The Tōdaiji priest Keijin composed a text listing twenty-eight errors Saichō allegedly made in his proposal. Baffled over the dilemma, the court turned the *Sōgō* response over to Mt. Hiei, and at that time Saichō wrote the *Kenkairon* and also submitted other works to counter the criticism. At the time of Saichō's death, the court remained unresolved as to how to handle the situation, but seven days after his death, the Bureau of Ministers decided to approve his request.

Although Saichō did not live to see his dream fulfilled, the ultimate success of his order vindicated his long struggle. It had been a labour that physically and mentally depleted him, and on the fourth day of the sixth month of the year 822, he died at the Chūdō-in on Mt. Hiei at the age of 56.

The twenty-sixth of the first month of the following year, the main temple of Hieizan was officially granted the title of Enryakuji and the first Tendai ordination was held there. Forty-four years after his death in the year 866, Saichō was the first person in Japanese history to be granted the posthumous title of *Daishi* (Great Master) by his admirer Emperor Seiwa, and became Dengyō Daishi to posterity.

Saichō's idealistic commitment founded the Tendai sect in Japan and established its independence by obtaining the right to build a Mahāyāna *kaidan*. It is unfortunate that in future generations the school was to depart from the founder's ideals by becoming aristocratic and eventually fall into institutional corruption. But despite the late Heian decline of Tendai, one of the greatest contributions of Saichō and his Mt. Hiei in the overall development of Japanese Buddhism, was the role Tendai assumed as the nourishing ground for the future spiritual leaders of the Kamakura period.

2. Historical Transmission

Chih-I had established two forms of devotional transmission for the T'ien T'ai sect in his introduction to the *Chih-kuan*, in which the teachings were traced back to the historical Buddha. But Saichō preferred what he termed a system of 'Textual transmission' for the Japanese Tendai school, commencing with Nāgārjuna, the founder of Mahāyāna Buddhism, and progressing through the master-disciple relationships that culminated with Saichō's own official reception of the teachings. The following is Saichō's version of Tendai transmission:

Nāgārjuna			
Sūryasoma	transmitters and translators of Nāgārjuna's writings and the *Lotus Sutra*		
Kumārajīva			
Hui-wen	(550–?)	technically the first Chinese founder	
Hui-ssu	(514–77)		
Chih-I	(538–97)	Popularly considered the founder and first patriarch since he was responsible for systematizing the doctrine of the sect.	
Kuan-ting	(561–632),	who compiled the three great works of Chih-I and is considered the second Chinese patriarch	
Chih-wei	(?–680)	third patriarch	Dark Ages of T'ien T'ai
Hui-wei	(634–713)	fourth patriarch	
Hsüan-lang	(633–754)	fifth patriarch	
Chan-jan	(711–82)	sixth patriarch and reviver of the school	
Tao-sui	(dates unknown)	seventh patriarch and Saichō's master	
Saichō	(767–822)		

3. Textual Basis

When Saichō transmitted the Tendai sect to Japan, the basic text for the school was the *Lotus Sutra* (Skt. *Saddharmapuṇḍarīka sūtra*), popularly known in Japanese as the *Hokekyō* (full title, *Myōhōrengekyō*). As translated by Kumārajīva during the late fourth or early fifth century, the sutra is composed of twenty-eight chapters. The first fourteen relate to the teaching of the historical Buddha as *upāya* (adapted teachings) for the purpose of leading all forms of sentient beings to Enlightenment. Chih-I entitled this, 'the section of Manifestation' (Jap. *Shakumon*). The Tendai emphasis was placed upon this half of the sutra, since it dealt with the means of realizing universal Enlightenment. The second half of the sutra, designated by Chih-I as 'the section of Origin' (*Honmon*), dealt with the essence of the teachings, idealized as the *Dharmakāya* in the form of an Eternal Śākyamuni, of which the historical Buddha was revealed to be but one manifestation. The inseparability of the Origin (Absolute Truth) and its manifestations, was ceaselessly reiterated by Chih-I.

In China, the T'ien T'ai sect was initially known as the Lotus school prior to assuming the popular name of its place of location, due to its complete reliance upon the *Lotus Sutra*. But in Japan, as the influence of Mikkyō (esoterism) increased, the *Lotus Sutra* gradually became eclipsed by the *Dainichikyō* (*Mahāvairocana sūtra*) until during the period of Annen (died 889 or 897), the latter was declared to be the superior text. As the Mikkyō influence once again waned, the *Lotus* resumed its dominant position. Other texts closely related to Tendai doctrine were the following:

Daihatsu nehangyō (*Mahāparinirvāṇa sūtra*)
Important to Tendai for it discloses that all sentient beings possess a Buddha nature (capacity for Enlightenment) that can be revealed by the practice of an ethical life.

Daihonhannyakyō (*Mahāprajñāpāramitā sūtra*)
Presents the interrelationship of the teachings of *ku* (emptiness), *ke* (temporary existence) and *chū* (middle way).

Bosatsu yōrakuhongōkyō (*Chin. P'u-sa-ying-lo-pen-yeh-ching*)
Sets forth the three views of *ku*, *ke*, *chū*.

Besides these, the *Daichidoron*, which was a commentary on the *Daihonhannyakyō* attributed to Nāgārjuna, and the three works of Chih-I devoted to the *Lotus Sutra* consisting of:

a. *Hsüan-i* (Jap. *Gengi*)—exposition of the meaning of the sutra.
b. *Wen-chü* (*Mongu*)—textual commentary.
c. *Chih-kuan* (*Shikan*)—manual for religious contemplation

were the basic texts of the sect, although since the Tendai maintained the doctrine of the Five Periods and Eight Teachings, they recognized all Buddhist texts as holy scriptures.

4. Classification of Teachings

In the Mahāyāna tradition, Chih-I created a classification of the development of Buddhist teachings to designate the philosophical position of the Tendai sect. This classification was somewhat unique in that it divided the life and activities of the historical Buddha into five chronological periods and the teachings themselves into eight varieties:

Five Periods

a) Time of the *Avataṃsaka*, immediately after the Enlightenment of the Buddha, when he taught the essence of his Enlightenment but was unable to be understood by his disciples. Comparable to the sun at dawn, whose rays touch only the highest mountain peaks.[6]

b) Time of Deer Park, when he preached the *Nikāyas*. This was also known as the time of 'inducement' or 'attraction' since the purpose of the teachings was to prepare the disciples for Mahāyāna. The sun at a point that illuminates the lowest valleys and canyons.

c) Time of the *Vaipulya*, when the Hīnayānists were converted to Mahāyāna. Sutras such as the *Vimalakīrti nirdeśa* and *Laṅkāvatāra* were preached. Comparable to the sun at 8 a.m., the time of the monk's meal.

d) Time of *Prajñāpāramitā*, when the doctrine of *śūnyatā* was emphasized. Comparable to the sun at 10 a.m.

e) Time of the *Saddharmapuṇḍarīka* and *Mahāparinirvāṇa Sūtras*. The *Lotus Sutra* was considered to be the supreme doctrine taught by the Buddha uniting the temporary teaching of the three vehicles (Śrāvaka, Pratyeka Buddha and Bodhisattva) into one vehicle. The ultimate objective of these five periods was to lead the Śrāvakas to the perfect teachings of the *Lotus*. The *Nirvana sutra* served as a resumé of the previous teachings and source of Enlightenment for those not included in the *Lotus*. Comparable to the sun at high noon, which illuminates the entire earth without distinction.

Eight Teachings

The first four doctrines are classified according to the method utilized in preaching (*kegishikyō*):

a) *Sudden Doctrine* (*ton*). The direct and penetrating method used when the Buddha teaches what he has conceived without adaptation to the audience (*upāya*). This is equivalent to the Time of the *Avataṃsaka*.

b) *Gradual Doctrine* (*zen*). The Buddha uses various *upāya* to induce his hearers into deeper thought. Time of Deer Park, *Vaipulas* and *Prajñāpāramitā*.

c) *Mystic Indeterminite Doctrine* (*himitsu*) Both mystical and indeterminite since the hearers are often concealed from each other by the Buddha's power and each believes he is being preached to alone. This method and the following are applicable to the first four periods, the Time of the Lotus transcends all four of these methods.

d) *Indeterminite Doctrine* (*fujō*) Non-mystical, yet although the hearers are aware they are listening together, each understands differently.

The next four doctrines relate to the nature of the teachings (*kehō*).

a) *Doctrine of the Three Piṭakas* (*zōkyō*) or Hīnayāna scriptures and related works that set forth an inferior form of *śūnyatā*.

b) *Doctrine Common to All* (*tsūgyō*). Common to the three vehicles and also an elementary doctrine of Mahāyāna. The *Prajñāparamitā sūtra* is most representative of this category.

c) *Distinct Doctrine* (*bekkyō*). Pure Mahāyāna and special to superior bodhisttvas. The bodhisattva views the three truths of Tendai (*kū*, *ke* and *chū*) separately or distinctly, progressing from Emptiness (*kū*) to the temporary (*ke*) and finally arriving at the Middle Way (*chū*). The *Avataṃsaka Sūtra* is most representative.

d) *Round Doctrine* (*engyō*), meaning the 'complete', 'perfect', 'all-penetrating', 'all-permeating' doctrine. The teaching of the principle that one dharma contains all the dharmas or 'the one is all and all is one.'

5. Threefold Truth (*kū, ke, chū*)

One of the key concepts in Tendai thought was the establishment of a threefold category of truth. This was an endeavour to transcend the dichotomy of the traditional Mahāyāna twofold truth (Absolute and relative) with its inherent dangers of elevating one at the expense of the other, and to set forth a synthesis in the form of the middle way. The philosophical basis for the origin of this idea is found in Nāgārjuna's *Mūlamadhyamakakārikā:*

> We declare that whatever is relational origination is *śūnyatā*. It is a provisional name (i.e. thought construction) for the mutuality of being and, indeed, it is the middle path.
>
> Chap. XXIV verse 18[7]

In other words, *śūnyatā* is equated with *Pratītya-samutpāda* and this is declared to be the middle path (*madhyamā pratipad*) or a temporary name for the expression of truth. Chih-I developed the thought in the following manner:

a) *Follow the temporary and enter into the realization of Emptiness* (*kū*). This awareness does not mean the acceptance of either the temporary or Emptiness as actual entities, nor does it mean the total abandonment of the one for the other. Emptiness is to be discovered within the relative world for it is identical to the temporary.

b) *Follow Emptiness and Enter the Temporary* (*ke*). Which stresses the movement from the realization of Enlightenment to actual functioning in the temporary world. But this step alone has an inherent danger of corruption if a return to the experience of Emptiness is not regularly effected.

c) *This is the Middle Way* (*chū*). The ideal balance between the realization and the actual application.

6. Ten Aspects of Existence (jūnyoze) and the Ten Stages of Man (*jikkai*)

The Ten Aspects or 'suchnesses' of existence form the basis of the popular Tendai concept 'one thought is three thousand worlds' (*ichinen sanzen*). The origin of the Ten Aspects is found in the Kumārajīva translation of the second chapter of the *Lotus Sutra* and since the complete listing does not appear in any other version of the text, it most likely represents an addition composed by the translator.

Based on the theories of *Pratītya-samutpāda* and *śūnyatā*, the Ten Aspects represent the manner in which the Enlightened One views the rise, fall and change of the dharmas. The aspects were applied by Chih-I to the viewing of all forms of existence embracing Enlightenment and ignorance, phenomena and principle, conventional and Absolute alike. The aspects are presented in the following cycle:

Potential

1) *Sō*—External appearance
2) *Shō*—Internal characteristics
3) *Tai*—Total body combining external and interior aspects

Manifestation

4) *Riki*—Inherent ability or power
5) *Sa*—Function
6) *In*—Direct cause or origin
7) *En*—Indirect cause, or circumstances and conditions

Present Result

8) *Ka*—Result of direct and indirect causes
9) *Hō*—External manifestation of result as a tangible fact

Consistency and Unity of Cycle

10) *Honmatsu kukyō*—Interrelatedness and consistency of former nine aspects. Essence of the aspects as *śūnyatā* (*kū*), which leads to the temporary (*ke*) and resides in the middle way (*chū*).

Chih-I interpreted the Ten Aspects of existence in four different manners: 1) as relating to the Ten Stages of Man (*jikkai*), 2) as applying to the Buddha's world (from the standpoint of Enlightenment), 3) as representing separation and unification (Absolute and conventional), and 4) as ten ascending stages of religious practice.

The Ten Aspects are linked to the Ten Stages of Man to form the Tendai concept of '*three thousand worlds*'. The Ten Stages consist of the traditional Buddhist Six Existences (hell, *preta*, animal, *asura*, human and *deva*) plus four Mahāyāna additions (Śrāvaka, Pratyeka Buddha, bodhisattva and Buddha). According to the Tendai view, these stages or psychological realms are mutually inclusive, each realm contains within it the other nine stages.[8] For example, the individual who may psychologically reside in hell, bears within him all the higher potentials for goodness ranging up to Buddhahood. In fact, the Tendai view of the *icchantika*, was simply an individual who had exhausted the ability to manifest his inherent goodness in actual practice. Likewise, the Buddha was regarded as an individual who had exhausted or overcome his ability to practice evil; as a human being, he still possessed human desires. In fact, if he completely lacked any potential for evil, he would not have any need to exercise virtue. Evil and goodness were considered to be mutually complementary, since a world lacking evil would also be devoid of goodness; just as Enlightenment and ignorance are complementary in Buddhism. The Buddha was believed capable of utilizing the knowledge of his own evil desires to assist others towards Enlightenment.[9] Although this view is theologically sound, the thought that a Buddha could possess inherent evil disturbed many devotional critics and potentially had danger of misinterpretation by those who would carry it to the opposite extreme. The subject created considerable controversy in Japan, particularly during the Tokugawa period, when the Jōdo priest, Fujaku Tokumon (1707–81) challenged it.

The Tendai view of '*three thousand worlds*' is formed by these ten realms with their mutually inclusive domains (each realm possessess the other ten, thus there are one hundred realms). These in turn are respectively viewed from the Ten Aspects of Existence (creating one thousand realms). Finally, each is further subdivided into: 1) subjective entity, 2) Five psycho-physical constituents, and 3) container world, making a grand total of three thousand realms.

The 'one-thought' (*ichinen*), which embraces these three thousand worlds refers to the most minute microcosm and may represent a fraction of a second of time, or a particle of space or temporary matter. The totality of the macrocosm is embraced within that infinitesimal real by the expression '*one thought is three thousand worlds*' (*ichinen sanzen*)

7. Concentration and Insight—*Shikan*

The form of meditation devised by Chih-I and imported to Japan by Saichō is known as *shi* (Skt. *śamatha*, tranquility or concentration) *kan* (*vipaśyanā*, right knowledge or insight), which means the 'immovable mind functioning in wisdom.' Chih-I applied the threefold Tendai truth to this meditation and the result was known as the *sanshi-sangan*. To give an example, the *sanshi* consisted of the following:

a) *Taishinshi*—to experience the truth of *śūnyatā* in this body and reside in it.
b) *Hōben zuienshi*—in accordance with direct and indirect causes or circumstances, to practice *upāya* in the midst of temporary existence.
c) *Soku nihenfunbetsushi*—to abandon either extreme of the foregoing and reside in the middle way.

These stages were explained chronologically but meant to be experienced simultaneously. The *sangan* were quite similar.

In actual practice, the *shikan* were divided into four varieties of meditation based upon the physical posture utilized in each form. These consisted of the following:

a. Jōza sammai—Perpetual sitting

To practice sitting for ninety days, during which the devotee physically faces the image of the Buddha in the lotus posture and assumes silence while meditating on reality as-it-is. When he becomes tired, ill or drowsy and can no longer silently meditate, he is allowed to chant the name of a single Buddha as a means of focusing the mind. Since the meditation consisted only of sitting, it is also known as the *ichigyō sammai* (meditation of one practice). It is based upon the *Monjusetsuhannyakyō* and *Monjumonhannyakyō* sutras.

b. Jōgyō sammai—Perpetual Practice (Walking)

In this form, the principal image was Amida and the meditation consisted of chanting the *nembutsu* for ninety days while circumambulating the image. Since the practice was believed to result in the visualization of the Buddhas of the Ten Directions, it is also known as the *Hanju* or *Butsuryū sammai*. It is based upon the *Hanju sammaikyō* and became the origin of Pure Land Buddhist development in Japan. During the meditation, the devotee either focuses his mind upon the Pure Land or Thirty-two marks of the Buddha.[10]

c. Hangyō hanza sammai—Half-walking, Half-sitting

Based upon the *Daihōtō daranikyō* and *Lotus Sutra*. Seven days are devoted to the first text and three periods of seven days (21 days) to the latter. During the first seven days, the devotee walks around the image of the Buddha, chanting the esoteric *dhāraṇī* and upon completion, sits in meditation. During the next twenty-one days, he spends his time venerating the Buddha, chanting the sutra and in particular, practicing repentance for his false notions of reality.

d. Higyō hiza sammai—Non-walking, Non-sitting

This form of meditation was practiced in daily life without restrictiions upon physical posture. The devotee could be walking, sitting, eating or lying down. Generally the meditation was of two varieties: sutra chanting, in particular the *Shōkannongyō*, or practicing ethical meditations upon the nature of good, evil and neutral.

In Japanese Tendai, the principal images for these various meditations differed in accordance with the vocal transmission of master to disciples, but generally, when the four varieties were practiced separately, the principal image for each consisted of the following:

Jōza sammai......Monju (Mañjuśrī)
Jōgyō sammai......Amida (Amitābha)
Hangyō hanza sammai......Fugen (Samantabhadra)
Higyō hiza sammai......Kannon (Avalokiteśvara)

When all four meditations were practiced together in one place, Amida was usually the principal image. In Tendai temples the most popular name for the meditation hall was the Jōgyōdō or Hokkedō. On Mt. Hiei, the Jōgyō sammaidō meditation hall built by Ennin in 848 became the major place of inspiration for the evolution of Japanese Pure Land Buddhism and later several other halls of the same type were built upon the mountain.

In preparation for these meditations, the monks carried out certain practices in daily life that were believed to condition the mind. These were known in Tendai as the twenty-five *upāya* and were broken down into five categories:

1) *Establishing the Five Causes* (*gugoen*)
   a) to control oneself, keep pure and maintain discipline
   b) to keep clothing and food in order
   c) to attempt to reside in a quiet environment
   d) to avoid miscellaneous affairs
   e) to make good friends
2) *Control of the Five Desires* (*kagoyoku*)
   sight, sound, smell, taste and sensation
3) *Elimination of the Five Hindrances* (*kigogai*)
   greed, anger, torpor, instability and doubt
4) *Control of the Five Affairs* (*jōgoji*)
   food, sleep, physical body, breathing and mind
5) *Practice of the Five Dharmas* (*gyōgohō*)
   a) intent
   b) endeavour
   c) to increase one's profundity of thought
   d) using one's wisdom well
   e) completing one's objectives

These were all actions to be practiced in daily life in order to prepare the mind for meditation. The meditations themselves had progressive stages with special subject matters designated in accordance with the individual's spiritual progress.

Ten Subjects of Meditation

1) Objects of daily life—to still the mind of the beginner
2) Human desires
3) Illness and the infirmities of the flesh
4) The manifestations of karma

5) Hindrances to Enlightenment
6) Dangers encountered in meditation (improper states, etc.)
7) Views acquired through meditation (testing their validity)
8) Pride (in one's own spiritual progress)
9) Hīnayāna state (false pride, opinions and such held by religious)
10) Dangers of the bodhisattva (who is submerged in working in the temporary world and apt to forget the spirit of *śūnyatā*)

Ideally, by following these guidelines, the individual should be able to be continually aware of his own spiritual level of advancement. Besides the foregoing subjects of meditation designed to assist spiritual progress, there were also ten interior characteristics to be maintained with each level of meditation. These were known as the *Jūjōkanbō* (Observation of the ten vehicles leading to Enlightenment). They ranged from: 1) the continual interior practice of *ichinen sanzen* or seeing the entire macrocosm in each dharma, 2) the continual practice of compassion, 3) the practice of constant tranquility, 4) freedom from clinging, 5) proper judgement of good and evil, 6) experimentation in actual life with the fruits of meditation, 7) eliminating hindrances by ethical practices, 8) constantly keeping aware of one's spiritual state and not falling into either the extreme of pride or an inferiority complex, 9) keeping the mind unmoved and stable at the next to highest level of meditation, and finally, 10) upon reaching the goal of perfection in a meditation, not to cling to it, since meditation should be regarded merely as an *upāya* itself.

In this manner the Tendai sect attempted to place equal emphasis upon practice and theory. Contrasted with the Nara stress upon scholastic studies, the Tendai applied their theory practically to daily life.

8. Taimitsu and Further Developments

Saichō's encounter with Tantric Buddhism in China had been quite fortuitous and as a result, he did not have time to gain either a thorough knowledge of the subject nor adequate texts to enable him to pursue his studies upon his return to Japan. Nevertheless, shortly after Saichō's return from China, he held an *abhiṣeka* or initiation ritual at the Takaosanji upon the request of Emperor Kammu. At that time Mikkyō (esoterism) became officially regarded as an integral part of the Tendai sect, but it still lacked a clear position. Theoretically, Saichō gave the Tantric teachings equal status with the *Lotus Sutra* by dividing Mt. Hiei into two study areas and assigning one of the two official *nembundosha* to study the subject. But Saichō did not live long enough to even systematize the exoteric teachings he had brought to Japan, let alone work out a clear relationship with Tantrism. At his death his followers were left in a dilemma, although ultimately decided advantages developed from the situation.

Saichō had attempted to incorporate the philosophy of the Nara Buddhist sects as well as esoteric thought under the mantle of the Lotus and Tendai *ekayāna*. Although the system was never completed, it was sufficient to offer a theological challenge as well as ample room for development by future scholars. Such eclectic freedom in conjunction with the stimulating intellectual atmosphere of Mt. Hiei, allowed the Tendai sect to become the mother of Kamakura Buddhism. Eisai, Hōnen, Shinran, Dōgen and Nichiren all were scholars on the mountain before initiating their own schools of Buddhist thought. And although Saichō's contemporary Kūkai disdained such emphasis upon theory over practice, the difference in viewpoint between the two schools resulted in the final triumph of Tendai. In their attempt to grant equal status to theory and practice, Mt. Hiei succeeded in becoming a thriving intellectual centre, whereas Kōyasan declined into a sacred mountain of religious practice with secret transmission from master to disciple. During his lifetime Kūkai completed the systematization of Shingon doctrine, there were few advances remaining for his disciples to make. The emphasis turned away from doctrine and as a result the danger crept in that the Tantric rituals would degenerate into worldly theurgic practices just as in the early days of Buddhism in Japan. In contrast, Tendai Taimitsu managed to continually maintain a strong emphasis upon doctrine. Both sects equally faced the problems of institutional corruption arising from affluence and aristocratic patronage, but the Shingon became slightly more susceptible due to their neglect of doctrinal study. Although Saichō's attitude towards study and the incompleteness of his system ultimately benefitted the Tendai sect, it did create a desperate situation immediately following his death.

Gishin (781–833) succeeded Saichō and became the first official Tendai abbot in the sixth month of 824. He had been ordination master in 823 when the first fourteen disciples were ordained on Tendai's Mahāyāna *kaidan*. But Gishin did not have time to worry about the systematization of Tendai doctrine; his principle concern was the financial survival of the institution and a solution for the poverty of the monks.

Despite Saichō's desire for the autonomy of his sect, he had ardently sought acceptance by the Ritsuryō government, since that was the established means of financial support for Buddhist institutions. But by the Heian period, the Ritsuryō government itself was in decline. The imported system of land nationalization and taxation had failed and as a result, the government faced a shortage of funds. Manorial estates (*shōen*) with tax exempt privileges, owned by the aristocrats had sprung up throughout the country and gobbled up land from the tax rolls; the older established temples and shrines built up their own *shōen* as means of support. It was a trying time for a new institution to attempt to establish a financial footing. The Fujiwara family, who dominated the government during the late Heian period, were among the worst transgressors of the Ritsuryō system. Yet despite the failure of government to raise revenue, the court glittered in abundant wealth derived from the income of the aristocrat's tax-free *shōen*. It took some time before the Tendai sect became aware of the potentiality of aristocratic patronage, and more time elapsed before they could convince the aristocrats to sponsor them.

During the lifetime of Saichō, certain relationships had already begun to be forged between Tendai and the aristocrats; his biography lists twenty-eight bureaucrats and patrons of the temple. But when Tendai consciously began to seek the assistance of the aristocracy, they quickly realized the key to attracting their interest was esoteric Buddhism and in this area, Tendai sadly lagged behind Shingon. In desperation during the year 831, a senior monk Enchō, who subsequently succeeded Gishin as the second abbot, submitted a request to Kūkai together with twenty-six direct disciples of Saichō to receive instructions in Tantrism. At this point, Tendai Taimitsu (Tantrism) was so inferior to that of the Shingon school, that Saichō's disciples evidently suffered from a severe sense of inferiority and sought to remedy the situation. Another attempt was to send their most outstanding scholars to China to study and ultimately this method succeeded in 846, the year which marked the cessation of Tendai financial struggles and the return of Ennin, after completing nearly ten years of study in China.

Ennin (794–864) had entered Mt. Hiei and become a disciple of Saichō's at the age of fifteen. He was only twenty-nine when Saichō died but had become one of his trusted disciples. In the sixth month of the year 838, he left with a group of *kentōshi* sent from Hakata, this was the last embassy from Japan to embark for T'ang China. When Ennin arrived, he requested government permission to make a pilgrimage to Mt. T'ien T'ai, but the Buddhist situation had already deteriorated to such a state in China that he was refused. The following year he resignedly decided to return to Japan but when his ship made a stopover, he was allowed to land at Hai-chou and with difficulty, made his way to Mt. Wu T'ai, the home of Mañjuśrī and esoteric arts, where he was able to study Tendai doctrine. In the eighth month of the year 840, he arrived at Ch'ang-an and spent three years there studying the *Vajradhātu* and *Garbhakośa* teachings from leading masters as well as studying the hitherto unknown practice in Japan of *susiddhi* (esoteric accomplishment).

While Ennin was in Ch'ang-an, the Buddhist persecution under Emperor Wu-tsung occurred in 745, and an edict was issued that all foreign priests be deported. In the fall of 847, Ennin returned to Japan without ever having been able to visit Mt. T'ien T'ai, but for the future of Tendai in Japan, it seemed as though destiny had guided his journey. Mt. Wu T'ai had been the home of the famous Tantric master Amoghavajra and the temples where Ennin had studied in Chang-an were also famous for their esoteric studies. Ennin had the opportunity not merely to study the the esoteric doctrines but also to engage in the complex practices that were essential for proper understanding. He was able to bring back to Japan the complete teachings of the *Vajradhātu*, *Garbhakośadhātu* and

Susiddhi, which united the former. This was a great *coup* for the Tendai sect. Besides, Ennin also acquired a sound knowledge of Sanskrit, which had also been an added source of Tendai inferiority. With the return of Ennin, the Tendai sect no longer had any feelings of inadequacy and they were able at last to equal and surpass the Shingon in esoteric Buddhism. Ennin received a triumphant welcome from the Imperial court upon his return and the new direction he guided Tendai quickly won over the aristocrats, who were now reaching the apex of their glory.

Besides his interest in esoteric practice, Ennin had also been attracted to the *Jōgyō sammai* meditation practiced on Mt. Wu T'ai and upon his return to Japan, encouraged the practice of this meditation as well as constructing a *Jōgyō sammaidō* meditation hall on Mt. Hiei. His efforts greatly popularized the practice not only at the Enryakuji but also at Tendai branch temples throughout the countryside; this eventually resulted in the development of the Pure Land sect in Japan.

Ennin's successor in further developing Tendai esoterism (Taimitsu) was his rival Enchin (814–89), who became abbot of the Enryakuji in 868. Enchin was a distant relative of Kūkai's from Sanuki province and he became a disciple of Gishin at the age of fifteen. He was an outstanding scholar and administrator, serving as abbot for twenty-three years. But Enchin also prefigured a rivalry with his predecessor Ennin that ultimately divided the Tendai order.

The rivalry that arose between the disciples of Ennin and Enchin was actually a result of the ill feelings generated at the time of the abbot Gishin's death. Gishin had been very close to his master Saichō and had accompanied him to China. But upon return to Japan, Gishin went to live in his home province of Sagami and failed to maintain cordial relations with the remainder of Saichō's direct disciples. After Saichō's death, upon his express desire, Gishin was made abbot of the Enryakuji but at Gishin's death, a serious dispute arose over his successor. In 833, Gishin entrusted the affairs of Hieizan to his own disciple Enshū (735–843), who promptly declared himself abbot. But the appointment was not accepted by Saichō's direct disciples, who felt the mantle should rightfully pass to one of their number and sought to expel Enshū and his followers. As a result of the bitter conflict that ensued, an Imperial edict was issued removing Enshū from the post and appointing Enchō (771–836) as abbot, a direct disciple of Saichō. Enshū, disgruntled and embittered, left Hieizan with his disciples for the Murouji temple, which belonged to the Shingon sect. The conflict did not cease at this point but latently continued during Ennin and Enchin's abbacy, becoming the origin of the later armed wars between the Sanmon (Ennin's successors on Mt. Hiei) and Jimon or Mii (Gishin and Enchin's disciples) branches of the sect at the time of the 18th abbot Ryōgen (912–85).

When Ennin went to China and returned to such a brilliant reception, Gishin's followers recognized the danger of losing all future influence on Mt. Hiei if they could not counter-balance the situation; thus they attempted to send their most brilliant scholars to China. Enchin left in the year 853 aboard a commercial ship, since the official embassies had ended. He first went to Mt. T'ien T'ai were he encountered a Japanese Tendai monk named Ensai, who had gone to China with Ennin, been caught in the anti-Buddhist movement and disguised himself as a lay Chinese to escape persecution. By the time of Enchin's arrival, it was too late for Ensai to hope to return to either the priesthood or Japan.

In 855 Enchin visited Ch'ang-an where at the Ch'ing-lung temple he received instruction in the *Vajradhātu*, *Garbhakośadhātu* and *Susiddhi* practices. On his return to his ship, he again stopped at Mt. T'ien T'ai and built a small temple at the Kuo-ch'ing for the benefit of Japanese student monks, no doubt thinking of Ensai.

In 858, after spending six years in China, Enchin returned to Japan and very shortly assumed an important role in the court of Emperor Seiwa gaining the patronage of Fujiwara Yoshifusa and his son Mototsune, who at that period controlled the Heian court. In 866, Enchin became the master of the Onjōji temple and in 868, the fifth abbot of the Enryakuji, a post he held until his death in 891 at the age of seventy-eight.

Both Ennin and Enchin brought about considerable developments in Tendai esoterism and successfully surpassed their Shingon rivals, but the person who was responsible for theologically systematizing the Tendai adaptation of Tantrism into Taimitsu was the priest Annen (841–89 or 97). For even though the practice of Tantrism had been smoothly effected on Mt. Hiei, it still was a challenging problem to resolve the differences between Tendai doctrine and Tantrism.

Previously there had been differing views on exactly where to classify Tantrism within the Tendai system. Saichō had believed the Lotus *ekayāna* and that of the Shingon were identical and the two teachings were equal. Ennin also maintained the concept of the two teachings being theoretically equal but in practice, considered Tantrism superior. Enchin had placed Tantrism in the Tendai Five Period classification along with the *Lotus* and *Nirvana sutras*, an opinion Saichō had shared. But Enchin was also convinced that esoterism was superior both in theory and practice. This was a difficult situation in a school that was nominally known as the Tendai sect.

Annen was the first to suggest that Tendai actually change its name to Shingon, not to ally itself with the existing Shingon sect, but to emphasize the importance of Tantrism in its teachings. Annen was also responsible for establishing what became known as the 'five teachings' in place of the 'four teachings' of Tendai that had been based upon the nature of the contents (*kehō*). After the 'Round doctrine,' he added Tantrism as the superior teaching. He further explained that all conventional classifications of the teachings were based upon the questions of 'who, when and where'. This he resolved by making the characteristic teaching of Taimitsu the notion that there is one Buddha (Dainichi Nyorai), one time and one place-with all the Buddhas equated to Dainichi, all times identical with the one time, all places the same as the one place, and all teachings equivalent to the one teaching. This view of 'all equal to one' became the distinguishing factor between Tendai Taimitsu and Shingon Tōmitsu. In his doctrine of *enretsu misshō*, Annen further declared the *Dainichikyō* superior to both the *Lotus Sutra* and *Kegongyō*.

Annen's systematization and influence was very important to the growth of Mt. Hiei. By the period of Emperor En'yū (969–84), the abbot Ryōgen could claim nearly three thousand disciples. This was a drastic change from the days of Saichō when the loss of a single disciple was a serious matter. Also the Tendai sect had received *betsuin* (branch temples) from the government. One of the earliest had been in 836, when the Ise Tado Daijingūji became an official Tendai *betsuin*; after that, they sprang up all over the nation.

Besides such government support, the Tendai sect received the patronage of Emperors and aristocratic families. The pious Emperor Uda visited Hieizan five times and was lavish in his donations. The Fujiwara family, traditionally close to the Nara sects since the Kōfukuji was their family temple, also established cordial relations with Tendai. In 929 Fujiwara Tadahira, minister of the Left, celebrated his fiftieth birthday on Mt. Hiei and one thousand monks were invited to the celebration. The Tendai sect had reached its apex of popularity.

The man who controlled the mountain during its greatest glory, who is also known as the rejuvenator of Tendai during its middle ages, was the abbot Ryōgen (Jie Daishi). Born in nearby Ōmi province, Ryōgen became abbot of Hieizan in 966 and laboured for twenty years to restore both the spirit and physical properties of the mountain. It was a difficult and chaotic time. The morals of the monks had degenerated and the temples of Mt. Hiei had been ravaged by a number of fires.

As early as 866 Emperor Seiwa had already issued a special court edict with four articles of prohibition directed against the monks of Mt. Hiei. This was the first example of an edict issued especially against Tendai and its tone was mild in comparison to those of future years. It was mainly concerned with the keeping and use of horses by the monks and the wearing of luxurious robes. But the situation worsened and by 964 an Imperial reprimand was directed against monks disrupting esoteric services by entering the sanctuary and brandishing swords. Besides such problems, the mountain had been swept by a series of fires. In 935 the Hieizan main complex had been damaged by its first major fire and these were repeated in 941 and 966. The causes of these fires were unknown but it can be imagined that they reflected the careless and corrupt style of living of the monks.

In an effort to control such moral laxness, Ryōgen enforced the rules of isolation and also sought to revive the spirit of learning upon the mountain. Among his disciples were such outstanding theologians as Genshin, Kakuun, and Kakuchō. But Ryōgen was never successful in controlling the *sōhei* (priest soldiers). These did not represent the real monks of Mt. Hiei, but rather those engaged in miscellaneous duties such as maintenance and cooking. They were not spiritually motivated and easily aroused to champion mundane causes, frequently acting as mercenaries. In 970 Ryōgen issued twenty-six articles referring to their conduct and use of weapons. He did not successfully quell the problem and before the end of his life he witnessed the bitter quarrel that permanently divided the Tendai order.

Ryōgen was the first powerful abbot to emerge from among Ennin's disciples.[11] For many years the rival Ennin-Enchin parties had been politically equalized and their hostilities rested at a deadlock, but when Ryōgen rose to power, the balance was upset and Ennin's group vaunted their superiority. Then, at the end of 981, Yokei of the Onjōji was officially appointed abbot of the prestigious Hōshōji temple in eastern Kyōto.

The Onjōji (popularly known as the Miidera), was originally the *uji-dera* (clan temple) of the famous Ōtomo family. It was given to Enchin to supervise upon his return from China and in 859 at the official dedication ceremony, he ironically invited Ennin to conduct the services. The temple prospered and in 866 became a *betsuin* of the Enryakuji. In later years the temple became the stronghold of Enchin's followers. When Yokei of this group was appointed to the Hōshōji, a leading temple of the Fujiwara regents, the followers of Ennin on Mt. Hiei were incensed and marched to hold a raucous demonstration before the mansion of the Fujiwara regent Yoritada. This was the first massive demonstration by monks of Mt. Hiei and the court subsequently punished their leader.

Four years later, adding further insult, Yokei received an Imperial order to become the abbot of Tendai. A large group of Ennin's followers successfully foiled the attempt of the Imperial messenger to deliver this edict and the *sōhei* stole it. Three such attempts were made before the court finally decided to punish the monks by reading an Imperial order at Ennin's sutra repository hall on Hieizan, in effect reporting the improper conduct of the monks to Ennin's spirit.

Yokei of the Miidera did become abbot of Hieizan, but he was forced to resign after three months since the monks of the mountain refused to accept him. The bitterness over this affair smouldered on for four more years and then in 993, Kaisan, a violent follower of Yokei, attacked and vandalized the memorial shrine of Ennin on Mt. Hiei dedicated to the Shintō deity Sekisan myōjin. This event marked the beginning of open hostilities between the groups. The same year Ennin's followers attacked and totally destroyed the complex on Mt. Hiei belonging to Enchin's followers and more than one thousand monks were forced to flee to the Miidera. After this, the Tendai sect was permanently divided into the Sanmon (monks of Mt. Hiei) and Jimon or Mii branches. This major split was the product of internecine institutional rivalry, there were also more subtle divisions made upon theological differences.

Tendai Taimitsu in its earliest stages had been centered around the development of esoteric philosophy. Technically, this form of esoterism was the first to arrive in Japan, but since Saichō had been restricted to spending less than a year in China, the Taimitsu he transmitted was inferior to Shingon. This doctrinal disadvantage was surmounted by Ennin, Enchin and Annen. After their endeavours, Taimitsu doctrinally was complete; future innovations were in the area of practice. The differences in ritual and practice initially split Taimitsu into three major schools, each claiming their own founder and lines of transmission:

1) Saichō ....Konpon daishiryū
2) Ennin ....Jikaku daishiryū
3) Enchin ....Chishō daishiryū

Among these, the most prosperous school was the Jikaku daishiryū, which further split into numerous branches, the most notable being the Taniryū founded by Kōkei (977–1049) and the Kawaryū founded by Kakuchō (960–1034). Ultimately out of the many schools that subsequently sprang into existence, scholars have selected thirteen as traditionally most representative of Taimitsu. Besides the foregoing three main schools, the others consist of the following:

4) Hōmanryū by Sōjitsu
5) Butchōryū by Gyōgon
6) Insonryū by Inson
7) Rengeryū by Eii
8) Chisenryū by Kakuhan
9) Sammairyū by Ryōyū
10) Anouryū by Shōshō
11) Ajiokaryū by Chūsai
12) Kudokuryū by Kaiga
13) Nashimotoryū by Myōkai

The mainstream of the Tendai sect following primarily the exoteric doctrines also experienced divisions. Initially these evolved from the two leading disciples of the abbot Ryōgen: Genshin and Kakuun.

Genshin (942–1017), founder of the Eshinryū, was also the author of the *Ōjōyōshū* (Essentials of Salvation), an important theological study that successfully impressed T'ien T'ai followers in China to such a degree that they erected a temple in its honour. Kakuun (953–1007) was the founder of the Dannaryū. Just as in the case of the Taimitsu, these schools later divided into numerous sub-sects. In an effort to clarify the vague philosophical differences between the two and provide them with antiquity, future disciples attributed the differences to Saicho's two T'ien T'ai masters in China. Genshin was believed to have carried on the traditions originated by Tao-sui and Kakuun, the transmission from Hsing-man. Ultimately eight schools developed from these artificial differences, which became known as the *Edanhachiryū* or 'Eight Schools of *e* (Eshinryū) and *dan* (Dannaryū). There were no solid scriptural bases for the differences between these schools and transmission became esoteric from master to disciple, in the manner of Taimitsu. The Tendai sect thus gradually splintered into fragments and reflected the general worldly atmosphere of Heian society during its days of decline.

The close of the 12th century was marked by bitter warfare throughout Japan making the Japanese concept of Armageddon known as *Mappō shisō* (Degeneration of the teachings) seem a reality. The struggle between the warrior families of Heike (Taira) and Genji (Minamoto) for the control of Japan, which began in 1159 (Heiji war) and culminated in 1185 (Gempei war) with the triumph of the Minamoto, created an atmosphere of violence that permeated the nation. A few individuals did manage to elude the situation and one such person was Shōshin (dates unknown), who allegedly never heard of the existence of the Gempei war. In 1204, with the assistance of his master Jichin, the current abbot of Tendai, Shōshin brought together 270 scholar-monks to hold an *ango* (summer retreat) to renew the discussion of Tendai doctrine. The bloody atmosphere of the nation was violently brought home to Shōshin when the common monks (*dōshū*) of the mountain attacked the scholars and Imperial troops had to be brought in for defence. The Heian era for Tendai thus ended as it had begun, with a quixotic idealist raising the banner for reform. Saichō had sought to reform Nara corruption but now his own sect had sunk into the quagmire induced by aristocratic patronage and prosperity. In keeping with the cyclic history of the rise and fall of Buddhist institutions and the regeneration of new thought, it was time for the rise of a new movement. But before proceeding to the gradual evolution of Pure Land thought within the Tendai sect, we will pause to examine the fate of the contemporary Shingon sect, who in union with Tendai dominated the Heian period.

B. SHINGON SHŪ, Esoteric Buddhism

1. Kūkai, the Founder

Kūkai was born in the year 774 to the scholar-aristocratic family of Saeki in Sanuki province on the island of Shikoku. At the age of fifteen, under guidance of his maternal uncle, Atō Ōtari, tutor to the Crown Prince Iyo, he went to the capital (Nagaoka) to study Chinese poetry and Confucian classics. Three years later he entered the government university, enrolled in the elite course for bureaucrats and devoted himself to the standard Confucian curriculum. What happened after that is something of a mystery, since for unknown reasons Kūkai suddenly abandoned his studies and turned to Buddhism.

It can be theorized that this is probably when he met Gonzō (758–827) of the Daianji and received from him the sacred *Kokūzōgumonjihō* (Mantra of Ākāśagarbha) practice, and became so fascinated by it that he abandoned all thoughts of a future bureaucratic career. In the introduction to his own work, the *Sangōshiki* (Indications of the Goals of the Three Teachings), which he wrote at the age of twenty-four, Kūkai states that it was the encounter with this practice that changed his life, although he does not mention the name of the master that introduced him to it.[12] It is most likely that he avoided such mention because he was at the time a privately ordained priest (*shidosō*), which was not legally sanctioned.

Kūkai's attraction to Buddhism from the start was related to practice rather than theory and this predilection characterized his entire life. Although he later completed a masterly systematization of Shingon doctrine, theology occupied a second place in his interests and he inculcated this attitude in his disciples.

After his initial decision to abandon the university for Buddhism, Kūkai lived for a considerable period in the mountains engaged in practice. It is quite possible that he spent time with the *Jinen chishū* (Sect of Natural Wisdom), which advocated the practice of meditation in accompaniment with the *Kokūzōgumonjihō*, as well as visiting other centers of esoteric and Shugendō practice. During these travels, Kūkai encountered the *Dainichikyō* and came to the conclusion that this work epitomized all that he sought in Buddhism. In order to properly comprehend the esoteric text, he decided to find a Tantric master in China to instruct him.

There is no reliable biographical account of how Kūkai was selected to be on one of the *kentōshi* ships sailing to China in the year 804. It was a considerable honour to be selected and certain court contacts were required but it is not certain whether Kūkai had such contacts personally or through his rather illustrious relatives. In any event, he was selected to sail on the first of the four ships in the company of the envoy to the T'ang court, Fujiwara Kadonomaro.

When he arrived in Ch'ang-an, after a period of search, Kūkai met the esoteric master Hui-kuo (746–805) of the Ch'ing-lung temple, who, according to legend, immediately upon encountering Kūkai claimed him as his long awaited disciple. Kūkai received his primary *abhiṣeka* initiation from the master and within three short months was deemed ready to receive the final *abhiṣeka*, and be ordained as a master of esoteric Buddhism. Shortly thereafter, Hui-kuo died and Kūkai, as his newest but foremost disciple, had the honour of writing the epitaph for his master's tomb.

At his late master's request, Kūkai returned to Japan in 806, to propagate the Dharma, despite the fact that his initial agreement with the Japanese government had been to spend twenty years as a student-scholar. When Kūkai did return after thirty months, he had successfully managed to become the eighth patriarch of esoteric Buddhism, learned Sanskrit, studied poetry, calligraphy and other minor arts. It had been a brief period of tremendous accomplishment.

When Kūkai returned to Japan, it was after the death of Emperor Kammu, and if he had enjoyed influence with the court prior to his departure, it no longer existed. The Tendai sect received two *nembundosha* in the year 806, but the Shingon sect had to wait until 835, the year of Kūkai's death to receive *nembundosha* and official recognition as a sect.

Immediately upon his return, Kūkai sent a report to the court (*Shōrai mokuroku*) listing the sutras and other items he had brought back to Japan with Takashina no Tōnari, a bureaucrat that he had met aboard ship. It took three years, until the end of Emperor Heizei's reign, before there was a reply. It was very difficult at that time for the court to assess the value of Kūkai's contribution, furthermore, Saichō was already recognized as an esoteric master and this sphere of activity was believed to be a prerogative of the Tendai sect. Another problem in evaluating the materials was due to the fact that the Tantric Buddhism Kūkai brought to Japan was so new even in China, that it was still theologically disorganized and unsystematized. Before a new sect could properly be established, the material had to be classified and this Kūkai accomplished in the year 830 with his masterly *Jūjūshinron* (Ten Stages of the Development of Mind). Still another difficulty the court faced was the tone of the report Kūkai drafted. Coming from an unknown student-monk it displayed a confidence that could be considered brash; this also may have been a reason why they decided to allow him to wait in Kyūshū rather then summon him immediately to the capital.

Although the court might have hoped Kūkai would learn a lesson in humility by being apparently forgotten in Kyūshū, he managed to put the time to good use. This was a period when he began to systematize and arrange the materials he had brought with him, copy and study the sutras and also make plans how to propagate Shingon in Japan. When the time came to be called to the capital, Kūkai was prepared.

By the year 809, Emperor Heizei retired due to ill health and Emperor Saga came to the throne at the age of twenty-four. Later during that year, Kūkai received notice that he was to henceforth reside at the Takaosanji temple, near Kyōto. He was finally summoned to action. The following year during the ninth month the retired Emperor Heizei instigated a revolt and after it was quelled, Kūkai capitalized upon the situation by submitting a petition to the court suggesting that he be allowed to perform esoteric rituals for the peace of the nation, similar to those he had witnessed in T'ang China. This petition was evidently not accepted.

During his stay at the Takaosanji, Kūkai made close friends with Emperor Saga. On a number of occasions he donated scrolls of calligraphy to the court, an art that greatly interested the Emperor. At that time, Saga was one of the three great calligraphers of Japan, the other two being Kūkai and Tachibana Hayanari. It appears that Kūkai exerted a strong cultural influence upon the Emperor but this was confined to the areas of the Classics, Chinese poetry, Sanskrit and calligraphy; the Emperor did not share Kūkai's devotion to esoteric Buddhism. And despite his friendship with Kūkai, Saga attempted to maintain a policy of fairness towards all the Buddhist sects.

During the seventh month of the year 816, Kūkai received permission from the Emperor to build a monastery on Mt. Kōya. The consecration ritual was held the fifth month of the year 819 and the Shintō deities Nifu Myōjin and Kōya Myōjin, as well as one hundred and twenty *kami* from throughout Japan, were invited to the ceremonies to become protectors of the mountain. The main temple was given the name Kongōbuji, after the *Kongōburōkaku issaiyugayugikyō*. This sutra in contrast to the *Dainichi-kyō* (source of the *Taizōkai mandara*) and *Kongōkyō* (*Kongōkai mandara*), expressed the non-duality of the two *mandaras*. As the symbolic name of the main temple, it represented Kūkai's ideal of uniting the Diamond and Womb realms upon the mountain.

The construction of the monastery was not an easy task and many buildings, including the great pagoda, were not finished during the lifetime of Kūkai. He was constantly plagued by financial problems, which eventually were passed on to his disciples. Another difficulty arose from the demands of his active life that did not permit him to personally remain on Mt. Kōya.

Emperor Saga retired in the year 823 at the age of thirty-nine, in order to devote himself to his cultural pursuits. He was succeeded by Emperor Junna, whose reign coincided with the most successful period of Kūkai's life. Just prior to Emperor Saga's retirement, Kūkai was notified that he would receive charge of the renowned Tōji temple, which had been begun by Emperor Kammu in 793, and now thirty years later was still under construction. This temple and its counterpart the Saiji, had been planned to follow the pattern of the great Tōdaiji and Saidaiji of the Nara capital and represented respectively, the eastern and western sectors of the new city. When Emperor Junna came to the throne he granted Kūkai permission to have fifty Shingon monks reside at the Tōji and henceforth made the temple belong solely to the Shingon sect. This restriction was unique at the time in Japanese Buddhism, since the great temples of Nara had housed many sects simultaneously and the government had not previously recognized any need for exclusivism. The same Imperial decree also contained the first mention of 'Shingon shū' in an official document, which finally offered the sect a measure of recognition as an independent institution, although they still had not been granted *nembundosha*. Kūkai made the Tōji temple the centre of the sect since Mt. Kōya was distant and far from complete. He also created a repository there to house the scriptures and tantric instruments brought from China, and put into practice a study plan for those who wished to enter the order.

During the drought of the spring of 824, Kūkai was requested by the court to perform a Tantric rain ritual. For his success, he was granted the honorary title of *Shōsōzu*.

In the year 828, Kūkai opened the first school in Japan to accept students from all stations of life. This was known as the Shugeishuchiin (School of Arts and Sciences). The curriculum consisted of Buddhist, Confucianist and Taoist studies with related topics. Not much is known regarding the success of the experiment but in 847, the Tōji temple finally sold it. The idea was noble but perhaps the period was still too aristocratic for such egalitarianism.

In 830, just five years prior to his death, Kūkai completed his greatest theological work, the ten volume *Jūjūshinron* (Ten Stages of the Development of Mind) in compliance with the request of Emperor Junna for a treatise on the essentials of the doctrine of each of the major sects of Buddhism. This work completed the systematization of Shingon doctrine. It later was summarized into a shorter form known as the *Hizō Hōyaku* (Precious Key to the Secret Treasury). Both of these works were based upon the essential Buddhist concept that the key to Enlightenment is the true recognition of one's own state of mind.

By 831, Kūkai was forced to resign from his official duties at the Tōji due to ill health and when his resignation was finally accepted by the Emperor, he went to Mt. Kōya with the intention of spending his remaining years there. But he still maintained Imperial influence and in 834 he received permission to establish a Shingon-in at Court and hold Tantric rituals from the 8th to the 14th of the first month of the year. The ritual, known as the *mishuhō*, which subsequently became annual, was for the peace of the nation and prosperity of the people as well as for a rich harvest of the five grains. It was similar to those held at the T'ang court and to a certain degree reflected the realization of the ignored petition Kūkai had submitted in 810. The date of this new year ritual is quite significant because it followed the official seven days of Shintō ritual for peace, prosperity and good harvest, beginning on New Years' day and served as a Buddhist counterpart. Kūkai himself participated in the services held in 835, just two months prior to his death.

Another of Kūkai's greatest achievements occurred the same month when the court finally granted permission for the Shingon sect to have three *nembundosha*. At last, this meant proper official recognition of his sect.

Finally, at the age of sixty-two, on the 21st day of the third month of the year 835, Kūkai entered into what his followers were later to describe as eternal *samādhi* on Mt. Kōya. He was interred in the Eastern Peak of the mountain.

Kūkai's death brought to an end, one of the most dynamic careers of the Heian period. His dominating personality lived on in legend and eventually served as a unifying factor to revive the Shingon sect during the tenth century.

2. Historical Transmission

The origin of Tantric Buddhism, due to its esoteric nature is obscured in a vast wilderness as yet impenetrable. Certain aspects and rituals are most certainly derived from Vedic influence and the *dhāraṇī* (Jap. *darani*), mystical utterances utilized to 'preserve' or 'maintain' Buddhist teachings in capsulized form, became exceedingly influential during approximately the fourth century A.D. in India.

Philosophically, Tantric Buddhism was a natural outgrowth of Mādhyamika and Vijñānavāda thought. Once the fallibility of reason was exposed and the role of human consciousness revealed as the pivot capable of tilting the world of ignorance into Enlightenment, the emphasis upon practice increased along with fresh explorations into the realm of consciousness. These new innovations led quite naturally to experimentation with the effects of sound, form and colour upon the consciousness, linked with faith. Mental transformation was induced by the 'gods of form' in the shape of divinities of every variety and type that could appeal to an individual's psychological needs and be utilized as *upāya* to lead to the 'formless' divine within.

The origin of Tantrism appears in India between the sixth and seventh centuries with the appearance of sutras such as the *Mahāvairocana, Guhyasamāja* and *Sarvatāthagata tattva saṃgraha.* By the mid-seventh century this form became the mainstream of Indian Buddhism and innovations began to spring up. In exploring the relationship between sensation and mind, it was observed that bombardment by unsublimated passions was as effective in negating clinging to the ego as physical discipline and control. This resulted in the creation of a variety of Tantrism which embraced the erotic and became known as left-handed Vajrayāna, considered by the Japanese Shingon school to be 'unorthodox'. During the Pāla Empire (8th to 12th centuries), Tantrism flourished in India and when the Moslem invasions struck during the twelfth century destroying it, in accompaniment with Hindu influences, it spread to Southeast Asia and Tibet. Southeast Asian Tantrism degenerated and was replaced by Hīnayāna (Theravāda) forms of Buddhism; only in Tibet did it survive in the form of Lamaism and mingled with the indigenous Bön faith.

Tantric forms were disseminated in China from the time of the inception of Buddhism as various *mantra* and *dhāraṇī* were translated. Generally these were studied and occasionally used to gain mystical powers. By the sixth century, practice became more common with the use of *maṇḍala, mudrā* and various rituals. These ultimately arrived in Japan during the Nara period and that form of Tantrism is now designated as the Ancient Tradition. The turning point in the development of the Chinese, and subsequently Japanese, Tantric tradition occurred in the eighth century with the arrival of three great Indian masters in China: Śubhākarasiṃha, Vajrabodhi and Amoghavajra.

Śubhākarasiṃha or Shan-wu-wei (637–735), was a central Indian who supposedly studied Tantric Buddhism at Nālanda after retiring as the King of a small principality. He was encouraged by his master to spread the teachings to China and after a difficult Central Asian journey, finally arrived at Ch'ang-an in 716 at the age of eighty. He translated the *Hsü-*

k'ung-tsang-ch'iu-wen ch'ih-fa (Jap. *Kokūzōgumonjihō*) the following year, which was soon imported to Japan, and then went on to Loyang, where he translated the *Mahāvairocana sūtra*. He died in China at the age of ninety-nine after being refused permission to return to India.

Vajrabodhi or Chin-kang-chih (671–741) was reportedly of either Central or South Indian royalty. He studied Mādhyamika and Yogācāra philosophy at Nālanda and then proceeded to South India to pursued Tantric studies under Nāgabodhi. He embarked by sea to China and reached Canton in 720. He is best known for his translation of the *Vajraśekhara*. He spent the remainder of his life working on this translation project and devoting himself to Tantric rituals and the construction of *abhiṣeka* platforms. He died at Loyang at the age of seventy-one.

The Chinese pupil I-hsing (683–727) was a student of both Śubhākarasiṃha and Vajrabodhi. He was responsible for combining their teachings and giving a philosophical foundation to Tantrism in China.

The third great master, Amoghavajra or Pu-k'ung chin-kang (705–774), was a native of Siṃhala (Ceylon), who first arrived in China at the age of ten. At fifteen, he became a disciple of Vajrabodhi. After the death of his master, Amoghavajra travelled to India and Ceylon, where he received national honours. In Southern India, he met Nāgabodhi and was able to bring back many Tantric texts to China, which he subsequently translated. Amoghavajra became the spiritual master of three Chinese Emperors: Hsüan-tsung (713–55), Su-tsung (756–62) and Tai-tsung (763–79). With his tremendous accomplishments, China witnessed its golden age of Tantrism during this epoch.

Hui-kuo (746–805), the master of Kūkai, was the successor to Amoghavajra, who lived in the famous Ch'ing-lung temple in Ch'ang-an. He claimed Kūkai as his successor and Tantric Buddhism did not further develop in China. During the 845 persecution it lost all court influence and suffered severely throughout the country. Later it gradually was assimilated into Chinese folk religion.

The official patriarchs, as recognized by the Shingon school in its transmission are:

1)	Mahāvairocana	(Jap. Dainichi Nyorai)
2)	Vajrasattva	(Kongōsatta)
3)	Nāgārjuna	(Ryūmō or Ryūju)
4)	Nāgabodhi	(Ryūchi)
5)	Vajrabodhi	(Kongōchi)
6)	Amoghavajra	(Fukūkongō)[13]
7)	Hui-kuo	(Keika)
8)	Kūkai	

3. Texts

Although the Shingon school is esoteric and does not base its teachings upon textual knowledge *per se*, it does rely upon certain Tantric scriptures and commentaries that are interpreted by its masters. The most important of these is the *Mahāvairocana sūtra* (*Daibirushana jōbutsu jimben kajikyō*, known popularly as the *Dainichikyō*) translated by Śubhākarasiṃha. This work reveals the *Garbhakośa dhātu* (Jap. *Taizōkai*) *maṇḍala* and also presents the *upāya* of the three Tantric principles (body, speech, mind) that allow the individual to enter into the Buddha nature inherent in all sentient beings. A series of related scriptures are used in conjunction with this text, the most important being the commentary by I-hsing.

The second important work is the *Vajraśekhara* or the (*Sarva-tathāgata tattva samgraha sūtra* (*Kongōchō issai nyorai shinjitsu shōdaijō genshō dai-kyōōkyō*, known popularly as the *Kongōchōkyō*) translated by Amogha-vajra. The complete text of this work does not exist but it forms the basis of the *Vajradhātu* (Jap. Kongōkai) *maṇḍala*. There are also a number of related works.

4. Classification of the Teachings

The basis of the Shingon classification of the teachings is found in two works by Kūkai: *Hizō Hōyaku* and the *Jūjūshinron*, both completed in the year 830. In essence, these outline ten stages of development in the awakening of the mind to Enlightenment and the following is a brief summary:

1) Those who live by instinctive impulse, existing blindly like

sheep. They have no conscious awareness of moral or religious values. There is nothing to differentiate them from animals.

2) Those who are ignorant and naïve yet ethical. These are basically humanistic individuals, capable of practicing simple Buddhist precepts and *dāna* (giving). This stage is equated with the Confucianist, for whom the ethical way of life is the ultimate perfection.

3) Those who have attained fearlessness due to their faith in rebirth. Here are classified those who believe in Taoism, the Hindu schools, as well as Buddhists who literally believe in rebirth. These are people who are attached to their own ego and its preservation.

   This stage and its two predecessors are known as the three worldly types of mind.

4) Those who accept the *anātman* theory and believe the self consists merely of the Five psycho-physical constituents (form, feeling, notion, activities and consciousness). These people still are ignorant of the *anātman* nature of the dharmas. Kūkai classifies this as the teaching of the Śrāvakas.

5) Those who have eliminated the origin of suffering or cause of karma and strive for Nirvana. These are the Pratyeka Buddhas, they lack the knowledge of *upāya* to aid others.

6) Those who act with compassion towards others. This is the first step of Mahāyāna and the Hossō school is placed in this category.

7) Those who realize the mind is unborn. This awareness is based upon Nāgārjuna's Eightfold Negation, and the mind that reaches this stage is able to comprehend the ungraspable Emptiness. The Sanron school falls into this category.

8) Those who are aware of the nature of reality as taught by the Tendai school.

9) Those who have the most profound exoteric thought that is aware of the Interdependent origination of the *Dharmadhātu*. This stage corresponds to the Kegon Sect.

Evidently stage 8 and 9 are considered still to be within the realm of ignorance because, according to Kūkai's interpretation, they represent merely theoretical arguments. As he explains in his tenth stage, man is a combination of mind and body, true Enlightenment must encompass the total being.

10) Those who have attained the stage of comprehending Shingon or the total union of the individual mind and body with that of Dainichi Nyorai, the Absolute truth or immanent Buddha nature. In particular, this stage relates to spiritual practice.

5. Exoteric versus Esoteric Buddhism

The Shingon sect is the only school of Japanese Buddhism that considers itself to be totally esoteric. A generalized definition of 'esoteric' in this instance, would entail the rejection of any definite scriptural or textual basis for the school's doctrine and the secret transmission of the teaching vocally from master to disciple relying greatly upon the use of symbolism, a stumbling block for the uninitiated. In effect 'esoteric' becomes a synonym for 'Tantric' although Shingon followers tend to avoid such an identification in an effort to disassociate themselves from the vast amount of superstitious and degenerative practices lumped together under that generic title.

Kūkai was quite convinced that esoteric Buddhism was superior to exoteric and the basis of his contention is found in the *Benkenmitsu nikyōron* (Treatise on the Difference Between Exoteric and Esoteric Buddhism). Here and elsewhere he differentiates four major points between the two:

1) Subject Preaching

Exoteric—preaching of *nirmāṇakāya* or manifestation body utilizing *upāya* suited to the audience.

Esoteric—preached by the *Dharmakāya* Buddha, Dainichi Nyorai without the use of *upāya*. This doctrine is set forth for the Buddha's own enjoyment and represents his innermost spiritual experience. Some might question how the *Dharmakāya*, the formless inconceivable Absolute Truth can be said to 'preach', and the answer is that this is termed 'preaching' from the standpoint of religious experience.

2) Quality of Preaching

Exoteric—the profound mystical experience of the Enlightenment of the Buddha is unpreachable since it transcends language.

Esoteric —preaching expressed by the 'True Words' (*shingon*), these correspond exactly to the reality of the *Dharmakāya* Dainichi. By means of the Shingon *mantra*, *mudrā*, *samaya* (symbol) and *maṇḍala*, it is possible to experience this.

3) Time Required for Effect

Exoteric—offers a gradual approach to Enlightenment that for the common man would require infinite lifetimes. Although the Kegon and Tendai theoretically discuss Enlightenment with this mind or body, they fail to offer actual practice.

Esoteric —by practicing the *sanmitsu* (*samādhi*, *mantra* and *mudrā* to occupy mind, speech and body), the individual can instantly unite with the *Dharmakāya* Buddha and attain Enlightenment. The Shingon view firmly sets forth the concept of Enlightenment now with this body.

4) Universality of Benefits

Exoteric—classifies sentient beings into various categories of spiritual capability, even denying the potentiality of Enlightenment to some individuals (*icchantika*). Also believes in the three periods of *Mappō* (*shō zō matsu*) during the last of which, no matter how great an individual endeavours, he will receive no benefit.

Esoteric—Dainichi perpetually works to aid all sentient beings and even those who follow the most rudimentary practices will be assured of benefit.

In this comparison, Kūkai sets forth the very typical Mahāyāna viewpoint that the written word or letter, symbol of human language itself, has limitations insofar as it represents a conceptualized notion of reality based upon human agreement. The Absolute Truth can never be directly expressed in human language since it transcends the discursive reasoning that constantly divides the universe between self, the attributes of self and other. Even the sacred scriptures when read literally by the unenlightened inevitably will convey false impressions. In contrast to this, the words of Dainichi transcend such limitations by representing the direct expression of experience itself; in effect, this is the immediate intuition of Enlightenment prior to conceptualization.

Although Kūkai clearly advocates the superiority of esoterism in his *Benkenmitsunikyōron*, he was also aware that the interpretation of an exoteric sutra depended upon the level of spiritual realization of the reader. Those with a profound religion awareness are 'capable of experiencing the esoteric truth from reading an exoteric text just as in the eyes of the Enlightened One, the roadside weed can be recognized as a medicinal herb or the jewel expert can visualize a gem within the unpolished stone'.[14] The value of a sutra is totally dependent upon the ability of the individual.

6. Dual *Maṇḍala* (*Ryōkai mandara*)

Central in Shingon ritual and symbolism is the *mandara* (Skt. *maṇḍala*). In India, this was originally a mystical circle or sphere drawn upon the ground or painted on a pedestal or dais to represent the psycho-physical universe. It generally was presented in the symbolic shape of an Indian castle, fortress against invasion and repository of worldly wealth and power. Accordingly, the *maṇḍala* will normally have its spiritual symbol of strength in the centre surrounded with walls guarded by numerous deities and gates in the four directions.

In meditation the *maṇḍala* is used as a projection of the interior life, a revelation of the subjective universe to enable movement from the multiple facticity of daily life to a focused concentration and the revelation of the limitless potentialities of Enlightenment. Conversely, it can also lead to the realization of the outflowing of Enlightenment to penetrate every sphere of phenomenal existence.

Shingon doctrine is based upon two *maṇḍalas:*

a. Garbhakośadhātu Maṇḍala (*Taizōkai Mandara*)

The 'Womb-realm' *maṇḍala* is an evolution of Indian cultural history representing Mahāvairocana (Dainichi) as the body of Principle (*rishin*), the *Dharmakāya* as-it-is or as it exists in the totality of phenomenal existence. It symbolizes the unfolding compassion, growth and potentiality

TAIZŌKAI MANDARA

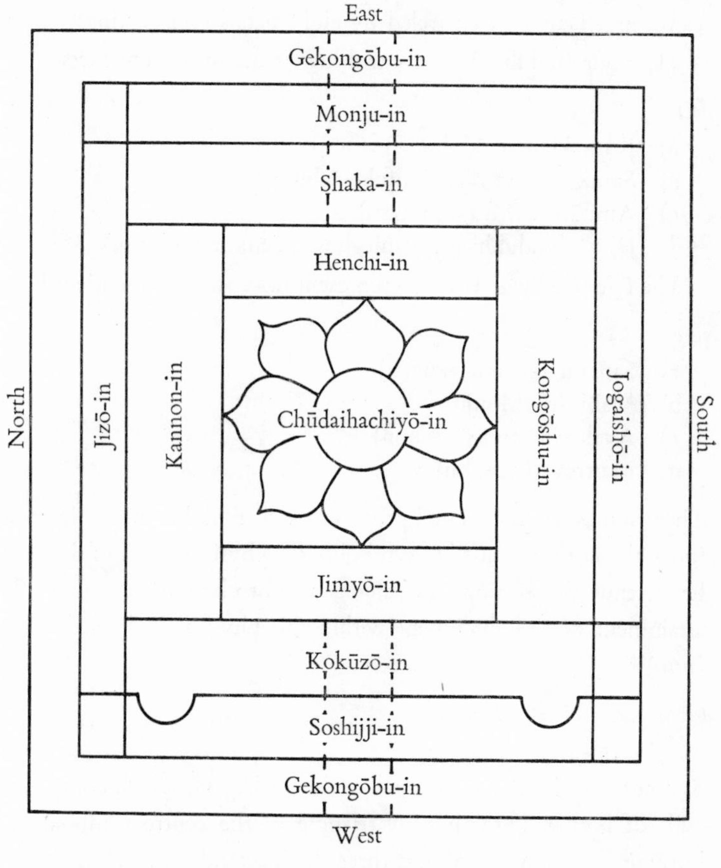

of the world of Enlightenment. Every sentient being is believed to have an inherent potentiality or seed (Buddha nature) that can be nourished in this womb of compassion to attain Enlightenment.

The *maṇḍala* is formed in the shape of an eight-petaled lotus with Mahāvairocana in the centre, surrounded by four Buddhas and bodhisattvas, symbolizing the nine consciousnesses.[15] It unfolds from its unitary centre to the diversity of its extremes in twelve sections:

1) *Chūdaihachiyō-in*

The foundation of the entire *maṇḍala* and direct centre with Mahāvairocana (Dainichi) encircled by eight petals representing:

The Four Buddhas who control his virtues or 'effectiveness'.

Effect

a) Ratnaketu (Hōdōbutsu)
b) Saṃkusumita-rāja (Kaifuke-ō butsu)
c) Amitābha (Muryōjubutsu)
d) Divyadundubhi-meghanirghoṣa (Tenkuraionbutsu)

The Four bodhisattvas who represent his vow to aid sentient beings.

Cause

a) Samantabhadra (Fugen)
b) Mañjuśrī (Monju)
c) Avalokiteśvara (Kannon)
d) Maitreya (Miroku)

These symbolize the eternal process to seek Enlightenment. In ancient India, the Lotus was used to symbolize the physical organ of the human heart, thus this section can be considered to be representative of the attainment of Enlightenment within this physical body (*sokushin jōbutsu*)[16]

Eastern Sector of the Maṇḍala

2) *Henchi-in*

Symbolic of the Enlightenment of the Tathāgata, which conquers the evils of human ignorance. A triangle in the centre symbolizes the burning fire of wisdom, and three deities stand on each side of it to make a total of 7 deities.

3) *Shaka-in*

Śākyamuni is the central figure, representing a manifestation of Mahāvairocana in the phenomenal world to save sentient beings. He is surrounded by his various disciples to create a total of 39 deities.

4) *Monju-in*

Mañjuśrī as the central figure, symbolizing the dynamic wisdom attained through practice. He sits in the middle of the eastern gate surrounded by bodhisattvas composing a total of 24 deities.

Western Sector

5) *Jimyō-in*

Prajñā bodhisattva symbolizing compassion surrounded by the four *vidyārāja* (Myō-ō): Acalanātha (Fudō), Trailokyavijaya (Gōsanze), Yamāntaka (Daiitoku), and Trailokyavijaya (Shōsanze), who by displaying the countenance of anger, subdue those who are difficult to save; a total of 5 deities.[17]

6) *Kokūzō-in*

In contrast to the wisdom of Mañjuśrī, this section represents worldly virtue and merit in the form of Ākāśagarbha (Kokūzō), the bodhisattva who acts as the storehouse of treasures. There are 28 deities in this section.

7) *Soshijji-in*

Again Ākāśagarbha, symbolizing that the various virtues of Mahāvairocana benefitting sentient beings have been 'wonderously achieved' (*soshijji*). 8 deities.

8) *Kongōshu-in*

Vajrasattva is the principle deity representing the Buddha's wisdom inherent in all sentient beings. 28 deities.

9) *Jogaishō-in*

Sarvanivaraṇaviśkambhin (Jogaishō) bodhisattva, symbolizing the elimination of the hindrances to Enlightenment. 9 deities.

Northern Sector

10) *Kannon-in*

Avalokiteśvara, symbolizing the compassion of the Buddha in contrast to the wisdom of the *Kongōshu-in*. 37 deities.

11) *Jizō-in*

Kṣitigarbha (Jizō) bodhisattva, who saves all sentient beings of the Six Existences (of the Realm of Desire), who live between the death of the historical Buddha and the arrival of Maitreya, the Buddha to come. 9 deities.

Periphery of the Maṇḍala

12) *Ge kongōbu-in*

The outer border of the *maṇḍala* containing a total of 205 deities all representing manifestations of Mahāvairocana as he infinitely creates the universe.

Total number of deities in the *maṇḍala*..................414[18]

b. Vajra-dhātu Maṇḍala (Kongōkai Mandara)

In contrast to the foregoing, this *maṇḍala* is a product of psycho-

KONGŌKAI MANDARA

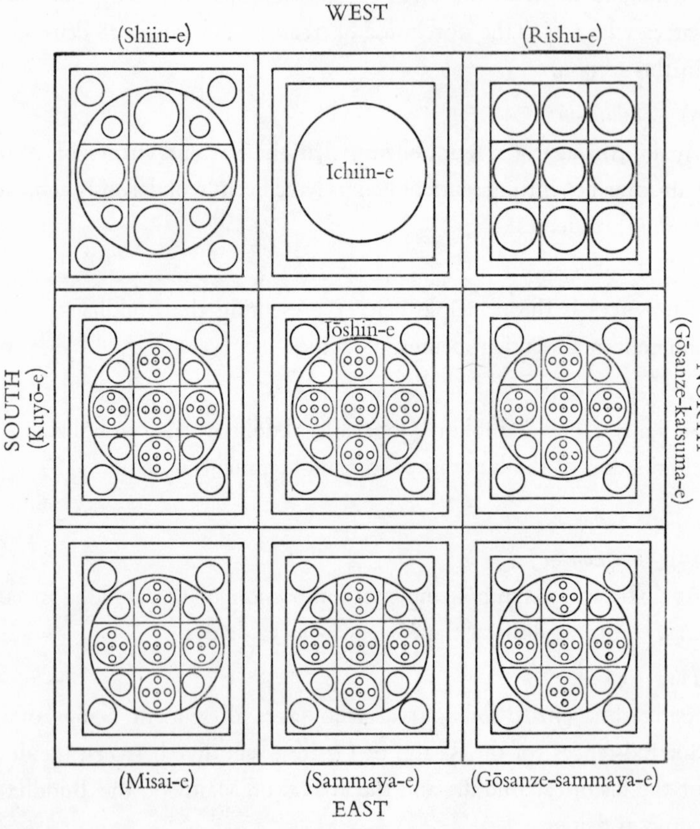

philosophical evolution and deals primarily with the spiritual practice that leads to Enlightenment. The *vajra* (diamond, adamantine or thunderbolt type of weapon) symbolizes the power to penetrate ignorance and achieve integration; it belongs to the Body of Wisdom (*chishin*). The *maṇḍala* consists of nine sections (*ku-e*) that can be interpreted from two directions: clockwise and counterclockwise. Clockwise, it demonstrates the dispersion of the function of Enlightenment from the centre (Mahāvairocana) to the extremities (his manifestation, Vajrasattva). Counterclockwise, it reflects the process of reintegration whereby the individual is led by the function of Enlightenment, to practice the teachings and ultimately to attain Enlightenment. There are a total of 1,461 deities in this *maṇḍala*. The following presents a brief summary of the nine sections or miniature *maṇḍalas:*

1) *Katsuma-e*

The direct centre of the *maṇḍala*. This section is also known as the Jōshin-e since the practice leads to Enlightenment. The *maṇḍala* section consists of Mahāvairocana displaying the *mudrā* of wisdom, surrounded by his four Buddha attendants (Akṣobhya, Ratna-sambhava, Amitābha, and Amoghasiddi) in a central and four encircling orbits making a total of 25 figures, plus 32 bodhisattvas, 4 female *deva* and on the periphery 1,000 Buddhas of the present aeon. The total number of deities is 1,061. The section expresses the interior peace and tranquility of the human mind beneath the tumult of worldly concerns.

2) *Sammaya-e*

In Sanskrit *samaya* literally means 'original vow' and it refers here to the various symbolic means that Dainichi uses to fulfill his vow to save all sentient beings, represented by Tantric instruments. These symbolize a total of 73 deities.

3) *Misai-e*

Demonstrates the Buddha's attempt to save sentient beings with delicate (*misai*) wisdom. Total of 73 deities.

4) *Kuyō-e*

Various deities making offerings for sentient beings in order to awaken their Buddha nature. The *sammayagyō* (symbolic objects) are carried to the Five Buddhas on lotus flowers. 13 deities.

5) *Shiin-e*

Symbolizes the inseparable oneness of the previous four sections as four *mudrā*, and also the four marks symbolizing the fourfold wisdom of the Buddha: Action, observation, equality and mirror-wisdom. 13 deities.

6) *Ichiin-e*

In this section, Mahāvairocana stands alone with a single *mudrā* of wisdom, symbolizing the unification of the previous four *mudrās* of the *maṇḍala* (*shiin*), as well as the unity between the life of the individual and the wisdom of the Buddha.

7) *Rishu-e*

Demonstrating the manifestation of Mahāvairocana in the form of Vajrasattva, the ideal image of man. Surrounding him are four female-formed bodhisattva attributes representing the human desires (avarice, touch, thirst and pride), to symbolize the transcendence of the ideal man over temptation—or in contrast, the fact that because of ignorance and pollution, the existence of Pure Enlightenment is possible. This section demonstrates the interrelationship between ignorance (*saṃsāra*) and Enlightenment (*nirvāṇa*). 19 deities.

8) *Gōsanze-katsuma-e*

For the benefit of saving obstinate sentient beings, Vajrasattva assumes the ferocious external appearance of Trailokyavijaya (Gōsanze myō-ō). 77 deities.

9) *Gōsanze sammaya-e*

Expressing the psychological function of the angry *vidyārāja*. 73 deities.

Besides the two great *maṇḍala*, the Shingon sect also recognizes four other forms of *maṇḍala:*

a) *Dai mandara* (*Mahā-maṇḍala*)

Representing Kūkai's view of the universe, as all existents, both material and spiritual, symbolizing Dainichi Nyorai. For the benefit of making the common people comprehend this fact, the Buddhas and bodhisattvas were expressed in iconography—all such representations form the expression of the total form of Dainichi Nyorai.

b) *Sammaya mandara* (*Samaya maṇḍala*)

The previous *maṇḍala* presented a total view of the universe. In contrast, this *maṇḍala* symbolically represents parts of the whole by means of esoteric instruments such as the lotus, sword, or gem. It also utilizes the *mudrā*, symbol of the wisdom and power capable of saving sentient beings.

c) *Hō mandara* (*Dharma maṇḍala*)

The Shingon sect emphasizes the symbolic function of language, insofar as it can serve as a medium to express the essence of the existents of the universe. The word is believed to contain within its being the actual reality itself, which can only be comprehended by meditation. To simplify this process, Sanskrit words and letters, *mantras* and sutras are utilized in an effort to awaken the individual to the reality behind the word.

d) *Katsuma mandara* (*Karma maṇḍala*)

All existents are viewed as constantly flowing and moving, without a moment's cessation, while the Buddhas and bodhisattvas ceaselessly manifest in different forms to save sentient beings. This form of *maṇḍala* depicts their movement in iconography and philosophically represents all the dynamic actions of the universe.

7. *Abhiṣeka* (Jap. *Kanjō*) and Other Rituals

The *abhiṣeka* ceremony in esoteric Buddhism was derived from the consecration or anointment of Indian kings upon their ascension to the throne. Later, in Buddhist literature it came to symbolize the attainment of Enlightenment, after the completion of the ten stages of the bodhisattva. In esoteric Buddhism it is first used when a master initiates his disciple into the doctrine. At that time the initiate receives the *Gakuhō kanjō*, which permits him to learn the *Taizōkai* and *Kongōkai* doctrines. The term *kanjō* in Japanese literally means 'aspersion with water.' Before the actual ceremony is performed, the initiate is given the esoteric *śīla*, usually in the morning. Then early and late at night, the *Kongōkai* and *Taizōkai* doctrines are imparted ritually. At these ceremonies the initiate is blindfolded with a red or white cloth and led to the *maṇḍala* altar where he throws a flower to determine the Buddha or other deity to henceforth venerate, and is instructed in the appropriate *mantra* and *mudrā* relating to the deity. He then is conducted through further symbolic rites and finally is sprinkled with holy water from five vessels, symbolizing the five wisdoms of the Buddha (Action, Observation, Equality, Mirror and *Dharmadhātu*-nature wisdom), at which time the sacred formula of each of the Buddhas is recited. The *Kongōkai* and *Taizōkai* ceremonies are very similar. The Tendai Taimitsu performs an additional rite, the *Soshijji*.

There are various varieties of *kanjō* in Shingon esoterism ranging from the simplest, which initiates the layman into the sect to the more advanced. The three most important *kanjō* consist of: the 'Affinity with the Buddhas (*Kechien kanjō*), designed for the purpose of bringing monks or laymen to select a deity for devotion by throwing a flower upon the altar, the *Gakuhō* or *Jimyō kanjō* for initiation into the religious life and lastly, the 'Transmission of the Law' (*Denpō kanjō*) permitting a monk to attain the position of master, or be allowed to teach others. These ceremonies are not to be found together in any single text and depend very much upon oral transmission. In fact, differences in conducting the rituals led to the split of both Tōmitsu and Taimitsu into separate schools or branches.

Besides the *kanjō*, countless other rituals form an integral part of Shingon practice. These consist of devotions to various deities for both spiritual and worldly benefits. The aristocrats of the Heian period were particularly interested in the latter, and Tantric Buddhism managed to infiltrate nearly every aspect of their lives. During his lifetime, Kūkai performed official rituals more than fifty-one times for such purposes as peace for the nation, prosperity, rain, good harvest and so on. Such mundane goals were hopefully viewed as *upāya* and coincided with the Shingon emphasis upon this life.

One of the most important types of ritual used for both spiritual and worldly purposes was the *goma* (Skt. *homa*) burnt offering. This was an archaic rite dating back to the days of the *Veda's* when Agni (symbol of fire) was considered to be the intermediary between man and the heavenly *deva*. In Shingon, the *Ge* (exterior) *goma* rites offered oblations for mundane benefits. The following are the most popular types and known as the 'four goma'.

1) *sokusaihō* (Skt. *śāntika*)—to calm or quell such calamities as war, famine, diseases, accidental death and natural disturbances.
2) *zōyakuhō* (*puṣṭika*)—to increase or extend happiness and prosperity
3) *kōshōhō* (*vaśīkaraṇa*)—to invite the protection and compassion of the Buddhas and bodhisattvas.[19]
4) *gōfukuhō* (*abhicāraka*)—to conquer evil.

In contrast to the foregoing the *Nai* (interior) *goma* were used to obtain spiritual benefits.

8. Further Developments of Shingon Tōmitsu

After the death of Kūkai in 835, Shingon influence began to wane. With the return of Ennin from China in 847 and Enchin in 858, Tendai Taimitsu possessed the latest developments in esoterism and an edge of superiority. Shinzei (800–60) and Shinnen (804–91) attempted to reach China in 836 but were prevented by shipwreck. In 862, Shūei (809–84), a former priest of Mt. Hiei, was successful and spent three years in China. But by this time, Chinese Buddhism was seriously in decline and although the scriptures and instruments brought back were significant cultural enrichments, there were no further theological innovations. The burden of Buddhist evolution now rested upon the shoulders of the Japanese sects, which had reached their maturity. What was lacking was individual initiative and leadership. The Shingon sect was particularly plagued with this problem as well as internal dissension.

Shinnen was entrusted with the affairs of Kōyasan after Kūkai's death and among the many accomplishments of his fifty-six years as abbot was the establishment of the *Denpō-e* (Service for the Transmission of the Dharma). This had begun with the official grant of three *nembundosha* to Mt. Kōya in the year 835 and represented the Shingon method of training monks. Applicants were screened by being required to pass a minimum of five out of ten questions and the names of successful candidates were submitted to the government. The official ordination was held at the Tōdaiji and after this, the monks were required to spend six years engaged in assigned duties on Mt. Kōya without being allowed to leave. Every spring and fall, the *Denpō-e* were held, these were actually seminars in Shingon doctrine. After nineteen years, in 853, this system was altered when Shinzei of the Takaosanji requested and received three more *nembundosha*, raising the Shingon total to six. Then, those who qualified from both Kōyasan and Takaosanji were initially examined at Tōji. As time passed however, due to the distance between Tōji and Kōyasan, the ordained monks ceased to go to the mountain. Disturbed by this state of affairs, Shinnen petitioned the court in 882 to henceforth examine and ordain the Kōyasan *nembundosha* on the mountain. This petition was granted two years later and initiated a battle between the two temples. In 897, Yakushin of the Tōji temple requested court permission to ordain all six Shingon *nembundosha* at Tōji but this request was not granted. Finally, in 907 the Retired Emperor Kampyō granted additional *nembundosha* and solved the dispute.

Gradually all the leading Shingon temples received permission to have their own *nembundosha* and this greatly added to the numerical prosperity of the sect but increased the general disunity. Numerous conflicts between individuals, groups and temples created constant dissension. One of the reasons for such disunity was the fact that unlike Tendai, Shingon had never developed a headquarters or heart of the sect. It had evidently been Kūkai's intention to make Kōyasan a counterpart to Mt. Hiei, but he did not live long enough to complete its construction and establish its role. The Shingon rivalries and intrigues are particularly complex due to the frequent changes in temple affiliations among members of the sect. During a lifetime a priest might reside at several temples and the disciples of one master generally dispersed to different locations. The types of disputes that arose were personal, ideological, institutional and even political, as in the case where a given individual or group would rally to support an aristocratic patron in the chaotic shifting of power between Emperors, Retired Emperors, the Fujiwara regents, and their enemies.

An example of the dissension is the bitter dispute between the followers of Jitsue (786–847) and Shinga (801–79), the younger brother of Kūkai. Jitsue was entrusted by Kūkai with the Tōji temple, while Shinga, a constant companion of his brother during his lifetime, was placed in charge of the repository of scriptures at Tōji. The interests of these men were completely divergent and led to the ultimate strife between their disciples. Jitsue, who was succeeded at Tōji by Shūei, was primarily concerned with the affairs of the temple. Shinga, on the other hand, had established interests at court, becoming a confidante of such personages as Emperor Seiwa and the regent Fujiwara Yoshifusa. His disciple, Shinnen, became the abbot of Kōyasan. The first dispute between the disciples Shūei and Shinnen was over the *nembundosha* problem, which we discussed earlier.

The second dispute occurred over the *Sanjūjō sakushi*. This was a collection of secret scriptures that Kūkai had handcopied and brought back from China. Originally it was kept in the Tōji repository. Since Shinga had been in charge of the repository, after his death, fearing for the loss of the precious text, Shinnen, had declared it to be the property of his master and brought it to Kōyasan. Tōji insistently demanded its return but Shinnen refused. During the lifetimes of Shinnen and Shūei the debate reached a stalemate. Later the text was passed on to a Kōyasan priest named Mukū (?–918) and when Kangen (854–925) became the abbot of Tōji, he had the Retired Emperor Kampyō expressly send an order to Kōyasan to return the text. Just before the order arrived, during the last month of the year 915, Mukū took the text without authorization and permanently departed from Kōyasan with his disciples for Iga province where he died. Eventually, after Kangen also became abbot of

Kōyasan, he was able to restore the text back to Tōji. Ironically, during the early Kamakura period a priest of the Ninnaji borrowed the text and it resides there today. Such complex disputes however, were commonplace.

Under Shinnen, Kōyasan prospered and gained aristocratic support. The buildings that Kūkai had originally envisioned were finally completed at this time and one of the means of accomplishing this was the development of the belief among the aristocracy that Kōyasan was a Pure Land. The idea was set forth by Shinga and also by Shinnen, who informed Emperor Yōzei in 883 that the Kongōbuji was the home of ancient manifestations (*kojaku*) of the Buddhas. In 900, one of the first events in the life of the Retired Emperor Kampyō as a *Hō-ō* (Retired Buddhist Emperor), was to make a pilgrimage to the mountain. The concept of Kōyasan as a Pure Land was to be revived in subsequent generations but its origin, during the life of Shinnen, brought sufficient financial assistance to complete the construction on the mountain.[20]

One of the most successful periods in Shingon development was between 889–923. At this time Shūei's disciple, Yakushin (827–906) was the successor at Tōji, and Shinnen's disciple Shōbō (832–909) established the Daigoji temple.

Yakushin ordained Retired Emperor Kampyō (the former Emperor Uda) at the Tōji in 901 and three years later the Emperor built a special temple called the Endō-in at the Ninnaji with a living quarters. He resided there as abbot and followed the life of a monk. The Ninnaji temple, located in the western sector of the capital, had originally been built in 888 in memory of Emperor Kōkō and entrusted to the monks of Mt. Hiei. After Retired Emperor Kampyō took up residence there it became a Tōmitsu temple under the influence of Yakushin. This temple became very popular among the Pro-Imperial aristocrats and an important source of Shingon wealth and influence.

In 874, Shōbō established the Daigoji temple in the eastern sector of the capital. Thirty years later this became officially a temple of Imperial patronage, sponsored by three emperors: Daigo (897–930), Sujaku (930–

46) and Murakami (946–67). It also became the major centre of Shingon Shugendō.

In this manner the Shingon sect prospered as an institution with Imperial and aristocratic patronage but lacked unity and centralization. The 915 desertion of Mukū and his disciples from Kōyasan marked the decline of that temple, which Kūkai had conceived of as the heart of his order. Yakushin and Shōbō successfully revived Tōmitsu popularity and prosperity in the capital but they were unable to unify the breaches existing within the sect or heal the rivalries; this was finally accomplished by Kangen of the Tōji temple.

Kangen (853–925), a disciple of Shōbō, was the first monk to become simultaneously the abbot of the Tōji, Daigoji and eventually Kongōbuji on Kōyasan. He successfully managed to unify the entire sect by turning attention away from existing conflicts to the personality of the founder, Kūkai. In the year 921, upon Kangen's petition, Kūkai was finally granted the posthumous title of Kōbō Daishi, fifty-eight years after his death. This was quite late in comparison to the founder of the Tendai sect. Saichō had received the honour of Dengyō Daishi in 866, forty-four years after his death, while Ennin became Jikaku Daishi the same year, merely two years after his death[21] and Enchin was to become Chishō Daishi in 927, thirty-eight years after his death. It would seem that Kūkai had been unduly neglected.

At the time Kangen received the posthumous honour for Kūkai, he carried the Imperial edict to Kōyasan and opened the vault where Kūkai was interred. According to legend, Kūkai was found still in the posture of meditation and when one disciple touched his knee, he believed that the flesh still felt warm. This event became the basis of the popular myth that spread throughout Japan, alleging that Kūkai still lived on Kōyasan in the state of perpetual *samādhi*. The popularity of this cult successfully united the Shingon sect and Kōyasan became the object of pilgrimages from Tōmitsu temples throughout the land.

With the assistance of tremendous political power, Kangen attempted to revive Mt. Kōya and restore its structures. He was nearly successful when in 933 and again in 952 lightning struck, damaging major buildings. These were ultimately restored by the succeeding abbot Gashin (died 999), who built shrines to the protector Shintō deities Nifu and Kōya to prevent such calamities in the future. Unfortunately, despite his efforts just prior to his death, lightning again struck in the 7th month of the year 994, destroying the great pagoda, main hall and the priest's quarters. Services and rituals had to be conducted outdoors and although the local governor interceded to help, eventually the monks were advised to abandon the mountain, since its edifices had been virtually destroyed. This desolate situation continued up until the year 1016 when a new restoration was attempted.

The priest Jōyo (957–1047), originally a Tantric monk of Nara, experienced a divine dream in which the Kannon of the Hasedera appeared to him and instructed him to rebuild Kōyasan. At the time, Jōyo was sixty years of age and dedicated to the *Lotus sutra* and filial memorials, for which he was popularly known as Jikyō Shōnin (for his devotion to the *Lotus*) and Kishin Shōnin (for his filial remembrances). Jōyo, assisted by Ninkai (955–1046), a former disciple of Gashin, worked to restore the mountain. It was at this time that the popular notion of Kōyasan as a Pure Land was revived in conjunction with the belief that Kūkai resided there in perpetual *samādhi*. Added to the legend was the fact that Kūkai had announced that upon his death he would enter the Tuṣita heaven to serve Maitreya, the coming Buddha. Because of this, Kūkai became regarded as an incarnation (*keshin*) of Maitreya and Kōyasan was believed to be part of the Tuṣita heaven. Such legends managed to attract the aristocracy back to the mountain.

In 1023, the Regent Fujiwara Michinaga visited Kōyasan to bury sutras and declared that he indeed had seen Kūkai in meditation. In 1048 his son, the Regent Fuijwara Yorimichi, visited the mountain. With the financial assistance of such powerful patrons, the restoration progressed and Kōyasan's prosperity returned. During the late Heian period, when it became popular for Emperors to retire into religion, and assert power behind the throne (known as the Insei system), Kōyasan became a popular site of pilgrimages. Emperor Shirakawa visited the mountain four times between 1088 and 1127, while Emperor Toba visited it twice between 1124 and 1132. Warriors, wearied of combat, such as the famous Yoritoki, who became a monk in 1180, sought spiritual peace there.

By 1156, the reconstruction of the great pagoda was completed and Taira Kiyomori, who was then engaged in a contest for the control of Japan, attended the dedication ceremonies. According to legend, the central Dainichi Nyorai of the *maṇḍala* of the pagoda's main hall was drawn in blood from Kiyomori's head, as an act of devotion.

During these tumultous years of political chaos, there is no record of the monks of Kōyasan swarming down upon the capital to press their demands upon the court, as was the case with Mt. Hiei and the leading Nara temples. Undoubtedly, a chief deterrent for the monks of Kōyasan was the distance to the capital that separated them from its political affairs. The meditative nature of the mountain perhaps ameliorated the situation, although it did not prevent internal conflicts. For over 140 years, up to the year 1288, a bitter war was waged between the established power structure of the main Kongōbuji temple and a group led by Kakuban (1094–1143) of the Daidenpō-in, who sought to reform Shingon.

Kakuban was the first to theoretically assimilate Pure Land teachings into Shingon theology in his *Gorinkuji myō himitsu shaku* (Treatise on the Five and Nine *Mantra*). In this work he rejected the notion of *mappō shisō* and identified Dainichi Nyorai with Amida, making the *nembutsu* one of the three practices of Shingon. Admittedly this was for those of inferior ability who could not accomplish the Shingon goal of attaining Buddahood in this body. Kakuban was extremely interested in the plight of the laity and the development of *sekkyō* (popular-style) preaching. His battle with the Kongōbuji however, was not theological.

In 1131, Kakuban petitioned the court to build the Daidenpo-in temple on Kōyasan and the following year, when the temple and a *nembutsu* hall were completed, they were granted five *shōen* (estates) through the patronage of the Retired Emperor Toba. This made the new Daidenpō-in vastly richer than the Kongōbuji and the resentful monks of that temple submitted a petition of opposition. In 1134, adding further insult to the smoldering embers of jealousy, Kakuban was made abbot of both the Daidenpō-in and Kongōbuji. Since the Kongōbuji had for some time been governed by the abbot of Tōji, the young Kabukan met with opposition from both the monks on the mountain and Tōji. The situation worsened until later that year when the Daidenpō-in complex was attacked and destroyed by monks of the Kongōbuji. Kakuban and more than 700 followers escaped to Mt. Negoro, where he elected to remain despite Imperial requests that he return to Kōyasan. In 1143 at the age of forty-nine, Kakuban died on Mt. Negoro, but his followers refused to make peace with Kōyasan and established a Shingi (Neo) Shingon movement. The conflict with the Kongōbuji continued sporadically until the year 1288, when the Daidenpō-in was officially transferred from Kōyasan to Mt. Negoro.

The question naturally arises why both the Shingon and Tendai sects endured so much dissension and degeneration by the close of the Heian epoch? Why did the quiet mountains of meditation and learning disrupt into violence and blood-shed, the very antithesis of their being? It is obvious that the weaknesses of human nature and natural tendency for prosperity to corrupt were factors, but another essential ingredient was the institutional role of Buddhism in society. Nara Buddhism had been a magical instrument of the ruling classes, an apperture of the Ritsuryō system. Although scholarly monks made important doctrinal contributions, the social institutional function of the sects was to protect the government. As the Ritsuryō system declined, the Buddhist institutions so closely allied with the system also experienced degeneration. For many of the Nara temples, already endowed with abundant lands, the government decline did not result in a financial burden, since they were able to follow the trend of the day and develop their own *shōen*, but it was morally corrupting. To a certain degree an analogous situation exists in modern Japan, where the temples of the great cities are able to create their own financial independence without relying upon popular support by selling or leasing their lands for parking lots and modern skyscrapers. This type of independence can offer the freedom for creativity, but in most cases it leads to moral laxness, since a religious institution has an obligatory role in society.

Saichō recognized the dangers of having the Buddhist sects institutionally bound to the Ritsuryō government and he witnessed the decline of the institutions with the Ritsuryō failure, but he still was faced with the difficult problem of finding a new financial basis for his sect. Nara temples that were unable to develop their own *shōen* encountered the same difficulty. It is most likely that Kūkai, with his political acumen, recognized the situation even earlier and perhaps this was the reason for his conciliatory attitude; a transition had to be made before the system could be changed. The new basis for the financial support of the Buddhist institutions during the Heian period became the aristocracy. They alone possessed the wealth of the nation, and just as Nara Buddhism had been inseparably bound to the fortunes of the Ritsuryō system, so Heian Buddhism became tied to the pretentiousness, naïveté, and superstitions of the aristocracy. When that class ultimately succumbed to the violent warriors, the Heian Buddhist sects endured a similar fate and the cycle had to be repeated once again.

C. Aristocrats and Heian Buddhism

While the Ritsuryō system was in effect, many of the temples were classified as *Jōgakuji* (Temple of set amount) or *Goganji* (Temple of Imperial Vow). The *Jōgakuji* received a set amount of financial support as well as *nembundosha* from the government, while the *Goganji* received favours from the munificence of their Imperial patrons. With the decline of the Ritsuryō, the *Jōgakuji* temples suffered a loss of revenue, while the *Goganji* lasted through the Heian period until the Emperors eventually became impoverished along with the aristocracy. To give an example, the following were established as *Goganji* during the period of Imperial reigns between 833–967:

Temple	*Emperor*
Jōshin-in	Nimmyō

Shiō-in	Montoku
Jōganji	Seiwa
Genkeiji	Yōzei
Ninnaji	Kōkō
Daigoji	Daigo
Enmyō-in	Sujaku
Dainichi-in	Murakami

Although Imperial patronage was an important source of temple revenue, the support of the Fujiwara family became equally advantageous. Between 857–1160, which is commonly termed the Fujiwara period, this powerful family controlled the government acting as regents to the Emperor. During their centuries of glory, Fujiwara support became even more sought after than Imperial patronage since the family had more wealth and prestige to bestow.

The aristocrats had a great deal to gain by supporting Buddhism. As the Ritsuryō government declined, legal justification for their role diminished. Without military power supporting their claim to rule, the sanction of the church, the most powerful institution of the day, became important. This was particularly true for those who sought to usurp power, such as the Fujiwaras. Furthermore, the aristocrats sincerely believed that esoteric Buddhism could offer them mystical means to combat their enemies in the shifting political maelstrom.

Heian aristocrats also became aware of a new function of Buddhism that their Nara predecessors had generally overlooked, the funeral service. Preoccupied with the benefits of the new religion in procuring happiness in this world, little thought was given during the Nara period to what Buddhism might offer after death. Services had been held throughout the land every seven days after an Emperor's death, but the purpose was not so much to benefit the deceased as to protect the nation from the pollution of death and anger of the deceased. By the Heian epoch this view changed and Emperors began to request Buddhist funeral services and to be buried near temples. In fact, by the mid-Heian period, Imperial tombs were built within temple confines. Emperor Saga was the first to announce that he could see no purpose in having his body placed in a burial mound at death, since he believed it would be contrary to the law of returning to Absolute truth. The practice for Emperors to chose cremation became quite common.

Not a great deal is known regarding the nature of Heian funerals services, but they seem to have been associated with Lotus meditation, which entailed a form of repentance and solemn melancholy chant. The nobles followed the Imperial precedent and also began to have Buddhist funerals. By the late 10th century, the most popular services were utilizing Pure Land sutras or the chanting of the *nembutsu*.

With the no-soul or non-self (*anātman*) doctrine, the Buddhist funeral service could hardly expedite a non-existent soul to a happy heaven, but it did serve as a tremendous *upāya*. The thought of one's own mortality was capable of affecting changes in even the most callous megalomaniac, and it signified the first step of Buddhist negation was beginning to take effect. But besides directing thought towards one's own demise, the funeral and memorial services performed an even greater and more lasting benefit for the friends and relatives of the deceased. It brought them together to hear the teachings of Buddhism and remember the merits of a loved one, not only at the time of death but also each seventh day, for the first forty-nine days, again on the 100th day after death, and periodically thereafter. In this respect much of the deceased's evil karma was transformed to good in the minds and lives of the survivors. Needless to say, funeral services came to be an important and lasting source of revenue for the Buddhist institutions.

But just as aristocratic support was a financial blessing, it also became a source of dissension and political intrigue within the orders and temples. Bound to espouse the causes of their patrons, many temples by the end of the Heian period were forced into rivalries and hostilities totally unrelated to religion. In particular as Fujiwara control began to waver during the latter part of the 11th century, temples found themselves enmeshed in quarrels between that family and the Retired Emperors, who sought to assert their authority behind the scenes under the *Insei* system. An example of such a case was the Shingon Ninnaji temple. Established under the patronage of its abbot the Retired Emperor Uda, who had tried to break Fujiwara control as early as the close of the 9th century, the Ninnaji became a rallying place for Pro-Imperial, anti-Fujiwara groups. Such political involvement drew many temples into the endless succession disputes closing the Heian period.

Besides the political handicaps resulting from aristocratic patronage, the temples also had to endure the aristocrats as abbots. Just as the Retired Emperor Uda became abbot of the Ninnaji other Emperors, princes and sons of nobles, possessing virtually no religious training or experience, were installed in the prestigious temples. By the time of the *Insei* period (late 11th to 12th century) these temples, designated as *monzeki*, were dominant. One of the reasons for such a development was the fact that the traditional method of selecting abbots had been wiped away with the collapse of the Ritsuryō government.

Another factor that strongly influenced Heian Buddhism was the somewhat frivolous and superstitious manner in which the aristocrats accepted the religion and integrated it into their daily lives. Since they offered donations for lavish rituals, colourful robes and glittering tantric instruments, the temples hastened to fulfill their expections of exotic mysteriousness. An entire liturgical year evolved to occupy their time. In fact, it was reported that the Fujiwara regent Michinaga, who dominated the court from 995 until his death in 1027, devoted more than six months each year to Buddhist rituals accompanied by other government officials, while national affairs languished. Every month of the year offered elaborate festivals and ceremonies. The following are an example of some of the liturgical functions mentioned in contemporary literature: (the dates and months of many were not standard and the lunar calendar ran 17–45 days in advance of the Julian calendar).

First Month

Shūshōgatsu-e. A ceremony derived from the *keka* (Rites of Repentance) mixed with Shintō purification ritual. Individual repentance was made to a Buddha, followed by purification and the promise of longevity.

Gosai-e (8th–14th day). Celebrated in the Daigokuden of the palace for the protection of the nation. In the morning, lectures were held on the *Konkōmyōkyō* and in the evening, a Kisshōten (Lakṣmī) *keka* was held. First of the three great Nara festivals.

Gohichinichi no mishuhō (8th–14th day). The esoteric ceremony devised by Kūkai for peace, the Emperor's health and a rich harvest of the five grains, held in the Shingon-in of the palace. This became a great festival in Kyōto and is frequently mentioned in Heian literature.

Second Month

Shūnigatsu-e, a *keka* ritual centered around Kannon, the most famous being held at the Tōdaiji Nigatsu-dō.

Nehan-e (*Nirvāṇa sūtra* service) of the Sangai-ji.

Ki no midokyō The reading of the first half of the 600 chapters of the *Daihannyakyō*, which lasted for four days.

Saishō-e. The reading of the *Konkōmyō saishō-ō kyō* of the Enshūji (14th–23rd day). One of the three Kyōto Imperial festivals.

Third Month

During this month famous temples in the vicinity of the capital offered special sutra chanting services. For example, the *Hokke-e* of the Takaosanji, the *Kegon-e* of the Hokkeji and the *Saishō-e* of the Yakushiji. The latter was usually held the 7th–13th days and was the second of the three great Nara festivals.

Denpō-e (Service for the Transmission of the Dharma) of Shiga.

Kangaku-e (Service to Encourage Learning) of Hiei Sakamoto.

Mandō-e (Service of Ten Thousand Lights) of the Yakushiji, a popular festival offered for repentance and the elimination of sin. It was often held in famous temples during the dark winter months.

Fourth Month

The month of the Buddha's birth celebrated by the *Kambutsu-e* ceremony at the palace and leading temples offering sweet tea to the infant Śākyamuni.

Daihannya-e (*Mahāprajñāparamitā sūtra* service) at the Daianji.

Jukai (acceptance of *śīla*) ordination on Mt. Hiei.

Shari hōonkō of Mt. Hiei, venerating the Buddha's relics that Ennin brought back from China.

Fifth Month

Bosatsu-kai (Bestowing bodhisattva *śīla*) at the Hasedera.

Semai (Rice offering). Rice and salt were offered by an Imperial envoy to the hermits of the mountainsides.

Sixth Month

Manke-e (Ten Thousand Flower Festival) of the Tōdaiji; a counterpart of the *Mandō-e*.

Seventh Month

Monju hannyakyō-e. Recitation of the *Saptaśatikā Prajñāpāramitā sūtra* at the Tōji and Saiji with rice and salt offerings for the poor.

Urabon-e (Avalambana festival) held the 13th–16th days of the month at all leading temples as a festival for the dead.

Eighth Month

Fudan nembutsu (Perpetual chanting *nembutsu*) and Hachiman *hōjō-e* held on Mt. Hiei.

Ki no midokyō (Reading of the second half of the *Daihannyakyō*) and a conclusion ceremony.

Ninth Month

Kanjō (esoteric) ordinations at the *kaidan* on Mt. Hiei.

Tenth Month

Yuima-e (*Vimalakīrti nirdeśa* service) at the Kōfukuji held the 10th–16th days. This was the third of the great Nara festivals.

Daijō-e (Service to honour the *Tripiṭaka*) of the Hōshōji held the 24th–28th days. This was the third Imperial Kyōto festival. The month did vary during the Heian period.

Twelfth Month

Butsumyō-e (Chanting of the names of the Buddhas service) held the 19th–22nd days. A *keka* practice featuring the perpetual chanting of the names of the Buddhas, the *Butsumyōkyō* sutra lists the names of 11093 Buddhas, bodhisattvas and Pratyekabuddhas to be invoked.

Many of these festivals are mentioned in the *Makura no sōshi* (*Pillow Book*) written by the court lady Sei Shōnagon. In her witty and sophisticated style, this typical product of the Heian aristocracy presents an sight into the attitude of her contemporaries as they attended such functions:

Now a couple of gentlemen who have not met for some time

> run into each other in the temple, and are greatly surprised. They sit down together and chat away, nodding their heads, exchanging funny stories, and opening their fans wide to hold before their faces so as to laugh the more freely. Toying with their elegantly decorated rosaries, they glance about, criticizing some defect they have noticed in one of the carriages or praising the elegance of another. They discuss various services that they have recently attended and compare the skill of different priests in performing the Eight Lessons or the dedication of Sutras. Meanwhile, of course, they pay not the slightest attention to the service actually in progress. To be sure, it would not interest them very much; for they have heard it all so often that the priest's words could no longer make any impression.[22]

In brief, the aristocracy was not so much motivated by religious piety in attending the magnificent ceremonies as in the sheer enjoyment of the sight of the silken robes and golden instruments, the smell of rare sandalwood and the sound of melodious chanting. It was a purely aesthetic enjoyment for members of a society motivated to seek the refinements of taste.

For the Heian woman, such functions offered a pleasant change from the tedium of daily life. In fact, their lives revolved around the choice of costumes to wear to special services and festivities, as well as gossiping days on end concerning the taste, or lack of it, of their rivals. Pilgrimages and retreats offered relief from the claustrophobia of being confined to their houses to await the visits of husbands or lovers. The trips could serve as diversionary escapes or even as a means of demonstrating frustration, as the authoress of the *Kagerō Nikki* (*Gossamer Years*) frequently used them. They could even be excuses for lover's trysts. In any event, they had to be aesthetically tasteful and the most disturbing happening was the encounter of the uncouth masses. As the ascerbic Sei Shōnagon wrote:

> It is very annoying, when one has visited the Hase Temple and has retired into one's enclosure, to be disturbed by a herd of common people who come and sit outside in a row, crowded so close together that the tails of their robes fall over each other

> in utter disarray. I remember once I was overcome by a great desire to go on a pilgrimage. Having made my way up the log steps, deafened by the fearful roar of the river, I hurried into my enclosure, longing to gaze upon the sacred countenance of Buddha. To my dismay I found that a throng of commoners had settled themselves directly in front of me, where they were incessantly standing up, prostrating themselves, and squatting down again. They looked like so many basketworms as they crowded together in their hideous clothes, leaving hardly an inch of space between themselves and me. I really felt like pushing them all over sideways.[23]

The authoress of the *Kagerō Nikki* was slightly more sympathetic:

> The beggars at the temple, each with his earthen bowl, were most distressing. I recoiled involuntarily at being brought so near the defiling masses. I could not sleep, and with little else to occupy my mind, I found myself fascinated, even moved to tears, at the prayer of a blind man, not very well dressed, who was pouring forth his petition, in a loud voice without a thought that someone might be listening.[24]

Buddhism offered the Heian woman at least an imagined alternative to the prospect of an unhappy arranged marriage or husbandly neglect. Few seldom actually did enter religion, but it was a pleasant daydream, and as one unhappy wife wrote:

> Around the middle of the Second Month there was a widely circulated rumor that he [her husband] had spent ten days running with his newest lady friend.
>
> Higan (Spring or Fall equinox observance) week came, and I prepared to go into a retreat—it seemed at least a fair alternative to this constant brooding and weeping . . . I thought too that I should like to go on a long retreat at some mountain temple. Such a retreat might make it easier for me ultimately to renounce the world. *Kagerō Nikki*[25]

But Buddhism certainly did not offer the Heian woman an equality far beyond the dimensions of her society. Women were not allowed to even enter the sacred confines of Mt. Hiei or Kōyasan, and Japanese Buddhism, tainted by its Chinese parent, offered somewhat less equality than

Indian Buddhism. One of the clearest examples of this transformation is found in the ethical obligations set forth by the *Siṅgālovāda Suttanta.* In India this famous text laid down five reciprocal obligations for both husband and wife. The Chinese maintained the husband's five duties towards the wife, but depending upon the translation, increased the wife's obligations to her husband to the number 13 or 14.[26] Such attitudes constituted a major difference between Indian and Chinese Buddhism. Still, although Indian Buddhism offered women more equality than granted by contemporary society, Heian Buddhism offered them at least no less than currently accepted. By the late Heian period the situation improved with the rise of Pure Land belief and the challenge of established institutions. Woman's place idealistically rose; the denial of the right to enter Hieizan was challenged and the prostitute was promised the same hope of salvation as the pious monk. But this idealism was once again crushed by the realism of feudalistic society which measured equality by physical prowess.

Life for the Heian noblewoman was generally pleasant, although perhaps by contemporary standards it might be judged as vain and empty. Besides the great liturgical festivals, certain other religious practices permeated the daily lives of the aristocrats. These were a syncretic blend of Buddhism, Confucianism, Shintō, *Yin-yang* (*Onyōdō*), *feng-shui* geomancy and astrology. The main concern was to avoid bad luck, hence on inauspicious zodiac days, the nobles would circumscribe their activities or even confine themselves to their houses. Directions played an important role in their lives, in particular the unpropitious north-east. Mt. Hiei faced this direction from the capital and was believed to guard the city from calamities. The Tantric Buddhist adaptation of Indian direction worship paralleled such beliefs and the practices mingled. Esoteric sutras such as the *Hokuto-hichisei-enmyōkyō* (*Sutra of Seven Stars Granting Longevity*) gained popularity as did Myōken bodhisattva, embodiment of the North Star. These devotions were extremely intricate and required preparation as well as regular consultations of a diviner; the sexagenary cycle formed the basis of *yin-yang* divination. During the lifetime of Emperor Saga public observances of this nature were frowned upon, but after his death, the Fujiwara regents Yoshifusa and his adopted son Mototsune, installed Tantric *yin-yang* practices at court.

Devotions such as these seem far removed from the spirit of Buddhism yet they became inextricably bound to Heian esoteric Buddhist development. As long as the aristocrats formed the basis of institutional financial support, the temples catered to their anxieties. Buddhist Tantric priests even acted as exorcists to remove Shintō inspired defilements and taboos as well as putting to rest the unappeased spirits of the dead. But it was not pure opportunism that motivated the priests to enter so wholeheartedly into practices that might appear contradictory to the spirit of Buddhism; a great number believed in them as much as the aristocracy. The popular Shugendō movement, which was affiliated with both Taimitsu and Shingon, was a tangled mass of Buddhist, Shamanistic, Taoist and Shintō practices. Further, the Shingon emphasis upon 'this world' made Buddhist participation an important *upāya* even in cases where the priests might consider practices to be superstitious. But it is difficult for 20th century man, who naïvely believes in the powers of science and materialism to the same extent that Heian aristocrats placed their faith in Tantric rites, astrology and geomancy, to properly judge whether these practices were indeed 'superstitious.' It also is unfair to describe them as a degeneration from 'original' Buddhism. Admittedly, they were contrary to the spirit the historical Buddha wished to *ultimately* inspire within his followers but they were similar to the *iddhi* (spiritual powers), *paritta* (prayers of safety) and other practices utilized to attract lay followers and even beginning monks. The Four Noble Truths and Doctrine of Interdependent Origination were reserved for the advanced monks in Early Buddhism and not set forth for the laymen, who still had to be weaned from the pablum of rebirth in a happy heaven before they could consider a goal as intangible as Nirvana. In this respect, Heian court members did not greatly differ from the aristocratic contemporaries of the historical Buddha.

Although the terminology was not used in Japan, the typical method for instructing the laity of the Heian era corresponded to the three *kathā* (graduated forms of discourse) of Early Buddhism consisting of *dāna* (giving), *sīla* (morality) and *sagga* (promise of a heavenly reward). By now, in place of rebirth in a *deva* heaven, the longed for goal became the paradise of Yakushi (Bhaiṣajyaguru), Miroku (Maitreya) or Amida (Amitābha) and sutra-burying became one of the means of attaining such bliss.

As early as the Nara period, sutra-copying had been considered a source of gaining merit but during the Heian, the emphasis shifted to placing the sutra in holy ground. In 1007 Fujiwara Michinaga reportedly climbed Kimpusen, the holy mountain of Shugendō hermits to bury the *Lotus Sutra* and other volumes. To date, more than 300 places have been uncovered as sites of sutra burials. These were often dedicated to either Miroku (Maitreya), in hopes of witnessing his coming, or to Amida with the desire of being reborn in his Pure Land. In fact, Michinaga in his burial on Kimpusen evinced the hope of waiting in the Pure Land until Maitreya's coming and then being able to come forth resurrected. The mountain hermits and lay followers known as *hijiri* and *shami*, popularized these practices during the late Heian with the growth of Pure Land devotion. Among some of the most popular sites for sutra burial were Mt. Hiei and Kōyasan, by now believed to be a Pure Land in its own right.

Heian aristocrats were strongly attracted to Buddhism by its views of the transitory and illusory nature of life. The theme of *mujō* (impermanence) perfumes Heian literature and underlies the famous *Genji Monogatari*. But it is not presented graphically in terms of the physical horrors of death, illness or old age, so often found in Indian Buddhism, but rather symbolized by nature as the scattering of cherry blossoms or fading of autumn leaves. The poets and writers passively viewed such happenings in a mood of bittersweet reflection, terming it *mono no aware* (the sadness of things). As the poet-priest Saigyō (1118–90), so popular at the Heian Court, reflected:

Even a priest who does not have a self	Kokoro naki
Can understand the sadness of things	mi ni mo aware wa
	shirarekeri
From the snipe's flight	Shigi tatsu sawa no
on an autumn eve.	Aki no yūgure

Shinkokinshū IV: 362

How clearly such a poem contradicts the popular misconception that a monk had to purify himself of all human desires and longings in order to lead a holy life. Even though Saigyō has abandoned clinging to a false notion of self, he has not renounced the nostalgic human feeling of loneliness that he experiences as the bird takes to flight, symbolizing the approach of the cold winter.

The Heian aristocrats were romantically inclined to think that religious life demanded complete abandonment of all pleasures of life but the writings of the monks and hermits of the day exhibit the same enjoyment of the seasons and nature that the nobles cherished. To the courtier it might have appeared to be a renunciation because the values were reversed, or as Kamo no Chōmei (1153–1216) wrote:

> The Three Worlds are joined by one mind. If the mind is not at peace, neither beasts of burden nor possessions are of service, neither palaces nor pavilions bring any cheer. This lonely house is but a tiny hut, but I somehow love it. I naturally feel ashamed when I go to the capital and must beg, but when I return and sit here I feel pity for those still attached to the world of dust. Should anyone doubt the truth of my words, let him look to the fishes and the birds. Fish do not weary of the water, but unless one is a fish one does not know why. Birds long for the woods, but unless one is a bird one does not know why. The joys of solitude are similar. Who could understand them without having lived here?[27]

Many nobles romantically spoke of renouncing the world to enter religion but few sincerely did so. Emperor Kazan and Fujiwara Michinaga both found that becoming monks did little to inhibit their social lives, it was up to the individual. Many Retired Emperors entered religion as an escape from the political intrigues and succession disputes of the court, since a strong feeling existed that the most damning crime was to take the life of a religious. In fact, entering religion tended to become the rule rather than the exception. Between the 9th to the 12th centuries, the following Emperors upon their retirement entered religion:

Uda	Kazan	Gosanjō
Daigo	Ichijō	Shirakawa

Sujaku	Sanjō	Toba
Murakami	Goichijō	Sutoku
En-yū	Gosujaku	Goshirakawa

The aristocrats quickly followed the Imperial precedents. And during the period of Fujiwara domination, the clergy offered an added inducement since it offered the singular hope for talented individuals unacceptable to the Fujiwaras politically. Superficially the institutions prospered under the situation but the quality of the clergy and faith declined. Still for some individuals, religious commitments were sincere since Heian society offered ample reasons to turn to religion.

Heian aristocrats could indeed observe the changes of the seasons with poignant emotions in a day when senescence began at current middle age. Life was fleeting and the plagues, wars and other calamities at the close of the Heian period never let that fact be forgotten. Buddhist karma (*sukuse*, *gō*, *en*, *inga*) was romantically misinterpreted in popular literature as fatalistic determinism. Man appeared as fragile as the cherry blossom with no recourse but to silently lament his fate. Such resignation spared the frustration of fighting the inevitable, but at the same time it frequently serve as a justification for succumbing to human weaknesses. The literary protagonists such as Genji could always rationalize that their lot was a result of karma, so why fight it? An encounter with a beautiful maiden that developed into a brief love affair was 'karma' and if it failed to meet social sanctions for endurance, that too was 'karma'. Ironically, such a view of karma served as the perfect excuse to evade personal responsibility and thus became the very antithesis of the spirit of Buddhism. Yet it is difficult to clearly draw the line. Western man tends to often challenge the inevitable recklessly, refusing to acknowledge the existence of conditions beyond his control. Such a failure to accept the inescapable is as life denying as passivity. The question remains whether Sisyphus can ever transcend his rock by his own efforts or if he would do better to passively submit and forget its very existence.

The popular interpretation (often misinterpretation) of karma has done a great deal to shape the Japanese character. At times it appears the constant failure to challenge the conditions of existence is a weakness, but such an attitude can also offer great strength, particularly in rising out of defeat. It has offered as well a balance to the somewhat inhuman demands of the work ethic. Succumbing to 'ineluctable fate' can negate the self-sufficient ego and often preserve the human being. In fact, the ability to accept and endure without complaint is often considered to be an ingredient of sanctity. Such stoic acceptance forms a part of the basic fibre of Japanese life and at the same time is intertwined with hedonism. 'Accept what cannot be and enjoy what is' offers a perfect motto for the 'floating world', which became a psychological reality during the Heian period, although the term was not applied to Japanese society until centuries later.

For westerners who take the aristocrat's laments on life seriously, it undoubtedly appears that Buddhism introduced a negative attitude to Japanese society. But the aristocrats themselves relished the bittersweet atmosphere that so heightened the experience of the moment. Instead of interpreting the negation of worldly life as a step leading to a higher spiritual affirmation, they too often viewed it as justification for the enjoyment of the moment, and by the close of the Heian period, the cultivation of taste began to crumble into sheer hedonism.

The aristocrats, aware of the impermanence and illusory nature of life demanded from Buddhism, just as during the Nara period, theurgic panaceas, longevity, peace and prosperity. What they little dreamt, was that their own aristocratic world was soon to be swept into obscure limbo as the new warrior class rose to establish hegemony by the sword. The nostalgic thought of *mappō shisō* ultimately became a harsh reality as natural calamities and violence reduced the bittersweet aesthetic appreciation of life to acrid ashes. Deluged by fires, whirlwinds, famines, earthquakes, political intrigues and long years of civil war, the poet at the end of the Heian period could truly ask?

> Whence does he come, where does he go, man that is born and dies? We know not. For whose benefit does he torment himself in building houses that last but a moment, for what reason is his eye delighted by them? This too we do not know. Which will be first to go, the master or his dwelling? one

> might just as well ask this of the dew on the morning-glory. The dew may fall and the flower remain—remain, only to be withered by the morning sun. The flower may fade before the dew evaporates, but though it does not evaporate, it waits not the evening. Kamo no Chōmei[28]

Ironically, the final suffering of the aristocrats in their decline offered a more fertile spirtual soil than the period of their opulence.

The Buddhist church also faced a crisis as the aristocratic world began to fade and men once more began to extol ideals such as Gyōgi bosatsu's —that the aim of religion was not to cater to the preservation of a national or aristocratic ego but to offer all men hope for salvation. Every Buddhist sect theoretically carried such a message. It was present in the speculative theology of the Nara Sects and in the ideals of Saichō and Kūkai; institutional corruption was the source of its defilement. Even the somewhat legendary biography of Ryōgen, the most successful Tendai abbot, reports that 12–15 years after his ordination he had the desire to seek Enlightenment and to leave the Buddhist order for the peace and sanctity of a mountain hermitage but his obligation to his aged mother forced him to remain in the pollution of Mt. Hiei. How far had matters progressed that the committed individual had to leave the Buddhist institution to seek Enlightenment. The time had come when Buddhism had to become free of the worldly life of the court and aristocrats and establish itself as a religion of the masses; the time had come when Buddhism had to become truly Japanese.

D. Rise of Pure Land Devotion

During the Heian period, Pure Land belief came to play an increasing role in the Tendai sect. Under Ennin, *Jōgyō sammai* (Perpetual chanting meditation) was considered to be equally as effective as Lotus meditation. The Tendai priest Ensai further popularized devotion to Amida by holding special *nembutsu* services on the 15th day of every month. As the faith spread among the monks, it also began to take root among the aristocracy who patronized them. Zōmyō (842–927), a disciple of Ensai, who shared his Pure Land devotion and subsequently became an abbot of Mt. Hiei, attracted the patronage of Fujiwara Tadahira (880–949), who not only sponsored Pure Land services on Mt. Hiei but also at the Gokurakuji temple in the Higashiyama section of the capital. Even members of the Imperial family embraced the devotion. Reportedly the elder sister of Emperor Kazan died peacefully while engaged in *Jōgyō sammai* and *nembutsu* services were subsequently performed on her memorial days.

Around 964 a group of Classical Chinese scholars and monks brought together by mutual feelings of the impermanence of life, began holding regular semi-annual 'Meetings to Encourage Learning' (*Kangaku-e*). Under Tendai influence, the *nembutsu* became the main event at these gatherings.

Particularly under the abbot Ryōgen, Pure Land influence spread on Mt. Hiei. The *Jōgyō sammai* became the dominant form of meditation and the abbot himself wrote commentaries on the Pure Land texts for the aristocracy. But Pure Land devotion on Mt. Hiei was becoming too aristocratic. Influenced by this fear and the violent atmosphere of quarreling between the Sanmon and Jimon, Ryōgen's disciple Genshin left Mt. Hiei and built a small Amida temple in nearby Yokawa. There he predominantly taught commoners and lower aristocrats and under his leadership, Pure Land devotion reached its apex within the Tendai sect.

Genshin advocated that beginners in Pure Land faith should meditate upon the physical image of Amida, chanting the *nembutsu* vocally, and attempting to visualize the Pure Land within their own mind as a means of experiencing reality. This form of meditation was derived from the Tendai *Jōgyō sammai*. Advanced students were to proceed in the same manner only meditation was directed to the formless *Dharmakāya* of Amida in place of a tangible figure. Although Genshin utilized *Jōgyō sammai* meditation, which in Tendai was directed towards the goal of Enlightenment, he was one of the first Tendai monks to declare that his goal was birth in the Pure Land of Amida. He presented the reasons for this desire in his famous treatise, the *Ōjōyōshū* (Essentials of Salvation), which became the first Japanese theological study on Pure Land as well as a foundation for the development of Pure Land schools in Japan.

The *Ōjōyōshū* represented a departure from earlier Japanese Pure Land devotion in that it was strongly influenced by the writings of Shan-tao. The work actually consisted of an apologetical compilation of all available references in the Buddhist scriptures to Pure Land faith, relying most heavily upon the writings of Chih-I. Although it was a theological treatise written in Chinese script, it became very popular among the aristocracy and in fact, has been a best seller throughout Japanese history up to modern times. The Fujiwara regent Michinaga, was particularly inspired by the *Ōjōyōshū* and his faith in the Pure Land was so great that it was described both in the *Genji Monogatari* and *Eiga Monogatari*. In 1022, Michinaga constructed a Muryōju-in hall at the Hōjōji temple as a replica of the Pure Land and he resided there. This hall was the antecedent of the famous Byōdōin of Uji, one of the oustanding works of Heian architecture, built by his son Yorimichi.

Another Tendai monk instrumental in propagating Pure Land belief was Ryōnin (1072–1132), who retired from the aristocratic atmosphere of Mt. Hiei to live in the quiet suburb of Ōhara and chant the *nembutsu*. He became the founder of the Yūzū Nembutsu sect, which is still in existence.

Although Pure Land devotion was predominantly associated with the Tendai sect during the Heian period, it also attracted important followers among other schools. On Kōyasan, Kakuban and Shōshin both set forth *nembutsu* practice in accordance with Shingon tradition. Even the Nara sects had adherents. Most notable were the Sanron priests Yōkan (1032–1111) of the Zenrinji and Chinkai (1091–1152) of the Tōdaiji, who both advocated the devotion and wrote treatises on the Pure Land.

The most important development in Pure Land devotion was its diffusion among the masses, and Kūya (903–72), was one of the first to initiate such a movement. It is believed that he was born into the Imperial family of a non-Fujiwara mother at the time when that family was rising to ascendency. He perhaps wisely decided to become a monk and was ordained at the *kokubunji* in Owari province. Subsequently in 948 he went to Mt. Hiei and received a proper Tendai ordination from the abbot Enchō. Although he received the new name of Kōshō, upon ordination, he chose to remain known as *shami* Kūya for the remainder of his life.

While he was young, Kūya travelled throughout the Japanese countryside performing social works such as constructing bridges, roads, wells and constantly chanting the *nembutsu*. Popularly, he became known as *Amida hijiri* (Amida sage) or *Ichi no hijiri* (Sage of the people). Unlike some of the corrupt *shami* and *hijiri* groups, Kūya followed a strict discipline and even though he primarily worked among the masses, he also managed to attract the aristocrats, who were ever on the alert for gifted and holy priests.

In the year 963, after fourteen years of travel throughout the provinces, Kūya completed copying the *Ninnōhannyakyō* sutra in golden ink and held a dedication ceremony along the banks of the Kamo river in the capital. Many ranks of nobility attended as well as commoners, and even the Imperial court offered a handsome donation. As a result of this success, Kūya constructed the Saikōji temple, later known as the Rokuharamitsudera. Despite the diversity of Kūya's appeal, there still remained many primitive theurgic elements in his teachings and style of preaching that were quite far removed from the goals of Hōnen and Shinran, the subsequent founders of the Pure Land sects of Buddhism. But Kūya's endeavours, in conjunction with the Pure Land developments of the Tendai sect paved the way for Hōnen (1133–1212), to begin his Jōdo sect of Pure Land teachings at the close of the Heian period. Another important factor leading to the rise of the Kamakura Pure Land sects, was the atmosphere of *mappō*.

E. Mappō Shisō

One of the most compelling impetuses in the popular dissemination of the extremely self-reflective Pure Land form of devotion was the theory of *mappō shisō* (Degeneration of the Dharma). Popularized by Genshin in his *Ōjōyōshū* and enforced by the social deterioration of the late Heian period, the idea caught the public imagination and affirmed the need for a new Buddhist reform. Evidently this period in Japanese history coincided with the Indian historical motivation for developing an eschatological forewarning of disaster.

Not a great deal of material is available regarding the origin of *mappō* (Skt. *Saddharma vipralopa*) thought in India but from the available sources, it apparently evolved as a sociological mixture of political chaos and internal disturbances within the Buddhist order.[29] The Pāli term '*Saddhamma*' (True Dharma) quite possibly came into existence during the lifetime of the historical Buddha as a means of differentiating between the 'true' teachings and unorthodox views.[30] After the death of the historical Buddha uncertainty existed regarding the true teachings of the founder and gradually sectarian opinions emerged. One of the first references that can clearly be classified as embryonic *mappō* thought is found in the *Saṃyutta Nikāya*, where it states that the neglect of certain practices will cause the true Dharma to pass away not long after the demise of the Buddha.[31] This *sutta* was directed against Devadatta and such false teachers. It is obvious that the term 'True Dharma' was used to enforce sectarian claims, by charging their rivals responsible for its loss. The following presents an example of such an internal struggle:

> Those monks who bar out both the letter and the spirit by taking the discourses wrongly and interpreting according to the letter, —such are responsible for the loss of many folk, for the discomfort of many folk, for the loss, discomfort and sorrow of devas and mankind. Moreover such monks beget demerit and cause the disappearance of this true *Dhamma* (*Saddharma*).[32]

The warnings of the possible extinction of the Dharma were not confined to merely sectarian quibbles and the concern regarding the diffusion of false views. There was a distinct fear as well that allowing women to enter the Buddhist order would reduce the lifespan of the Dharma.

> If Ānanda, women had not been allowed to go forth from the home to the homeless life into the discipline of *Dhamma*, declared by the Tathāgata, then long would have lasted the godly life; for a thousand years would *Saddhamma* have lasted.

> But now Ānanda, since women have gone forth . . . not for long will the godly life last; now, Ānanda, just for five hundred years will *Saddhamma* last.[33]

Later the Sarvāstivādin *Mahāvibhāṣā* corrected this date back to one thousand years despite the admission of women to the order,[34] but all Buddhist sects did not follow suit.

The Sangha also saw internal corruption foreboding the end of the Dharma and it is in relation to such a situation that the first clear example of Simulated doctrine (Pa. *Saddhamma patirupaka*) appears:

> When members decrease, and the true doctrine disappears, there are more precepts, and few brethren are established as Arahants. There is no disappearing of the true doctrine, Kassapa, till a counterfeit doctrine (*Saddhama patirupaka*) arises in the world; but when a counterfeit doctrine does arise, then there is the disappearance of the true doctrine.[35]

The five elements that are considered in this text to make the doctrine disappear were: irreverance and unruliness towards: the Buddha, Dharma, Sangha, training and study. But interior corruption was not the only danger threatening Indian Buddhism.

The Early Buddhists had a preview of how political tyranny and disabuse of power could bring the Buddhist Dharma to an end in the "Cakkavatti-sīhanāda Suttanta" of the *Dīgha Nikāya*.[36] This clever allegory parodying contemporary social decay was a prediction of things to come. The Buddhist sangha enjoyed relative peace and prosperity until the early sixth century invasion by the Epthalites or White Huṇas and the violent anti-Buddhist reign of the Huṇa King Mihirakula between 518–529 made the 'End of the Dharma' appear to be an imminent reality. As the Chinese pilgrim Hsüan-tsang later wrote, in Gandhāra alone, Mihirakula "overthrew *stūpas* and destroyed *saṇghārāmas*, altogether one thousand and six hundred foundations."[37] The role of this King was described in a contemporary work entitled "Sutra Spoken by the Buddha on the One Called the Lotus-Face" (Jap. *Bussetsu Rengemengyō*), alleging that before the Buddha entered Nirvana, he foretold that in the future a Lotus-faced one would 'break the bowl of the Buddha' or destroy the Order.

This first destruction, an antecedent of the complete destruction of Indian Buddhism by the Muslims in the 12th century, created an atmosphere of *mappō*. This was portrayed in two crucial sutras composed at that time, the *Sūryagarbha* (Jap. *Daihōtō nichizōkyō*) and *Candragarbha* (*Daihōtō gatsuzōkyō*) translated by Narendrayaśas into Chinese during the mid-sixth century. Subsequently these views were incorporated into the *Mahāyānābhisamaya sūtra* (*Daijōdōshōkyō*), which became the basis for the development of *mappō* thought in China and Japan.[38]

In Indian Buddhism, the three periods of the decline of the Dharma were never assigned consistent dates, and they could vary from 80–800 year spans or even 300 year spans. Hui-szu (515–77) of the T'ien T'ai sect was the first in China to clearly distinguish the periods and assign them definite dates. In the *Li-shih-yüan-wen* he arranged them as follows.[39]

True Teachings (*Jap. Shōbō*)—500 years
After the death of the Buddha, when the teaching, practice and attainment of Buddhist doctrines were possible.
Simulated Teachings (*Zōbō*)—1,000 years
When only the teaching and practice remain.
Degeneration (*Mappō*)—10,000 years
When the teaching alone remains and there is no longer any practice or attainment.

But at the time when Hui-szu first attempted to systematize *mappō* thought in China, the Chinese merely grasped the theoretical aspect of the concept. A short while later with the persecution of Buddhism during 574–77 under the reign of Emperor Wu of the Northern Chou dynasty, *mappō* assumed a concrete form for the Chinese just as it had in India. The thought was so awesome and the arrival of the new Indian sutras on the subject so timely that Hsin-hsing (540–94) established the Sect of the Three Stages (San-chieh-chiao) based upon the concept of *mappō*. Hsin-hsing believed that the age had actually begun and his view was shared by the Pure Land masters Tao-ch'o (562–645) and Shan-tao, who both believed that they had been born during the period of *mappō*.

The concept of *mappō* arrived in Japan during the Nara period. The Sanron sect advocated the same view as Hui-szu, but the Hossō divided the first two periods into one thousand years each. The term *mappō* began appearing in popular literature such as the *Sanbō-e kotoba* composed in 984, but *mappō* thought did not become a living reality in Japan until the late Heian period.

During the mid-Heian period, the dominant theory of the time spans was that the periods of True Dharma (*Shōbō*) and Simulated Doctrine (*Zōbō*) each lasted for one thousand years; thus the first year of *mappō* was believed to commence in 1055, the year before Fujiwara Yorimichi dedicated the Phoenix hall of the Byōdōin.

The raging civil wars between the Minamoto and Taira families at the close of the Heian period as well as the rampages of the *sōhei* (priest-soldiers) were construed as tangible signs of *mappō*, but these were not the only calamities to strike the nation. Kamo no Chōmei, in his *Hōjōki* speaks of a great fire in 1177 that devastated the capital, a whirlwind in 1180, destroying a large portion of the city, famines in approximately 1134 and 1181, an earthquake in 1185 and also the attempt of Taira no Kiyomori to move the capital in 1180, which wasted the existing city. These were the calamities occuring within his remembrance. Undoubtedly it was a period of grave social and political instability. No wonder the scenes of hell depicted in the opening of Genshin's *Ōjōyōshū* captured public fancy and were made into popular hell screens. Also, in contrast, the *raigō* paintings of Amida descending to receive his faithful adherents and lead them to the peaceful bliss of the Pure Land grew popular during this era of destruction. The same type of feeling was evinced by the aristocrats in literature of the day.

The reign of Emperor Goreizei (1045–68) was popularly believed to mark the commencement of the era of *mappō* in Japan. Actually the chronology was not important, for the soteriological significance of *mappō* lies in its subjective application to the individual. For the aristocracy it represented the recognition of the absurdity of the values that they had hitherto cherished. Ceremonies, proprieties in dress, fine calligraphy and clever poetry suddenly became hollow meaningless—pastimes as society crumbled, and even those who attempted to continue life as in the days of past glory, became strained and artificial, creating a near parody of what had been. *Mappō* in this respect, represented in one word all the sufferings arising from social chaos combined with natural disasters and it represented as well, the singular desire to transcend such ugliness and suffering.

Religious, who had already experienced a realization of the repulsive hollowness of Heian society lurking beneath its facade of luxurious sophistication, could discover an even deeper comprehension of *mappō* in the form of the dawning and fearsome awareness that although all men might theoretically be capable of attaining Enlightenment, a sincere and introspective examination of one's own life made such a hope seem extremely remote. *Mappō* was in effect, the recognition of human defects and weaknesses as the ultimate cause of social imperfections and the disharmony with nature; in other words, it represented a profound self-reflection.

Exteriorally, the atmosphere of *mappō* outlined the necessity for Buddhist reforms. The Nara sects, by now also dominated by the influence of esoterism, attempted to respond but other factions sought new teachings applicable to the era, teachings that in themselves reflected the search for individual purity and self-reflection. On the other hand, national and personal calamities served to create among the masses the desire for a more perfect life that could only be attained through spiritual goals; for them, Buddhism appeared to be a stabilizing factor at a time when material and social goals had to be abandoned. Thus, the nascence of a new period emerged, an era when Buddhism began to assume the role of a truly national religion, rather than merely the pawn of the rulers and aristocracy. Of crucial significance in this new development was the faith of the masses, and the means by which they accepted the alien religion that was attempting to conquer the nation.

F. Developments in *Shinbutsu Shūgō*

The indigenous Pre-Buddhist folk beliefs remained the dominant faith of the masses up to the Kamakura period, but as earlier discussed, these had already fallen under the influence of Buddhism. The first step in the assimilation of the native *kami* into Buddhism had been their transformation into either guardians of the new religion or suffering sentient beings in search of Enlightenment. During the Nara period the construction of *Jingūji* (Shrine temples) and practices of sutra chanting before the *kami* were common. But Nara Buddhism was exceedingly formalistic and on the whole, disinterested in propagating the faith among the populace. The only natural and spontaneous developments that occurred to assimilate the native beliefs were actually outside the sphere of official state Buddhism, such as the activities of Gyōgi and others who illegally worked among the masses. But the official Buddhist attitude drastically changed during the Heian period and *shinbutsu shūgō* became a deliberate policy of the Tendai and Shingon sects. There were a number of reasons for this development.

First, it appears that both Saichō and Kūkai sincerely believed in or respected the native *kami*. Undoubtedly such faith must have been nourished by their early contacts with mountain *hijiri* and *shami*. Later, the choice of locating their new forms of Buddhism in the mountain areas that for centuries had been regarded as sacred places to the native faith, must have also been a factor. Before embarking for T'ang China, Saichō visited the deity of Kimpusen and the Usa Hachiman and Kahara shrines in Kyūshū in order to obtain blessings for a safe journey. He also made the gods Ōhiei and Kohiei guardians of Mt. Hiei. When Kūkai opened Kōyasan, he reportedly had a revelation from the diety Nifu myōjin, whom he subsequently made protector of the mountain. The Tōji temple, he entrusted to the deity of the Inari shrine. Some of these events probably were contrived to win political support, but the respect of Saichō and Kūkai for the native gods appears to have been genuine.

Secondly, the Indian *deva* played an important role in Tantric Buddhism, thus it was natural to assume that if alien gods could achieve such status, the native *kami* should also be assimilated. This led to the development of *shinbutsu shūgō mandaras* focusing upon the *kami* and indigenous scenery.

Thirdly, both the Shingon and Tendai sects wished to extend their hegemony. In order to accomplish this, they had to obtain at least a measure of support from the masses. The remote provinces and villages offered impenetrable conservative social groups, the only means for Buddhism to gain entrée was by means of *shinbutsu shūgō* or the utilization of native folk beliefs. A similar situation existed upon the great temple *shōen*, where the mingling of beliefs was necessary to create a harmonious working atmosphere with the farmer cultivators.

Lastly, a very obvious need arose for cooperation between Buddhism and the native faith in order to cope with certain uniquely Japanese problems, which in a large part were actually caused by *shinbutsu shūgō* developments in folk religion, such as the new concept of spirits. This cooperation greatly influenced the 'Japanization' of Buddhism.

1. Spirit Worship

From the very earliest periods of Japanese society, the dead were treated with a mixture of awe and fear. The *kussō* form of burial found during the Jōmon period in which the corpse was folded into a fetal position and often with a stone placed upon the chest, attests to the quality of fear existing in early beliefs. For the native faith, death was regarded as a defilement and even today funeral services are not held within the Shintō shrines. Prior to the Nara period, even the capital was moved after the decease of an Emperor to avoid the impurity of death. At the same time the Japanese also had an early history of ancestor worship.

Initially, Japanese ancestor worship considerably differed from the Chinese concept. The traditional *ujigami* or clan ancestral deity was at its primeval stages totemic and generally derived from natural forces such as sun, mountains, thunder, streams and so on rather than a human progenitor. At an early stage the indigenous cult fell under continental influence and even though it is too sweeping and dangerous a generalization to state that the humanization of the *kami* or creation of the *hito-gami* (man deities) was totally a result of this influence, it is quite obvious that the movement greatly increased as a result of it. One of the most powerful factors was undoubtedly the arrival of Buddhist iconography depicting the human form of the Buddhas and bodhisattvas. Up until their arrival, no efforts had ever been made to carve or paint the native *kami*, but by the Heian period it became a popular art.

Another important influence was Chinese ancestor worship that had already been assimilated into Buddhism prior to its entry to Japan. This form of ancestor worship was quite different from the Japanese totemic cult. It was based upon the view that the souls of the ancestors were immortal, dwelling among their living relatives, in control of the fortunes of the family and dependent upon offerings from the living. Confucianism made it a moral obligation for the living to venerate their ancestors and discharge duties to them as filial piety. Even this form of ancestor worship was strongly rooted in fear, since it was believed that if neglected, the ancestors could wreak havoc upon the family or person responsible. Such a notion began early to influence the Japanese.

Another factor in this complex process, was the traditional Indian *śrāddha* (funeral rites) that had already influenced Buddhist-Chinese ancestor worship. The Indians had believed in the *pitṛyāna* (way of the fathers) after death, leading to the heaven of Yama, the first ancestor. Before one could enter this road, he had to complete the early stages of *preta* (deceased), during which his relatives would offer him food for sustenance. If they failed to do so, the deceased would suffer in the afterlife and perhaps even fail to achieve the status of *pitṛ*. Woe to those who left no progeny or had their lines cut off. If the transition was successfully completed, the deceased would be allowed to join the *pitṛ* and the earthly relatives would hold a special service with offerings, songs and dancing and later the tomb-stone would be erected. Even the *pitṛ* regularly received offerings of sesame, *piṇḍa* (balls of rice or dough) and other foods.

By the rise of Buddhism, doubts had already come into existence regarding the desirability of Yama's heaven for the departed ancestors and it became viewed as the path of smoke and darkness (*dhumarga*), in contrast to the way of the *devas* (*devayāna*), which culminated in union with Brahmā. Yama also began to be associated with the idea of justice, as one who decided the fate of the deceased.

Since the teachings of the historical Buddha were directed towards the present life rather than life after death, the Early Buddhist community had very simple funeral services or at times turned funerals for the monks over to the lay devotees. In the case of the historical Buddha, his funeral was handled by wealthy and noble followers. Their efforts to preserve his memory by erecting stupas (Jap. *sharitō*) for his relics became the source of an important form of devotion that spread even to Nara Japan.

In Early Buddhism the *pitṛ* and *preta* had already begun to be mixed. This was furthered in China where both were translated as *kuei* (ogre, demon). The *preta*, viewed as 'hungry ghosts' were either confined to the Preta-realm, one of the Five (or Six)[40] Existences, or else forced to wander among the living, constantly seeking food to fill their large bellies but thwarted in their attempts by the minute size of their needle mouths. Although the Five Existences were philosophically designed to represent the psychological state of the human mind, to the laity, who accepted the notion of a literal rebirth, they assumed the qualities of real places.

The imported concepts of ancestor worship, offerings for the deceased and fear of the *preta* existence and hells, captivated the Japanese imagination and began to mingle with indigenous folks beliefs. As early as the seventh century we find inscriptions that clearly illustrate Chinese ancestor worship mingled with Buddhist devotion. For instance, in an Amida inscription of 658, the widow Asemaoko dedicates the image in honour of her deceased husband and the generations of ancestors. The following year, an Amida inscription at the Sairinji dedicates the image to 10,000 years of happiness for the living and seven generations of ancestors. Such inscriptions were very common and they indicate Amida's Pure Land was regarded as a popular resting place for deceased relatives.

In effect, it offered a place where one could safely hope to deposit the deceased or place them where they could live peacefully and not entertain notions of interfering with the living. The Pure Land literally became a place of purification for the defilement of death.

Vengeful Spirits

By the end of the Nara period, spirit worship assumed a new form when the notion of the wronged deceased transforming into an evil spirit began to become popular. Most likely this idea originated out of folk beliefs combined with public sympathy towards political figures who had met with unjust treatment. Attributing calamities befalling the perpetrators of their injustice or even national disasters was one method of effectively challenging unpopular political decisions. The oldest such political case was Fujiwara Hirotsugu, who was forced into rebellion by the priest Gembō and put to death in 940. His subsequent revenge upon Gembō became a popular folk tale. The second such figure was Prince Sawara, the Emperor's younger brother who in 745 assassinated Fujiwara Tanetsugu, the Imperial advisor blocking his future succession to the throne. The Prince was banished to Awaji and either murdered on the way or allowed to die of starvation. After his death, the Imperial family was plagued with misfortune until finally in 799 the prince was posthumously made Emperor Sudō and reinterred in an Imperial mausoleum in the Yamato area.

The *Nippon Reiiki*, generally believed to have been composed during the Kōnin era of Emperor Saga (810–23) by Kyōkai, a priest of the Yakushiji, relates the story of Nagaya Ōkimi, the most significant vengeful spirit.[41] According to this tale, Nagayaō was the Chancellor (*Dajō daijin*) under Emperor Shōmu and in the spring of 729 placed in charge of supervising offerings for the monks at a grand service held at the Gangōji. While the food was being served, one shabby monk failed to heed the order and took his rice out of line. Nagayaō saw the incident and became so incensed that he immediately began to berate and beat the poor monk with his ivory stick until the monk's head was cut and bleeding. Chagrined, the monk wiped the blood and disappeared. Monks and laymen witnessing the event, secretly whispered to each other that the Chancellor had incurred bad luck. Two days later, those jealous of Nagayaō reported secretly to the Emperor that he was plotting a rebellion to overthrow the government. In anger, Shōmu sent troops to have him arrested. Upon their arrival, Nagayaō considered that since he was about to be arrested without having committed a crime, he would surely be executed. He then had his wife and children drink poison and followed suit. When the Emperor heard of his action, he ordered the bodies of Nagayaō's family to be thrown out of the capital, burnt and the ashes scattered in the river and ocean. Nagayaō's body was ordered to be exiled to Tosa province.

Not long after the arrival of Nagayaō's remains, the peasants of Tosa began to mysteriously die and finally requested the government to do something about the spirit of Nagayaō before they all died. The remains were then transferred to Okinoshima island. The moral of the *Reiiki* tale was that respect should be shown for all monks, even those shabbily attired for one never knew when a holy man might be hidden among them. Of course this story was contrived to grant the clergy a respect they might not have deserved, but the story of Nagayaō was historical. And despite his improper conduct, his unjust treatment must have aroused public sympathy sufficient to attribute his spirit with the power to create calamities. Other tales report that the area of his final burial at Okinoshima island henceforth became haunted ground. This story ushers in the Heian belief in the vengeful spirit.

According to the *Sandai Jitsuroku*, on the 20th day of the fifth month in the year 863, a special *Goryō-e* (service to calm the spirits) was held in Kyōto in order to placate various victims of political persecution, who were believed responsible for plagues, epidemics and other such disaster. Soon such services were held throughout the provinces during the summer and autumn. Mainly these were festivals in nature, entailing Buddhist services and popular preaching (*sekkyō*) as well as mixed Shintō and yin-yang rites, also singing, dancing, sumo wrestling, horse-racing and other events.

By this time six major vengeful spirits were recognized:

1) Fujiwara Hirotsugu
2) Sudō Tennō
3) Emperor Kammu's younger brother, Sara Shinnō
3) Iyo Shinnō
5) his mother, Fujiwara Yoshiko
6) Tachibana no Hayanari

Many more existed and it is not clear why these six were particularly popular. The number was increased to eight when the upper and lower Goryō jinja were erected in Kyōto and such shrines spread to other areas as well.

One of the classic *goryōshin* (spirit god) cases of the Heian period was the brilliant scholar, Sugawara no Michizane (845–903), later to be known as Tenman Tenjin. Michizane incurred the wrath of the Fujiwara's and subsequently was exiled to Kyūshū where he died. Undoubtedly anti-Fujiwara forces must have sympathized with his cause and when the crown prince died suddenly in 923 and the Imperial palace was struck by lightning in 930, as well as other calamities, they were attributed to Michizane's vengeful spirit. In 947 the court dedicated Kitano Tenjin Shrine in Kyōto to him in an effort to appease his ghost. Subsequently other shrines sprang up such as the Temmangū dedicated in 949 in Ōsaka to his memory with four other deities, and the Egara Tenjin shrine in Kamakura honouring him as the patron of learning. He was also linked with various Buddhist figures.

One of the clearest examples of a Shintō *kami* as a *goryōshin* is found at the Gion Tenjin shrine. According to the legends, during the early tenth century, the Kōfukuji priest Ennyo transferred the Kasuga mizuya, a temporary building for the god of plague, to the Yasaka (Gion) shrine. This subsequently became the place where permanent *goryō-e* were held and the polymorphous Gozu Tennō came to be enshrined there. This unusual deity with 342 arms and a cowhead crown was a mixture of Buddhist and indigenous beliefs. It was known as early as the Nara period and even then believed to be identified with Susano-o no mikoto, the brother of the Sun Goddess.[42] The reason for this identification is unclear but may have been due to the fact that both deities were capable of curing diseases, as well as demonstrating violent behaviour when aroused. Later Yakushi Nyorai, the healing Buddha became regarded as the *honji* (true nature) of Gozu.

In the year 970, the first public *Goryō-e* service was held on the 14th day of the sixth month at the Gion shrine. This subsequently became an annual custom and is mentioned by Sei Shōnagon in the *Makura no sōshi*. It was the origin of the famous Gion *matsuri*, which is still one of the main festivals of the city of Kyōto.

Esoteric Buddhist rites soon became the dominant means of calming the *goryōshin*, just as they had already been proven successful in handling other calamities. In the year 994, a great *Goryō-e* was held combining Tantric and Shintō rites; a purification ceremony and the chanting of various sutras. The general belief among the populace was that the Buddhist power was more potent than Shintō purification.

The Tamamatsuri (Welcoming the Spirits Festival) for the benign departed also came to be assimilated into Buddhism. Originally this festival was held twice annually, on the last day of the year and during the end of the summer. It was a time when the ancestral spirits of the fields, water and so on were welcomed in hopes that they would respond by granting good planting conditions and an abundant harvest. The festival of the last day of the year eventually disappeared but the late summer Tamamatsuri was assimilated into the Buddhist *Obon* (*Avalambana* or *Ullambana*).

Avalambana

The origin of the Avalambana (Buddhist Festival of the Dead) in India is somewhat obscure but is generally believed to have been derived from the tale of the ascetic Jaratkāru, found in the *Mahābhārata*.[43] According to this account, one day Jaratkāru was astonished to encounter a large pit above which a number of men were hanging upside-down suspended by a single grass root that was just about to be gnawed away by a rat. Upon inquiring their identity, Jaratkāru found that these hapless creatures were his deceased father and ancestors hanging upside-down (*avalambante*) in a precarious position because Jaratkāru was unmarried and childless, having no one to succeed him to offer services for the dead. According to the story, Jaratkāru was so impressed by the incident that he temporarily abandoned his celibacy long enough to marry and produce an heir.

The Buddhist version of the ceremony is based upon the *Avalambana Sūtra* and the story of Maudgalyāna rescuing his mother from suffering in the *preta* world. There is no existing history of the ceremony being celebrated in Indian Buddhism but it did become very popular in both China and Japan, mingling with indigenous beliefs and ancestor worship.

Urabon observances began in Japan during the Nara period. The *Nihonshoki* reports that on the 15th day of the 7th month in 606, a *sai-e* (vegetarian repast) was held for the first time and on the same date in the year 657 an *Urabon* festival was held at the Asukadera. The event was first officially observed at Court in 733, during the reign of Emperor Shōmu and held annually thereafter. The legend of Maudgalyāna first appears in popular literature in the *Sanbō-e Kotoba* written in 984, although the sutra had been introduced even prior to the Nara period. The festival is frequently mentioned in works relating to the Heian period such as the *Engishiki*, *Genji Monogatari*, and *Eiga Monogatari*. It has continued to be a popular festival up to modern times.

2. Cult of Jizō and the Ten Kings

One of the most influential forms of Buddhist folk belief imported to Japan was the cult of Jizō (Kṣitigarbha). This deity is generally believed to represent the Buddhist assimilation of the Indian earth goddess Pṛthivī. The bodhisattva arrived in China during approximately the latter half of the third century. An independent cult unaffiliated with any particular sect emerged that represented a fusion of Buddhist, Taoist and Confucian concepts. Jizō (Chin. Ti-t'sang) became regarded as a saviour of the dead and patron of longevity. He was also affiliated in China with the popular notion of the Ten Kings or judges of the dead.

The Taoists had early entertained a belief in the underworld of T'ai-shan, ruled by T'ai-shan-fu-chün, a deity attended by ten kings in charge of summoning the souls of the deceased to account. In time, due to the similarities in character, this god became identified with the Buddhist Yama and gave rise to the Buddhist concept of hell in China. A number of forged sutras such as the *Yü-hsiu-shih-wang-sheng-ch'i-ching* of the Five Dynasties period (907–60) supported this claim, although the devotion itself appears to have originated about the time of the Six Dynasties (222–589), shortly after Buddhism began to flourish in China. Some efforts have been made to trace the concept back to an Indian origin but this has not been successful and the names and appearances of the Ten Kings are Chinese. Each of the kings is believed to judge the deceased during a specific period after death:

1) Ch'in-kuang-wang —first seventh day
   Jap. Shinkō-ō
   honji—Fudō myō-ō
2) Ch'u-chiang-wang —second seventh day
   Shokō-ō
   honji—Shaka
3) Sung-ti-wang —third seventh day
   Sōtei-ō
   honji—Monju
4) Wu-kuan-wang —fourth seventh day
   Gokan-ō
   honji—Fugen
5) Yen-lo-wang (Yama) —fifth seventh day
   Enra-ō
   honji—Jizō
6) Pien-ch'eng-wang —sixth seventh day
   Hensei-ō
   honji—Miroku
7) T'ai-shan-wang —seventh seventh day
   Taizan-ō
   honji—Yakushi
8) P'ing-teng-wang —hundredth day
   Byōdō-ō
   honji—Kannon

9) Tu-shih-wang —first year
Toshi-ō
honji—Seishi

10) Wu-tao-chuan-lun-wang —third year
Godōtenrin-ō
honji—Amida

The dates of these judgements were made to coincide with the Buddhist memorial services for the dead.

Originally Yama was regarded as the leader of the Ten Kings and in Japan the buildings dedicated to the kings were generally named Emma-do (Hall of Yama). But the figure of Yama had already mingled with Kṣitigarbha (Jizō) in China and it was believed the bodhisattva by his vows was capable of rescuing the deceased. In the *Nippon Reiiki*, Jizō is said to be the name by which (Emma) Yama is known in Japan.[44] During the A. Stein expedition to the cave of the Thousand Buddhas in Tun-huang, a representation of the Ten Kings was discovered dating from the Sung dynasty (960–1126). In this depiction, Kṣitigarbha is seated in the center on a rock with the Ten Kings gathered to his left and right. The Kings are dressed in Taoist robes and before each there is a desk bearing the records of the deceased.[45] A similar grouping is found in the Shin Yakushiji in Nara.

Honji (true nature) for the Ten Kings were created in the *Jizō bosatsu hosshin innen jūōkyō*, a popular sutra believed composed in Japan during the late Heian period. The only one of the Kings to enjoy independent veneration besides Yama was T'ai-shan-wang (Jap. Taizan-ō), believed to have been the deification of a sacred mountain in China. The Japanese aristocrats venerated this deity for longevity and as a cure for misfortunes. The belief particularly became popular among those who followed the yin-yang practices and this festival is clearly depicted in the early 12th century *Konjaku Monogatari*.[46]

Besides the affiliation with the Ten Kings as saviour of the dead, many other forms of devotion to Jizō also sprang up in Japan. In Pure Land faith, Jizō was regarded as one of the twenty-five bodhisattvas who descended from the Pure Land with Amida to welcome (*raigō*) the deceased. The *Engishiki* also mentions *keka* (Rites of Repentance) held to Jizō in mid-March and October.

One of the most popular Japanese devotions became the Jizō Ennichi held on the 24th day of the month with flowers and offerings made to the bodhisattva.[47] Jizō was also regarded as the patron saint of travelers and small shrines were erected in his honour along the roadsides. The devotions to Jizō did not decline with the popularization of Pure Land beliefs but rather increased during the Kamakura and Muromachi periods.[48]

3. The Deceased as Hotoke (Buddhas)

Besides devotion to Jizō and the Ten Kings, a popular belief also developed whereby the deceased themselves entered the ranks of the Enlightened and could be referred to as *hotoke* (Buddhas). To a certain degree, this was equivalent to the western euphemisms of 'gone to heaven' or 'joined the saints.' It is impossible to set a date for the origin of this notion, but it must have been an early development and it does bear a certain theological validity.

The essence of Buddhahood is the attainment of Nirvana, which refers to the perfect experience of Reality, freed from the desires, projections and attachments of the individual ego. And in Early Buddhism a distinction was made between the Buddha's Nirvana during his lifetime and (Pāli) *Mahāparinibbāna* at the time of his death. The latter was considered the most perfect form of Enlightenment, completely free from the hindrances of the physical body, although the body was regarded as inseparable from the consciousness or mind. A similar term, *parinibbuta* was applied even to the condition of Arahants who had committed suicide.[49] Under the circumstances, it became logical for laity aware of such teachings to hope that their deceased might also achieve final emancipation.[50] The development of the Mahāyāna concept that all sentient beings would ultimately attain Enlightenment must have been a further factor to increase optimism, for it was obvious that the deceased had abandoned the *saṃsāra* of the relative world and surrendered their attachments; it was natural to assume that they had entered a higher pathway.

As early as the Nara period in Japan, Prince Shōtoku was pictured as having attained the bliss of the 'Land of Heavenly Longevity' in the *Tenjukoku mandara*, and by the Heian period he was already identified with the Buddhas and bodhisattvas. Having the knowledge that a contemporary or near contemporary had achieved such a status undoubtedly stimulated Japanese aspirations. The Shingon concept of Enlightenment during the present life (*sokushin jōbutsu*) made the goal appear more attainable to all, but the most compelling factor was the rise of Pure Land belief. According to this faith, everyone who sincerely called upon the name of Amida Buddha could be assured of attaining the Pure Land. In Japan the notion of the Pure Land assumed a role similar to that which the *deva* heavens had held for the laity during the time of Early Buddhism, with the exception that the sensual comforts of this form of 'heaven' were not emphasized. In Fujiwara Michinaga's sutra burial of 1007, he clearly expressed the hope of leaving the Pure Land and being reborn again upon Maitreya's coming. Such a desire sounds more in keeping with the notion of a *deva* heaven than the usual conception of the Pure Land.

The Japanese belief regarding the status of the deceased was strongly influenced by ancestor worship and the indigenous faith. It has become as common to refer to the dead as *kami* as *hotoke*. But certainly it would be incorrect to generalize that whenever the deceased are referred to as either *hotoke* or *kami*, the sincere belief exists that they have actually achieved such a status. The terms are used just as euphemistically as their western counterparts. On the other hand, a germ of truth underlies the folk belief.

It cannot be denied that the knowledge of one's approaching demise can have a soteriological effect and lead to the experience of Enlightenment. It must have been in recognition of this fact that the historical Buddha, able to view the attitudes of mind of Godhika and Vakkali at the last moment, could state that the two suicides had attained Nirvana. The state of mind at the approach of death was an important concern in Early Buddhism and the sutras frequently depict the Buddha preaching to the sick or seriously ill, not merely to assist them in overcoming their physical sufferings, but to calm their minds. The sickbed or deathbed was always recognized as an important moment to touch even the most calloused individual. The *Milindapañha* states that although a man should live a hundred years of evil life, the thought of Buddha at the moment of death will lead him to rebirth in a *deva* heaven.[51]

Raigō paintings depicting Amida descending to welcome the dying became exceedingly popular during the Heian period. These were undoubtedly executed with the soteriological nature of the knowledge of approaching death in mind. These paintings were based upon the *Larger Sukhāvatīvyūha* and *Meditation* sutras, but similar notions of Buddhas or bodhisattvas appearing to those about to die can be found in the *Avataṃsaka*, *Lotus* and *Bhaiṣajyaguru* sutras. Of course in Buddhism, as in other religions, the fear of death was also capable of inspiring conversion to a religious life. The *Ōkagami* relates that in the year 1019, after suffering sharp chest pains during the night, the Fujiwara Regent Michinaga at the age of 54 abruptly entered the priesthood.

One interesting point regarding the belief in Amida's *raigō* is the fact that the Sanskrit version of the *Larger Sukhāvatīvyūha Sūtra*, which presents the textual basis for the idea, speaks only of Amida's vow to stand before the sentient being at the moment of death if he has been invoked with a sincere mind. It does not mention the Buddha leading the deceased to his Pure Land after death, an item which was apparently added by the Chinese translators.[52]

Besides the potentiality of the moment of death to lead to Enlightenment, the nature of the funeral and memorial services in drawing together the relatives and friends of the departed in his memory, gave the deceased an attribute of the bodhisattva—the ability to lead the living in the world of *saṃsāra* to Enlightenment. His memory became a sustaining factor in his family's relationship with the Buddhist temple through holding regular memorial services.

The folk belief of the deceased as *hotoke*, which is still popular today, can thus properly be viewed from three interrelated levels: 1) as a simple optimistic euphemism for death, 2) as an expression of the sincere hope of the laity for the departed, 3) the theological view of the soteriological natures of both the moment of death and the love of family and friends for the deceased.

G. The *Honji Suijaku* Theory

One of the most interesting developments in the Japanese assimilation of the indigenous faith was the evolution of the *honji-suijaku* (True nature—manifestation) theory. According to this concept, the native *kami* actually represented manifestations (*suijaku*) of the various Buddhas and bodhisattvas. The first written appearance of such thought occurs in Japanese history during the early part of the tenth century, but its philosophical origin is much earlier.

1. *Theoretical basis*

The terminology *honjaku* (Chin. *pen-chi*) was first used by Seng-chao (374–414) in his refutation of the Neo-Taoist concepts that had infiltrated early Chinese Buddhism, in particular the notion that a dichotomy existed between the Absolute truth and relative truth with a superior and inferior aspect; the goal being the transcendence of the phenomenal or relative world for the Absolute. In his commentary on the *Vimalakīrti Nirdeśa sūtra*, Seng-chao refuted such dualism by declaring that both Origin (Absolute) and Manifestation (relative) were 'different but unthinkable oneness.'[53]

In the eighth century, Chih-I of the Chinese T'ien T'ai sect applied the terminology to the *Lotus Sutra*. The first half of the sutra he entitled *chi-men* (Jap. *jakumon*) since it deals with the role of the historical Buddha, or the phenomenal manifestation of the teachings. The second half, which he termed *pen-men* (*honmon*) represents the Absolute in the form of an Original Buddha or the idealization of the teachings themselves. Chih-I quite deliberately used the *honjaku* terminology to demonstrate the inseparable unity of both views. But the terminology was not solely confined to the Tendai sect in Japan. It also played an important role in the esoteric *Dainichikyō*, where an elaboration of the *Lotus Sutra's honmon* was set forth in the concept of Dainichi Nyorai as the *honjishin* (Original body).

The Japanese practical application of the *honjaku* theory to the relationship between Buddhist deities and the indigenous *kami* is unique although quite in the Buddhist tradition of assimilation. Its singularity lies in the fact that with the *honjaku* application, the *kami* or *suijaku* is afforded a philosophical equality with its Buddha or bodhisattva *honji*. The Indian Buddhists had assimilated native deities but these only achieved a degree of equality to the Buddhas and bodhisattvas with the rise of Tantrism. The germ of the *honji-suijaku* concept was latent in Early Buddhism however, both in the attitude towards the *deva* as temporarily elevated mortals, and in the popular teaching to the laity that Indra, the King of the *deva* had been converted to Buddhism.[54] If the *deva* were mortals capable of being converted, they were also capable of attaining Enlightenment. The Japanese immediately grasped such an idea and by the end of the eighth century, certain *kami* converted to Buddhism had attained the title of 'bodhisattva'. The first to receive this honour was Hachiman, but soon Tado and others followed suit.

A popular supposition held today is that the concept of *suijaku* in Japan is derived from the Indian *avatāra*. Certainly there are soteriological similarities between the concepts of 'incarnation' in nearly every great religion, but the Buddhist view must reject the type of monotheism found in the *Bhagavadgītā* (IV, 7ff.), which sets forth the essence of the *avatāra* theory and an implied duality between natural and supernatural or divine and human. The subject requires lengthy philosophical and linguistic discussion, but it is this author's opinion that the Japanese concept of *suijaku* cannot be regarded as equivalent to either the Indian *avatāra* or *vyūha* (emanation).

2. *Practical Application*

Although the *honji-suijaku* theory represented the final step in the elevation of the native gods and their complete assimilation into Buddhism, an intermediate step to its final evolution consisted in the elevation of the Japanese gods and historical personages. We have already mentioned the rise of Hachiman and Tado to bodhisattvahood. One of the first historical figures to be so honoured was the cultural hero, Shōtoku Taishi. Although Prince Shōtoku was not granted the title of bodhisattva directly, he was considered to be the after-body (*goshin*) or reincarnation of Hui-szu, the second patriarch of the Chinese T'ien T'ai sect by the end of the Nara period.[55] During the next era, he was regarded as the *suijaku* of Dainichi Nyorai and Kannon. By the end of the Heian era, his legendary popularity increased to such a degree that he was considered as the *honji* of such historical personages as Emperor Shōmu, Kūkai and Shōbō, the Shugendō leader. The usage of the *honji-suijaku* theory in this manner became a common occurrence but not as significant as its application to the indigenous gods.

The earliest extant lists of *kami* identified with their *honji* Buddhas and bodhisattvas date back to the early 12th century. One interesting point regarding these lists is their lack of consistency. The *honji-suijaku* theory was propagated as a general philosophy and the actual application tended to be made by local priests and devotees based upon such factors as the regional popularity of the various cults, similarities in character, attributes and so on. But even lists composed by a single shrine over different periods of time would alternate or change *honji* as a result in the increase or decrease of popularity of the various Buddhas and bodhisattvas. For instance, the Kasuga shrine in the year 1175 listed the *honji* for its deities as follows:

Suijaku	*Honji*
Ichinomiya—Kashima	Fukūkenjaku Kannon (Amoghapāśa Avalokiteśvara)
Ninomiya—Katori	Yakushi Nyorai (Bhaiṣajyaguru)
Sannomiya—Hiraoka	Jizō bosatsu (Kṣitigarbha)
Shinomiya—Aidonohime	Jūichimen Kannon (Eleven-faced Avalokiteśvara)
Wakamiya	Monjushiri (Mañjuśrī)

But by the Kamakura period, the following changes had been made in this listing:

Ichinomiya—Kashima	Fukūkenjaku Kannon or Shaka (Śākyamuni)
Shinomiya—Aidonohime	Jūichimen or Guze Kannon
Wakamiya	Monjushiri or Jūichimen Kannon

The popular figure Jizō, at one time or another was listed as the *honji* for twenty-two different *kami*.[56] But one unusual feature of the *honji-suijaku* application was the inclusion of India *deva* as *honji*, which offered them an equivalency with the Buddhas and bodhisattvas that they had not generally received in Indian Buddhism, except in certain Tantric cults. For the Japanese masses, the origin of deities imported in the alien faith could not have been a matter of significance and undoubtedly, it was difficult to differentiate between them. The simple criteria for respect must have been based upon familiarity and believed efficacy. Popular *devas* that appeared as *honji* were: Bishamonten (Vaiśravaṇa), Marishiten (Marīci), Bonten (Brahmā), the Myō-ō (vidyārāja)[57], Kisshōten (Śrī Lakṣmī) and Benzaiten (Sarasvatī).

The popularization of *honji-suijaku* thought was natural and spontaneous among the masses but the same cannot be said of the clergy who propagated it. Many mixed motives were involved such as gaining entrée to new areas, extending the hegemony of existing sects, creating harmony on the temple *shōen* and even efforts made by Shintō shrine priests to become associated with popular Buddhist cults. It was a complex process that popularized and developed even further with the evolution of Ryōbu shūgō Shintō and Sannō Ichijitsu Shintō during the late Kamakura and Tokugawa periods respectively.

H. Shugendō (Way of Mystical Practice)

Ever since the legendary Ninigi no Mikoto, grandson of the Sun Goddess descended to earth on Mt. Takachiho and married the daughter of a mountain god, mountains have played an important role in Japanese folk-beliefs. Shugendō represents the syncretic religious movement centering around mountain religious practices.

Traditionally, the founder of Shugendō is believed to be the semi-mythical En no Gyōja (or En no Ozunu), who is first mentioned in a historical record in 699, when he was exiled to Izu on the charge of misusing his magical powers. At that time, his activities were generally in the areas of Mt. Kimpu and Katsuragi. Later, in the *Nippon Reiiki*, he was treated as a miraculous figure combining elements of esoteric Buddhism, Taoism, Shamanism and native folk-beliefs. His legendary personality served as an important factor in unifying the Shugendō movement, but it is not historically accurate to state that Shugendō had a real founder.[58] The basis of the movement is found in the indigenous attitude towards mountains combined with the later imported concepts of Taoism, Indian asceticism and in particular, esoteric Buddhism (which was also very Indian in nature).

1. *Mountain Religious Activities* (*Sangaku shinkō*)

From earliest periods, the Japanese held a deep veneration and awe for their lofty and mysterious mountains, so often shrouded in mists and penetrating the very heavens. Once gifted with the art of writing, they ceaselessly praised their majesty and sacredness. In the *Mannyōshū* countless poems relate to the mountains dealing with such topics as the beauty of Fuji, Yoshino or Kagu, the passions of Miminashi and Kagu, or the loneliness of Miwa. It is evident from these numerous and diverse descriptions that the mountains were personified, considered to be the dwelling places of the gods, and at times believed to be divine themselves. The *Mannyōshū* poems also frequently mention the mountains as places of burial. And just as they had been considered the dwelling places of the gods, since they entered into the heavens, so they came to be linked with the afterworld and spirits of the dead. The *Nihonshoki* even states that the god of *Yomi no kuni* (the land of the dead) was buried on Mt. Kumano.[59] Such a belief added further mystery and awe to the deeply isolated mountain.

With the arrival of Buddhism and Taoism, both of which had developed close affinities to the mountains of China, a spontaneous syncretic movement arose uniting these beliefs with the indigenous faith.

One example of the Taoist-Buddhist fusion is found in the name of the Chōgosonshiji temple nestled on Mt. Shigi. This temple, popularly known as the Shigisanji, bears a Taoistic name that is unique in Japan.

The process that ultimately evolved into the Shugendō movement during the Heian period was complex and lacks historical documentation. But we must conclude that some of the impetus must have arisen out of the desire to escape the confines and ultimately the corruption of Nara Buddhism.

The Ritsuryō regulations severely circumscribed the activities and freedom of the monks and nuns, particularly in their relations with the masses and being allowed to live in hermitages. To escape such a formalistic religion, many individuals illegally fled to the mountains during the Nara period. There they could practice in peace and solitude the devotions of their choice in company with the small groups who had always preferred the seclusion of the mountains. Their ranks were joined by *shidosō* (privately ordained priests), as well as many other varieties of social dropouts. Small amorphous groups were formed that quietly engaged in practice such as the *Jinen chishū* (Sect of Natural Wisdom). Among these religious were *shami* and *ubasoku*, who practiced Buddhism following the lay life and *hijiri*, who were usually monks, often following strict discipline. But by the Heian period, the lines often crossed and some of the *hijiri* even married, in a few cases to female shamans. With the popularity of magical beliefs, most of these groups were devoted to the acquisition of supernatural powers. Those who emphasized mountain austerities were also known as *yamabushi* (lit. those who lie down on the mountain). There were no clear class distinctions among the early groups and some monks, such as Kūya, propagator of the *nembutsu*, chose in either humility or in rejection of Buddhist institutionalism to be called *shami* although being ordained. There were also yin-yang (*Onyōdō*) practitioners who dealt with the arts of geomancy and the prediction of auspicious directions and even undesirable elements such as thieves who sought disguise among the religious. Since the movement was predominantly illegal during the Nara period, respectability could only be acquired through personal holiness or magical skills. Undoubtedly Saichō and Kūkai became acquainted with many of these religious during their mountain sojourns.

With the new Buddhism of the Heian era, the religious outcasts dwelling in the mountains and preaching among the masses won acceptance for the very idealism that had driven them from Nara society. Shingon and Tendai esoterism, with its natural affinity for mountain retreats greatly stimulated the further evolution of such movements. Saichō required his monks to spend twelve years of practice on Mt. Hiei and Kūkai opened Shingon centers at both Takaosan and Kōyasan. Enchin even followed En no Gyōja's footsteps by making a pilgrimage in the mountains of Katsuragi and Kumano. The aristocrats naturally followed suit and immediately became interested in the skills of such rugged individualists who chose to forsake the refinements of life in the capital. In the summer of 856, the government tested monks for supernatural powers in the presence of the Emperor at the Jinsen-en and a search was initiated for gifted individuals. The arts long practiced secretly among fellow religious or laity in remote areas were now attracting government interest. Naturally many charlatans quickly emerged but sincere interest was generated as well. Just as Kūkai and Dōkyō, whose paths were ultimately so divergent, had both initially been attracted to the potent *Kokūzō gumonjihō*, now with further respectability granted to the magico-ascetic arts, numerous adherents appeared. The aristocrats made pilgrimages to the mountains themselves in hopes of acquiring special merit or meeting holy sages. During the Early Heian period the retired Emperors Seiwa and Uda visited Kumano and by the close of the era, both Emperor Shirakawa and Go Shirakawa had made numerous visits to the mountain. The *yamabushi* and *hijiri* acted as their spiritual guides or leaders (*sendatsu*) on such journeys.

One of the first mountains to attract attention was the lofty and mysterious Kimpusen (also known as Mitake), mentioned in poetry and writings from earliest times. By the Heian period the entire general area from Kimpusen to Kumano became recognized as a place of Shugendō activities. One of the early attractions to Kimpusen was the belief in the ferocious Zaō gongen.

According to legend, Zaō gongen is a manifestation of Shaka (Śākyamuni).[60] When Shaka appeared to En no Gyōja as he was practicing in Yoshino, the ascetic told the Buddha that his form was not suitable for Japan. Shaka then assumed the appearance of Miroku (Maitreya), but En no Gyōja found this embodiment also unsatisfactory. Finally, Shaka manifested himself in the ferocious shape of Zaō gongen and En no Gyōja exclaimed that this form was ideal.

The dynamic appearance of Zaō gongen is quite unique in Japanese iconography. The appearance itself supposedly symbolized the deity's magical function of granting longevity and the fulfillment of requests. Zaō gongen evolved from the mingling of mountain faith, esoteric and Pure Land Buddhism, coupled with the very mundane hope of the aristocrats of finding gold in the mountains. He is depicted with an angry countenance, blue and black in colour with either two or three eyes. He usually wears a *sanko* (three branched) crown and assumes a trampling posture; the left foot resting on a pedestal with the right lifted high. The left hand is held in the sword *mudrā*, symbol of conquering ignorance and his right hand holds a *sankosho* (three-branched vajra) above his head. The body is generally blue to denote his conquest of Māra, the Tempter.

Zaō gongen (also known as Kongō Zaō bosatsu) became an extremely popular figure among the aristocracy. In 1007 when regent Fujiwara Michinaga visited Kimpusen, he buried copies of the *Lotus* and *Maitreya sutras* beneath the lantern before the Zaō-dō (hall). This popular shrine became the mother temple of numerous Zaō gongen shrines erected throughout the country. The figure even became known in China. The majority of *mishōtai* (engraved mirrors),[61] so popular during the Heian period, bear the image of Zaō gongen.

In modern times only the major peaks of the Yoshino mountain range are known as Kimpusen, but in early days the entire Yoshino range was known by that name. Both Shingon and Tendai temples eventually spread across the mountains in a vast complex that became known as the Konrinnōji; today it is under the jurisdiction of the Enryakuji of Mt. Hiei. The early pilgrimages to Kimpusen required an elaborate three month period of purification prior to their undertaking, during which the devotee would abstain from meat eating, drinking and sexual relations. Women were not allowed to enter the mountain.

Another important mountain area was the Kumano *sanzan* (three mountains of Kumano), which became a centre of Heian religious activities. Popular Kumano deities were Hayatama shin and Kitsumiko shin. The latter was believed to be derived from Ki no miko, the god of trees, of Kumano. The misty Nachi waterfall was also recognized as divine. By the 11th century three deities were recognized as the *gongen* (manifestations) of Kumano:[62]

gongen	*honji*
Kitsumiko	Amida
Musubi	Kannon
Hayatama	Yakushi

In popular legend, Kumano was identified with Amida's Pure Land.

A Shugendō pilgrimage route was established from Kumano to Kimpusen, ultimately uniting the religious activities of both areas and Zaō gongen came to be enshrined at Kumano. The fusion of mountain practices gave an apparent unity to the great mountains themselves and they were identified with the dual *mandara:* Kimpusen representing the *Kongōkai* and Kumano, the *Taizōkai*. A special Kumano *mandara* was created to demonstrate this relationship.

Aristocrats were also drawn to the religious practice of the mountains and in approximately 987, the retired Emperor Kazan spent 1,100 days (nearly three years) of practice at the Nachi waterfall area in Kumano. The Tantric monks primarily served as spiritual directors for such activities and eventually it was under the auspices of esoteric Buddhist that the Shugendō movement was organized.

2. *Honzan and Tōzan branches of Shugendō*

With regular pilgrimages made to the mountains and the growing popularity of mountain practices, an organization gradually came into being. In 1049, a priest of the Kōfukuji was appointed overseer of Kimpusen and that mountain became legally a branch of the Kōfukuji, although this was subsequently disputed by the monks of Kimpusen.

As pilgrimages gained popularity and esoteric rites relating to the mountains further developed, a need for organization and control became apparent. Kumano *sanzan* was among the first to devise a system of guides (*sendatsu* or *oshi*) and those who provided lodging (*zaichō*). The organization was extremely loose since the mountain practitioners naturally resisted any movement that would regiment them in the manner of the Nara temples, but it was effective since it became socially accepted. This system subsequently spread throughout the Shugendō areas of Japan.

By the late 10th century, Kumano shugendō had established an organization. Zōkō was appointed the first administrator (*bettō*) of the *jingūji*. The post was passed on to his younger brother and subsequently, after intermarriage with a branch of the Fujiwara family, became hereditary. It is interesting to note that the *jingūji* (shrine-temples), a *shinbutsu shūgō* development of Buddhism, antedated the established sects in the recognition of clerical marriage and hereditary succession, following the example of the Shintō shrines.

In 1090 when Emperor Shirakawa visited Kumano, accompanied by the Tendai priest Zōyo (1032–1116), he created the post of overseer for the entire Kumano *sanzan* and placed Zōyo in the post. When Zōyo became abbot of the Onjōji temple, headquarters of the Jimon branch of Tendai in 1100, Kumano shugendō became permanently associated with that school. Zōyo later built the Shōgoin and made that the headquarters of what developed into the Shōgoinryū or Honzan branch of Shugendō during the Kamakura period. The Kumano *gongen* were enshrined at the Shōgoin and the post of overseer for the Kumano *sanzan* became a permanent function of the abbot of that temple.

The Sanmon branch of Tendai also established their own form of mountain religious practice known as Katsuragawa *shugen*. This is not as well known as the Honzan-ha, but it played an important role on Mt.

Hiei. The movement was founded by Sō-ō (831–918), a disciple of Ennin. Sō-ō became a very popular figure among the Fujiwaras at court and was believed to have miraculous powers. In 858 he made a retreat at the Katsuragawa waterfall on Mt. Hiei. He sought mental purification by meditation upon the concept of hell, repentance and chanting the *Butsumyōkyō* (Names of the Buddhas sutra), as well as performing ascetic devotions such as standing under the icy waters of the fall. During his retreat at Katsuragawa, Sō-ō was inspired to carve an image of Fudō Myō-ō and enshrined it in a small temple subsequently known as the Myō-ō-in of the Mudōji. Sō-ō's movement attracted many followers and the Myō-ō-in temple prospered. The illustrious Tendai abbot Jien temporarily resided there and during the Muromachi era, the Shōgun Ashikaga Yoshimitsu practiced meditation at that peaceful spot.[63]

It is obvious that Pure Land devotion influenced Shugendō activities on Mt. Hiei. Sō-ō was active in establishing *nembutsu* practice during his later years and died chanting the name of Amida. The Pure Land emphasis upon self-reflection and mental purification coupled with the chanting of the *nembutsu* or meditation upon the Buddhist hells, strongly appealed to Shugendō practitioners everywhere. And faith in the mountains became aligned with the desire to establish a Pure Land there free from the pollution and corruption of life in the capital or court. This attitude very easily was reconciled with indigenous Shintō concepts of purification. We can observe the unity in practices such as the three month period of purification and preparation to enter Kimpusen. The aristocrats experienced the same desire of uniting the quest for purification with their search for a Pure Land. This was evinced by their own practice of mountain asceticism and the burial of sutras on the mountain sides. But at the same time esoteric Buddhism was an extremely influential force in the development of Shugendō.

Shōbō (832–909) is considered to be the founder of the Shingon Sambōinryū of Shugendō popularly known as Tōzan-ha.[64] Shōbō is also regarded as the first major regenerator of the Shugendō movement after En no Gyōja. This is undoubtedly because he was the first illustrious historical figure to personally be interested in mountain practice and thus draw the attention of Heian society to that form of religious activity.

In his early years, Shōbō studied Sanron, Hossō and Kegon doctrines in Nara and was ordained at the Tōdaiji temple. He later received Tantric ordination from Shinga. By his late thirties he had become a well-known figure at the capital and received the patronage of the powerful Fujiwara Yoshifusa. In the year 874, he established the Daigoji temple, which became a centre for esoteric activities and the future headquarters of Tōzan Shugendō. Shōbō was also known as the restorer of the Sanron school at the Tōdaiji, where he established the Tōnan-in for the teachings of that sect.

Shōbō had numerous honours during his lifetime, becoming abbot of both the prestigous Tōji and Tōdaiji temples and founder of the Ono-ryū school of Shingon. He is considered the founder of Tōzan Shugendō due to his own pilgrimages in the area of Kimpusen, which set a precedent for the monks of the Daigoji. He was also the author of many works relating to *shugen* (mystical practice). His success in esoteric rituals was so great that he is even credited with obtaining the birth of a son for Emperor Daigo. And his fame and respect was so immense that the retired Emperors Yōzei and Uda reportedly visited his bedside as he was dying.[65] In the year 1707, Emperor Higashiyama granted him the posthumous title of Rigen Daishi.

Shōbō was succeeded by his disciples Kangen and Joken. Kangen, the Shingon abbot, as earlier discussed, closely matched his master's fame and accomplishments but also shared his interest in Shugendō. In 919, he became the abbot of the Daigoji. The disciple Joken became the overseer of Kimpusen in the year 900.

Both Tendai and Shingon forms of Shugendō had little ideological differences since the movement emphasized practice rather than theology. They followed the esoteric traditions of Taimitsu and Tōmitsu respectively but this was blended with the syncretic practices of Shugendō. Both groups followed the philosophy of Enlightenment with this physical body (*sokushin jōbutsu*) and visualized the mountains themselves as forming the great *maṇḍalas*. The peaceful serenity these retreats offered was the ideal place for self-reflection and the undefiled stones, trees, streams and vegetation of the mountains appeared to be part of the great body of Dainichi Nyorai or Enlightenment itself.

Besides the Shugendō activities in the area of the capital, other movements developed in places such as Hikosan of Kyūshū, Ishizuchi in Shikoku, Taisen in western Honshū, Hakusan in the middle of northern Honshū, Haguro, Gassan and Yudono in northern Honshū and elsewhere.

During the Kamakura period, the movement prospered and attracted the interest of the samurai. The popular Honzan and Tōzan branches were established and also newer movements came into being such as the Yakushiji and Nichiren forms of Shugendō. At the same time independent movements sprang up developing in accord with local folk-beliefs and practices. The Shugendō movement cannot properly be classified as "Buddhist" although Buddhism certainly played a major role in its formation. The movement does represent a perfect example of the unique Japanese religious phenomena known as *shinbutsu shūgō*.

I. EPILOGUE—The Heian Role in the Development of Japanese Buddhism

One of the major contributions of the new Buddhism of the Heian era was its search for autonomy and freedom from the bureaucratic confines of the Ritsuryō government. This movement was not wholly initiated by the Tendai and Shingon sects, since Emperor Kammu, upon transferring the capital to Kyōto was well aware of the dangers of the involvement of the Buddhist institutions in government. By his controls and edicts he severely circumscribed the political activities of the Buddhist sects, but this was still a far cry from autonomy. To a certain degree, the Ritsuryō government had been responsible for its problems with Buddhism at the close of the Nara period. The government's effort to control ordinations and create minor bureaucrats of the clergy was a corrupting influence and its pragmatic approach to religion completely negated the idealism necessary to create good religious. The government was not concerned about individual Enlightenment, but merely in acquiring benefits for the state. Nara Buddhism tended to stifle individual religious expression and goals and the net result was naturally institutional and individual corruption.

When Kammu moved the capital to Kyōto, he had no real solution for the Buddhist problem. His efforts were punitory rather than visionary and left the Buddhist institutions themselves in a quandry. They naturally made attempts to reform but it is exceedingly difficult for those sunk in quicksand to objectively deduce a means of escape. Saichō was one of the first to truly appreciate the situation and take action. His pressure for the establishment of a Mahāyāna *kaidan* was in effect an indictment against Nara corruption and at the same time a revolt against the government control of Buddhism. Only when the Buddhist institutions were free to set forth the goals of individual salvation could they properly function as religious organizations. This did not mean that Saichō sought to abandon the role of Buddhism in protecting and furthering the interests of the nation. Nothing could have been further from his intentions, since he was not only personally nationalistic but also cognizant of the practical need for some form of continued government patronage for the survival of the Buddhist institutions. Saichō's unceasing demand for the development of a Mahāyāna *kaidan* ultimately provided the Buddhist order with a form of autonomy. The control of ordinations granted the right to select and ordain monks for religious rather than secular goals. Gaining this privilege was one of the greatest accomplishments of the Heian era in terms of Buddhist development. On the other hand, freedom ultimately proved to be as conducive to institutional corruption as undue control.

Both the Tendai and Shingon sects contained the seeds of their ultimate degeneration from their inception. Tendai placed more emphasis upon theological development than Shingon and the intellectual stimulus of Mt. Hiei generated the Kamakura sects. But Tendai philosophy stressed universalism in the form of the omnipresent Buddha nature in all existents, coupled with the recognition of endless *upāya* to achieve the realization of that nature. Such an orientation made it difficult to draw a clear distinction between traditional Buddhist practices and peripheral syncretic developments. The lack of such delination is even more pronounced in Tendai Taimitsu and the Shingon sect, both of which placed emphasis upon practice rather than theology. Such an orientation perhaps had greater soteriological benefit for contemporaries than theological speculation, but it ultimately led into syncretic forms of assimilation that appear to be quite far removed from the spirit of Buddhism. The same problem had arisen with Tantrism elsewhere. For example, the Shingon sect in Japan strictly avoided any form of sexual practice, yet the Tachikawa group that developed in the early 12th century did encourage such activities as proper religious practice. In fact, the sect claimed its teachings originated with Ninkan of the Shingon Daigoji temple, who was also an adept in Shugendō. His views were transmitted to a Yin-yang master, who combined this form of male-female application to Buddhist esoterism and formed the Tachikawa sect. Although in Japan such a development was the result of a combination of Yin-yang and esoterism, in India and Tibet the so-called 'left-handed' Tantrism independently developed. There is no question that such practice was extremely dangerous, yet theologically, the basic doctrines and symbolism did not greatly differ from orthodox esoteric Buddhism. Syncretism and eclectism made abuses in practice difficult to control, particularly when theological study was reduced to a minor role. Other factors such as institutional disunity added to the confusion. By the end of the Heian period practically every major Shingon temple had developed its own school, emphasizing minor differences in practice and ritual. Tendai Taimitsu was simultaneously dividing into countless small sects unaccountable to a central authority. Such diversity provided a fecund breeding ground for corruption.

During the late Nara and early Heian periods, despite the pragmatic use of Buddhism to obtain prosperity for the Imperial family and nation, certain controls had been placed upon extremes in magico-supernatural practices. Emperor Saga in particular, as a philosophical rationalist, placed strict supervision over what he considered to be superstitious practices. All of this restraint was removed by the Fujiwara regent

Yoshifusa, who credulously encouraged any form of practice that might conceivably benefit his aims. The self-seeking aristocracy emulated his example and in those days a priest, no matter how idealistic, who hoped to achieve aristocratic patronage to further his goals, had to prove competent in theurgic powers.

The hedonistic attitude of the Heian aristocracy also proved to be an undermining factor for Buddhism. With the failure of the Ritsuryō system, the aristocrats became the basis of institutional financial support, their desire for affirmative supernatural powers and the perpetuation of their lifestyle had profound influence upon the temples and priests they patronized. Their inclination to place their sons as abbots further embroiled the leading temples in all the political intrigues of the day. Yet, they alone were not to blame for the corruption of the Buddhist institutions.

The vast land acquisitions of the temples in the form of *shōen* (estates) created a need for numerous individuals engaged in maintenance rather than religious functions in the great temples. These *dōshū* (maintenance priests) were separated immeasurably ideologically from the *gakushō* (scholarly monks), who played a major role in the development and transmission of Buddhist doctrine. It was from the ranks of the *dōshū* that the *sōhei* (soldier-priests) evolved. Such individuals were spawned as a product of irregularities in the ordination system. Many represented the survival of the pragmatic government ideal of ordination, while others represented the natural tendency of mediocre and corrupt individuals to surround themselves with followers incapable of pointing out their shortcomings. At the close of the Nara period many religious had illegally fled the Ritsuryō system and Buddhist temples of the capital for idealistic reasons. The *sōhei* represented the opposite extreme, using arms to sustain the temporal power of factions and institutions. On Mt. Hiei the period of the abbot Ryōgen witnessed the rise and eventual dominance of the *sōhei*, not because Ryōgen sanctioned them, but because he was powerless to deal with their violence.

As early as 866 the first decree had been issued against Mt. Hiei for the improper behaviour of the monks. The problem festered for a long time.

In 914 a document describes peasant efforts to evade taxation by assuming the tonsure and Buddhist robes and in the worst case, becoming monk-bandits. The presence of such individuals undoubtedly worsened the situation and made it more uncontrollable. Incidents in 949 and 968 exhibited the power of the Nara *sōhei* in enforcing their claims upon the court in Kyōto. But the major event in the creation of the marauding *sōhei* of Mt. Hiei was the conflict between the disciples of Ennin and Enchin evolving into the Sanmon and Jimon branches of Tendai. All types of undesirable elements entered into this dispute. There is no question that the lay monks had gotten out of hand, and the idealism of Tendai scholars was not adequate to resolve the situation. If Heian society had been stable, the court would have been able to handle the matter but the rise of the *sōhei* was also indicative of the degeneration of the general society.

The *shōen* (estate) system had completely undermined the Ritsuryō form of government and the Fujiwara regents, ostensibly in charge of government policies, numbered among the largest *shōen* owners. To protect *shōen* of absentee aristocratic landowners, the warrior class (*bushi*) were employed, but soon they too became a political force, championing Imperial succession causes and other disputes. In time they began to replace the ineffectual aristocratic *shōen* owners. The mood of the society became violent and unstable. Natural calamities that coincided with this political chaos increased the general attitude of hopelessness and despair; it indeed appeared that the age of *mappō* had arrived.

The breakdown of moral values became apparent in the grotesque extremes found in the literature at the close of the era. Heian refinement of taste began to crumble into sheer vulgarity. The need for reforms was painfully obvious, yet Japanese society had to relentlessly proceed on to the catharsis of the Gempei wars before a semblance of order could be restored, and then it became order under the stern hand of military control. The golden days of the aristocracy were to end with the close of the Heian era but their trials and sufferings were just commencing. Religion, which they had tended to regard as an amusement during their days of affluence, became a source of comfort and solace during their days of ignominy. They turned to the type of religion that could be practiced individually in private, a faith that did not require great learning, massive ceremonies or rituals.

The masses who possessed no golden memories of affluence, nor great heights to topple from and in fact, had little to lose except life itself and the burden of taxation, also had recourse to religion during such uncertain times. Their lot was not about to appreciably worsen during the feudal ages but they did need spiritual comfort to help them accept it and above all, they needed some hope for the future—an expectation not offered by the existing society. At the close of the Heian period, Pure Land Buddhism emerged as the faith to fulfill their needs. Its practices were simple enough for them to follow in daily life, and hope was offered in the form of future birth in the Pure Land, which became the near equivalent for Japanese laity of what the *deva* heavens had offered Indian lay Buddhists. In this respect, the masses and aristocrats found something in common to sustain them through the close of the Heian era and into the harsh beginning of the Kamakura period.

In accompaniment with the growing need for private religious practice among the aristocrats and masses, another form of regeneration also gave impetus to the Pure Land movement. Besides the obvious need for institutional reform, there also existed the need to purify Buddhism of its entanglement with superstitious elements of folk-belief that were in effect nearly strangling it. As we have earlier discussed, the assimilation of native beliefs and use of *upāya* are integral features of Buddhism, yet such assimilation must always be controlled. Any organism which allows growth or assimilation to develop unreined ultimately loses control of its own destiny. The danger that assimilated beliefs and *upāya* might degenerate into ends in themselves, destroying their proper function, was particularly inherent in esoteric forms of Buddhism. By the end of the Heian period, such a situation had arisen. Undoubtedly there were still groups of idealistic priests practicing in accord with the aims of the founders of their sects, but they had become a minority. The Nara sects had in fact yielded to esoterism and the doctrines of the once powerful Hossō and Sanron sects were falling into neglect. The centers of esoteric Buddhism at the new capital, the Shingon and Tendai sects, had succumbed to institutional rivalries and corruption. The effective line between magical practices, supersition and Buddhism had disappeared for a majority of the aristocracy and clergy. Some form of restoration had to be made if Buddhism was to survive.

Ironically, one movement towards reform began to develop in a very strange areas. The *hijiri* and *shami* had been among the first to mingle Buddhism with magical practices. These men had an extremely important sociological impact upon Heian society and were instrumental in making assimilation a living practice. Although the *hijiri* and *shami* were composed of numerous types of individuals, they roughly could be classified into two groups: the secluded hermits living in isolation and the wandering priests who travelled throughout the provinces among the people. During the early Heian period, even those known to be dedicated to a single devotion, mingled it with magical practices, as can be seen in the case of Kūya and the *nembutsu*. On the other hand, we can notice that among the diverse practices followed by these religious, belief in Amida Buddha and the *Lotus Sutra* were generally present accompanied by other such devotions as *darani* (*dhāraṇī*), rituals, sutra-copying, image carving, Tantric and magical rites and various popular sutras. Eventually, with the passing of time, more emphasis was placed upon devotion to Amida and the *Lotus sutra* until these became single practices, purified even of magical rites. Such a trend towards the purity of a single practice among these influential people, was a harbinger of Kamakura Buddhist developments that arose from a very unusual quarter.

A similar attitude was evolving within the Tendai sect itself. As a result of Tendai universalism and broad acceptance of different soteriological pathways, it was possible for a monk such as Genshin to retire and devote himself to a single practice with official sanction. In fact, the Tendai emphasis upon doctrinal development even made it possible for a whole new sect emphasizing a single soteriological method to evolve within its confines. This is exactly how Tendai became the 'mother sect' of the three single-practice movements of the Kamakura period: Pure Land (Amida), Nichiren (*Lotus Sutra*) and Zen (meditation). Each of these practices had played an important role within the broad boundaries of the Tendai sect.

The truly national Buddhism of the Kamakura period did not evolve overnight. The elements of each of the new sects had been present as early as the Nara period. The search for purity resulted in remolding them into the form of a unitary practice. Yet the philosophy of assimilation, which had been a characteristic of Heian Buddhism was not to be wholly abandoned. Hōnen, Shinran, Nichiren and Dōgen, in their writings clearly indicated that the native gods were incorporated within their unitary soteriological pathways. To recite the *nembutsu* or name of the *Lotus Sutra* was in effect honouring the gods and obtaining their protection.

Once more Buddhism had completed the cycle from idealism to stagnant corruption, the time had arrived for another renewal. Such cyclic movements have characterized the entire history of Buddhism commencing with the idealism of the founder, stagnated by Abhidharma scholasticism and renewing itself with the rise of Mahāyāna. Like the phoenix rising from its ashes, the Buddhist sects had risen, stagnated and undergone regeneration in China, and now in Japan. The Tendai and Shingon sects made immense cultural contributions to Japanese society and they succeeded in opening the gates for the development of a truly Japanese form of Buddhism. Out of the ashes of their decay, idealistic young men were to come forward with awakened religious consciousnesses to effect the succeeding stages of regeneration. In our next volume we shall see how their idealism remolded the Nara and Heian foundations into the new sects of Kamakura Buddhism and revived the Tendai and Shingon schools themselves to create the present stage of Japanese Buddhism.

FOOTNOTES

CHAPTER I—INTRODUCTION

1 cf. Ienaga Saburō, *Nipponbunkashi* (Tōkyō: Iwanami, 1962) pp. 14–16.

CHAPTER II—INCEPTION OF BUDDHISM

1 *Fusō Ryakki* in *Kokushi Taikei* Vol. VI, pp. 483–4.

2 Contrary to the *Nihonshoki* and later chronologies based on the *Shoki*, the reign of Emperor Kimmei is now believed to have begun in 531, rather than 539. The reigns of his brother predecessors, Ankan and Senka, as well as his father Keitai, also have been adjusted. Cf. Ienaga Saburō ed. *Nipponbukkyō-shi* (Kyōto: Hōzōkan, 1967) pp. 47–8.

3 *Nihonshoki* in *Nippon Koten Bungaku Taikei*, vol. 68 p. 154.

4 Preserved in the *Tenjukoku shūchō* or *Tenjukoku mandara* of the Chūgūji Temple.

5 Cf. Fukui Kōjun "Sangyō gisho no seiritsu o utagau" in *Indogaku Bukkyō-gaku Kenkyū* (8) IV, no. 2 (March 1956) pp. 308–20 and J. H. Kamstra, *Encounter or Syncretism* (Leiden: E. J. Brill, 1967) pp. 407–17.

6 Hanayama Shinshō, "Sangyōgisho ni tsuite" in *Indogaku Bukkyōgaku Kenkyū* (8) IV, no. 2 (March 1956) pp. 321–30.

7 Recently Fujisawa Kazuo has initiated an entirely new system of dating roof tiles. Previously, scholars used the lotus-flower design as the basis for dating tiles but Prof. Fujisawa has demonstrated that the style of the inner and outer peripheries are crucial in determining the precise period. Cf. Ienaga, *Nipponbukkyōshi* pp. 88–9.

8 Cf. *Asukadera Hakkutsu Chōsa Hōkoku* published by Nara Kokuritsu Bunkazai Kenkyūjo (1958) p. 47; also, "Asukadera" in *Encyclopaedia of Buddhism* Vol. II, pp. 285–6.

9 Cf. "Bhaiṣajyaguru" in *Encyclopaedia of Buddhism* Vol. II, p. 662.

10 There is currently a debate whether the existing Yakushi triad was the original dedicated in 697. The Yakushiji was first located in Fujiwarakyō, a temporary capital prior to Nara, and in 718 moved to its present site on the outskirts of modern Nara. The Yakushiji and Kawaradera temples represent the most

famous examples of Hakuhō (645–710) architecture.

11 Cf. M. W. de Visser, *Ancient Buddhism in Japan* (Leiden: E. J. Brill, 1935) pp. 293–308; 533–571.

12 In the 624 edict, Empress Suiko created the priestly offices of *sōjō* and *sōzu* with a lay office of *hōtō*, a form of superintendent. Later the priestly office of *risshi* was added. By the 11th century the board increased to fifty-three offices, which had become predominantly honorary positions. It was officially abolished during the Meiji period and each sect established their own governing board.

13 Ienaga ed. *Bukkyōshi* p. 94.

CHAPTER III—NARA BUDDHISM, THE FOUNDATION STONE

1 E. Frauwallner, *On the Date of the Buddhist Master of the Law Vasubandhu* Serie Orientale Roma III (Rome 1951) p. 54, however, Hattori Masaaki and Ueyama Shunpei, *Ninshiki to Chōetsu in Bukkyō no Shisō* Vol. IV (Tōkyō: Kadokawa, 1973), p. 21 maintain that Vasubandhu, the author of the *Abhidharmakośa* was the founder of Vijñānavāda philosophy.

2 For a detailed discussion see Sakurabe Hajime, *Kusharon no Kenkyū* (Kyōto: Hōzōkan, 1969) pp. 65–92.

3 See A. K. Warder, *Indian Buddhism* (Delhi: Motilal Banarsidass, 1970) pp. 272–5.

4 Cf. Theo. Stcherbatsky, *Buddhist Logic* Vol. I (N. Y.: Dover, 1962), p. 111.

5 Cf. Funahashi Issai, *Gō no Kenkyū* (Kyōto: Hōzōkan, 1961) pp. 374–381 and Sakurabe, *op. cit.* p. 108–110.

6 The *Abhidharmakośa* XII offers the following definitions:

120 kṣaṇa = 1 tat-kṣaṇa
20 tat-kṣaṇa = 1 lava
30 lava kṣaṇa = 1 muhūrta
30 muhūrta = 1 day and night

According to this, one kṣaṇa would relatively equal 0.013 seconds of conventional time.

7 Prof. Funahashi believes that Vasubandhu erred in his criticism of the Sarvāstivādins in the *Abhidharmakośa* by confusing the two views (past → present versus future → past). The Sarvāstivādins failed to take him to task and merely claimed the eternally existing dharmas were nevertheless impermanent. See *op. cit.* pp. 378–9. For an English summary of Vasubandhu's argument see Theo. Stcherbatsky, *The Central Conception of Buddhism* (Delhi: Motilal Banarsidass, 1970) pp. 76–91.

8 Hattori, *Ninshiki to Chōetsu* pp. 78–81; Sakurabe Hajime and Ueyama Shunpei, *Sonzai no Bunseki in Bukkyō no Shisō* vol. II (Tōkyō: Kadokawa, 1973), pp. 84–88. For a description of the Vaiśeṣika theory see D. N. Shastri, *Critique of*

Indian Realism (Agra; Agra Univ. 1964) pp. 158–164.

9 Besides these minute atoms, the Kusha sect is also known to recognize three visible atoms beyond the dust mote in the sun ray, consisting of the size of: 1) a nit, 2) a louse, 3) a grain of wheat.

10 It is classified as belonging to this school because it supposedly alludes to the Buddha's transcendental teaching indicated by the five doctrines of: impermanence, suffering, emptiness, non-soul and emancipation. This was a Bahuśrutiya characteristic. See Warder, *Indian Buddhism* p. 278 and Andre Bareau "Bahuśrutiya" in *Encyclopaedia of Buddhism* Vol. II, p. 502.

11 Since the original Sanskrit of this work is no longer extant, there has been some question whether *Satyasiddhi* is a proper translation. In particular, the correctness of rendering the character *jitsu* 実 as *satya* has been challenged. Such a translation is not uncommon (cf. Mvy 1920) and in view of the proper purpose of the text, appears to be most accurate.

12 The following four categories are divided into degrees of cause and effect.

13 These refer to the psychological states known as the Three Worlds:

Kāma dhātu (Realm of Desire)	—domination of the senses
Rūpa dhātu (Real of Pure Form)	—primary stages of meditation where the lower sense functions have been eliminated
Arūpa dhātu (Realm of non-form)	—planes of pure meditation

It is possible to frequently move among these realms although the more spiritually advanced will remain in the higher levels. The goal of Nirvana transcends all Three Worlds.

14 *nirodha samāpatti* (meditation of extinction) is the stage of meditation transcending the Three Worlds.

15 Bukkyō Gakkai ed. *Hasshū Kōyō Kōgi* by Gyōnen (Kyōto: Hōzōkan, 1968) p. 133.

16 *Ibid.* p. 139.

17 Cf. Andō Kōsei and Kamei Katsuichiro, *Ganjin Wajō* (Tōkyō: Shunjūsha, 1963) pp. 169–202.

18 For a complete discussion see Hirakawa Akira, *Genshi Bukkyō no Kenkyū* (Tōkyō: Shunjūsha, 1964) pp. 372–391.

19 Bukkyō Gakkai ed. *Hasshū Kōyō Kōgi* p. 186.

20 R. Taya, E. Ōchō and I. Funahashi, *Bukkyōgaku-jiten* (Kyōto: Hōzōkan, 1961) p. 187.

21 1) touch one's robe,
2) enter a secluded area together,
3) stand with such a man,
4) talk with him,
5) walk together,

6) Lean against each other,
7) or make a promise together.

22 There is some question whether Piṅgala and Āryadeva were possibly the same person, the dominant consensus is that they were not. Cf. Mochizuki, *Bukkyōdaijiten* Vol. 3 p. 2793; Richard A. Gard "On the Authenticity of the Pai-lun and Shih-er-men-lun" in *Indogaku Bukkyōgaku Kenkyū* (4) Vol. II no. 2 (March 1954) pp. 6–7; "Āryadeva" in *Encyclopaedia of Buddhism* Vol. II p. 114; R. Robinson, *Early Mādhyamika in India and China* (Ann Arbor: Univ. of Wisconsin, 1967) p. 29–30.

23 When we use the term Hīnayāna philosophically, we are not referring to the historical or geographical form of Southern Buddhism currently represented by the Theravāda school, but rather to a philosophical attitude that places emphasis solely upon the goal of personal salvation without concern for the Enlightenment of others. At the time when Mahāyānists originated the pejorative term "Hīnayāna", they were primarily attacking certain Abhidharma schools that had seemingly become so devoted to the goals of scholastic analysis and personal salvation that they had lost the spirit of Early Buddhism, or the Buddhism existing at the time of the historical Buddha. The philosophical usage of this term can apply to anyone, including those professing to be Mahāyānists, who are concerned only with their personal salvation.

24 Cf. Mochizuki, *Bukkyōdaijiten* Vol. 2, p. 1702.

25 *Ibid*. p. 1703.

26 Fukuryō, prior to becoming a priest had been a married layman in China.

27 Ienaga ed. *Bukkyōshi* Vol. I, p. 134–5.

28 Trans. by Kenneth Inada, *Nāgārjuna: A Translation of his Mūlamadhyamakakārikā with an Introductory Essay* (Tōkyō: Hokuseidō, 1970) p. 114.

29 trans. by Inada, *op. cit.* p. 146.

20 *Ibid.*

31 Bukkyō Gakkai ed. *Hasshū Kōyō Kōgi* pp. 308–10.

32 For a discussion of Nāgārjuna's view of the three simultaneous inseparable aspects of Enlightenment: *Śūnyatā* (Emptiness), *Śūnyatāyām prayojanam* (the function of Emptiness) and *Śūnyatā artha* (practice of Emptiness in the conventional world) see Daigan and Alicia Matsunaga, *The Buddhist Concept of Hell* (NY: Philosophical Library, 1971) pp. 55–9.

33 Derived from the *Issai-hossōbon* chapter of the *Gejin Mikkyō*.

34 See our earlier footnote, Chap. III, f. 1.

35 This variety of Vijñānavāda philosophy replaced the earlier She-lun school which had been based upon Paramārtha's (449–569) translation of the *Mahāyāna samparigraha śāstra* of Asaṅga.

36 *Chung-pien-fu-pie-lun* (*Madhyānta vibhāga*) T. Vol. 31, p. 451.

37 Other translations that have been given for *vāsanā* (*vāsana*) are: impression, result of past deeds and experience on the personality; imprégnation, les appétits en tant que résult d' actes antérieres (Sylvain Lévi); perfuming impressions, memory, habit-energy (D. T. Suzuki); habit inclination, propensity. See Franklin Edgerton, *Buddhist Hybrid Sanskrit Dictionary* pp. 478–9.

38 Saeki Ryōken, *Nippon Bukkyō no Shūha*, in *Kōza Bukkyō* Vol. 6 (Tokyō: Daizō Shuppansha, 1959) pp. 38–9.

39 Cf. Yamaguchi Susumu et al. *Bukkyōgaku Josetsu* (Kyōto: Heirakuji. 1961) p. 182 and Hattori, *Ninshiki to Chōetsu* p. 174.

40 The Ti-lun sect of the Northern Wei regarded it as a pure consciousness identical to the *tathatā*, while the She-lun, based upon Paramārtha's views established a ninth consciousness they considered pure, classifying the Ālaya vijñāna as dualistically pure and impure. The Fa-hsiang (Hossō) view as set forth by Hsüan-tsang, considered the Ālaya impure.

41 D. T. Suzuki in his *Studies in the Laṅkāvatāra Sūtra* (London; Routledge and Kegan Paul, 1930) p. 182 was mistaken in this regard when he stated:

> . . . "the *Laṅkāvatāra* differs from the Yogācāra in one important point, i.e., that while the latter maintains that the *Ālaya* is absolutely pure and has nothing to do with defilements and evil passions, the *Laṅkāvatāra* and Aśvaghoṣa maintain the view that the tathagata-garbha or the *Ālaya* is the storage of the impure as well as the pure." . . .

See Walpola Rahula "Asaṅga" in *Encyclopaedia of Buddhism* Vol. II, p. 139.

42 For a practical application of this view see Matsunaga, *The Buddhist Concept of Hell*, pp. 71–2.

43 Shimizu Kōshō, *Nippon Bukkyō no Shūha, Kōza Bukkyō* vol. 6 (Tōkyō: Daizōshuppansha, 1969), p. 79.

44 *Ibid.*

45 The Shih-ti ching-lun (Daśabhūmika śāstra) school, popularly known as the Ti-lun was based upon this commentary on the sutra of the Ten Stages (*Daśabhūmika sūtra*) attributed to Vasubandhu. The sutra has been incorporated as a chapter of the *Avataṃsaka sūtra*.

46 Shimizu, *op. cit.* p. 97.

47 Hui-yuan did not accept Fa-tsang's critical classification of Buddhist teachings into five categories and devised his own system of four categories.

48 Shimizu, *op. cit.* p. 100.

49 *Mahāvibhāṣā*, T. Vol. 27, pp. 865 ff.

50 The Pāli Three *kathā* (graduated forms of discourse): *dāna kathā* (a discourse on the benefits of giving), *sīla kathā* (discourse on proper discipline or morality) *sagga kathā* (discourse on birth in a *deva* heaven) See AN IV, 209 ff.

51 According to Fa-tsang, the two *yānas* (Śrāvaka and Pratyeka Buddha) of

the Āgamas and *Abhidharmakośa* were 'ignorant' of the doctrine of Emptiness (*guhōjō*) in contrast to the two *yānas* of Mahāyāna, which were aware of Emptiness.

52 There were two versions of these Ten Profound Principles, an Ancient and New. The older was set forth by Chih-yen and transmitted by Fa-tsang; the later by Cheng-kuan, based upon an interpretation of Fa-tsang. The later theory is presented here. The major difference is in order and the clarification of #2 and #10.

53 The Ten *bhūmi* form stages 41–50 in the grand scheme of Fifty-two Mahāyāna stages to Enlightenment based upon the *Bosatsu Yōraku Hongōkyō*. These indicate the entire process to Enlightenment by means of the following categories:

10 Varieties of faith (mind to believe).
10 States of mind based upon the realization of the *śūnyatā* nature of Absolute truth.
10 States of practice.
10 States of return—After attaining the realization of *śūnyatā* by means of the former virtuous practices, the bodhisattva now returns his virtues back to the conventional world, to benefit others.
10 Bodhisattva *bhūmi*—where the bodhisattva maintains and resides in the wisdom of Enlightenment while carrying the burden of sentient beings on his shoulders just as the earth (lit. *bhūmi*) supports a tree.
1 Enlightenment of equality.
1 Wondrous Enlightenment—completing all the aspects of Self-Enlightenment, the Enlightenment of others and the practice of Enlightenment in the conventional world . . . representing the supreme incomprehensible Enlightenment of the Buddha.

54 Cf. Kamata Shigeo and Ueyama Shunpei, *Mugen no Sekai in Bukkyō no Shisō* Vol. VI (Tōkyō: Kadokawa, 1971), pp. 64–6, 246–69; also Suetsuna Joichi, *Kegongyō no Sekai* (Tōkyō: Shunjūsha, 1967) pp. 61–70. For an English version see Har Dayal, *The Bodhisattva Doctrine in Buddhist Sanskrit Literature* (Delhi: Motilal Banarsidass, 1970) pp. 283–91; Garma C. Chang, *The Buddhist Teaching of Totality* (University Park: Penn. State Univ., 1971) pp. 28–47; L. de La Vallée Poussin, "Bodhisattva" in *Hastings Encyclopaedis of Religion and Ethics* Vol. II, pp. 743–48; and Junjirō Takakusu, *The Essentials of Buddhist Philosophy* (Honolulu, Office Appliance Co., 1956) pp. 124–5.

55 *Tō-daiwajō-tōseiden* in *Gunshoruijū* Vol. IV, p. 511.

56 Hashikawa, *Gaisetsu Nippon Bukkyōshi* pp. 72–3.

57 Ienaga ed. *Nippon Bukkyōshi* p. 141 ff.

58 *Ibid.*

59 In his prelude to poem 794, Okura expresses his desire to escape this polluted

land and by means of Amida's Original Vow to attain the Pure Land.

60 Hashikawa, *op. cit.* pp. 67–76 was one of the first modern scholars to recognize the significance of the presence of these movements during the Nara period.

61 T. Vol. 24, p. 997. This text is also known as the *Bosatsu Kaikyō* or *Bommōkyō Roshana Bussetsu Bosatsu Shinji Kaihon*. It was the tenth chapter of the Sanskrit *Bodhisattva Hṛdayabhūmi*.

62 This seems to be the basis of Sir Charles Eliot's account in *Japanese Buddhism*, (London: Routledge and Kegan Paul, 1969) p. 220.

63 *Fusō-ryakki* p. 95.

64 Cf. Tsuji Zennosuke, *Nippon Bukkyōshi* (Tōkyō: Iwanami, 1945) p. 223.

65 Ienaga ed. *Bukkyōshi* vol. I, p. 176.

66 *Zoku-nihongi* p. 360.

67 *Ibid.* p. 3.

68 Cf. Takatori Masao "Nara Bukkyō" in *Nippon Bukkyōshi* Vol. I, p. 168 ff.

69 *Nippon-reiiki* in *Gunshoruijū* Vol. 25, p. 18.

70 *Muchimaroden in Gunshoruijū* Vol. 5, p. 352.

71 *Tadojingūji-garanengi-shizaichō* in *Zoku Gunshoruijū* Vol. 27, p. 350.

CHAPTER IV—HEIAN BUDDHISM, DEVELOPMENT OF A NEW DIMENSION

1 *Nembundosha* were official priests appointed annually to a particular sect. The custom began in 696 under Empress Jitō and became an important practice during the Heian period. In 798 the concept of the *nembundosha* changed and the priests were no longer responsible for merely sutra chanting but also required to learn the doctrines of the school. Eventually these monks became leading scholars. In 803, ten priests were appointed: five each to the Sanron and Hossō sects. In 806 the number was increased to twelve with the following dispersements: Kegon 2, Tendai 2, Ritsu 2, Sanron 3, Hossō 3. Among the Sanron and Hossō appointments, one priest in each category was assigned respectively to Jōjitsu and Kusha doctrine.

2 The full title of this commentary upon the *Dairaku Kongō Fukū Shinjitsu Sammaya Hannyaharamita Rishukyō* translated by Amoghavajra between 746–71, is the *Dairaku Kongō Fukū Shinjitsu Sammayakyō Hannya Haramita Rishushaku*.

3 For a full discussion of the relationship between Saichō and Taihan see Miyasaka Yūshō and Umehara Takeshi, *Seimei no Umi in Bukkyō no shisō* Vol. 9 (Tōkyō: Kadokawa, 1972) pp. 238–57.

4 This sutra contains the ten cardinal and forty-eight minor precepts of Mahāyāna Buddhism. For an English translation of the precepts see Alicia Matsunaga, *The Buddhist Philosophy of Assimilation* (Tōkyō: Sophia Univ., 1969) pp. 152–4.

5 Tsuji, *Bukkyōshi* p. 270.

6 Chih-I also used the analogy of milk for these periods, ranging from fresh milk at the time of the *Avataṃsaka* to completely fermented milk represented by the time of the *Lotus*.

7 Inada, *Nāgārjuna* p. 148.

8 According to Prof. Andō, this theory of mutual inclusion is derived from the *Avataṃsaka sūtra*. Cf. Andō Toshio, *Tendai-gaku* (Kyōto: Heirakuji, 1066) pp. 153–4.

9 The concept that the Buddha also possessed an evil nature was adopted by Ch'eng kuan, the fourth patriarch of the Hua-yen school.

10 The thirty-two characteristics of a great man (*Dvātriṃśam mahāpuruṣa-lakṣaṇāni*) were an Indian devotion incorporated within Buddhism describing the Buddha's physical perfection.

11 The abbots of the Tendai Enryakuji temple from Saichō to Ryōgen were as follows:

	Saichō	最澄	(767–822)	
1	Gishin	義真	(781–833)	First Abbot
2	Enchō	円澄	(771–836)	
3	Ennin	円仁	(794–864)	
4	Anne	安恵	(794–868)	
5	Enchin	円珍	(814–891)	
6	Yuishu	惟首	(826–893)	
7	Yūken	猷憲	(827–894)	
8	Kōsai	康済	(? –899)	
9	Chōi	長意	(836–906)	
10	Zōmyō	増命	(844–927)	
11	Ryōyū	良勇	(855–923)	
12	Genkan	玄鑒	(? –926)	
13	Soni	尊意	(866–940)	
14	Gikai	義海	(871–946)	
15	Enshō	延昌	(880–964)	
16	Chinchō	鎮朝	(884–964)	
17	Kikyō	喜慶	(888–966)	
18	Ryōgen	良源	(912–985)	

12 For a translation see Yoshito Hakeda, *Kūkai, Major Works Translated, with an Account of His Life and Study of His Thought* (NY: Columbia Univ., 1972) pp. 101–39.

13 Saichō's transmission of Tendai Taimitsu is identical up to this point, his esoteric master Shun-hsia, was a disciple of Amoghavajra.

14 *Hannya Shingyō Hiken* For a translation see *Hakeda, op. cit*. pp. 272–75.

15 The ninth consciousness is the *amala-vijñāna* or 'purified consciousness' repre-

senting the conversion of the *Ālaya vijñāna.*

16 See Miyasaka, *Seimei no Umi* pp. 79–80.

17 Trailokyavijaya was often divided into two forms in Japan. For a discussion of the dispute over this deity see Mochizuki, *Bukkyōdaijiten* Vol. 3, pp. 2616–7.

18 Some *maṇḍalas* of this variety have a slightly different arrangement.

19 When five or six *goma* rites are held instead of four, this ritual is designed to invite benevolent deities and the fifth *goma* rite (*kyōaihō* or *keiaihō*) requests the protection of the Buddhas and bodhisattvas. When six *goma* rites are held, the last (*enmeihō*) is offered for longevity.

20 As a result of his accomplishment, Shinnen was granted the posthumous title of Dentō Kokushi on the 1,050th anniversary of his death in 1940.

21 Some sources report that it was in 864, the year of his death, which would make him the first to receive the honour. Cf. Mochizuki, *Bukkyōdaijiten* Vol. I, p. 313.

22 Ivan Morris trans. *The Pillow Book* (NY: Columbia Univ., 1967) pp. 34–5.

23 *Ibid.* p. 258.

24 Edward Seidensticker trans. *The Gossamer Years* (Tōkyō: C. E. Tuttle, 1964) p. 67.

25 *Ibid.* p. 95.

26 The *Shan-sheng tzu-ching* T. Vol. I p. 254 lists fourteen duties and the *Chung-a-han* version T. Vol. I, p. 641 lists thirteen.

27 Trans. by Donald Keene "An Account of My Hut" [*Hōjōki*] in *Anthology of Japanese Literature from the Earliest Era to the Mid-nineteenth Century* (NY: Grove Press, 1958) p. 211. The 'Three Worlds' refer to the Realms of Desire, Form and Non-form.

28 *Ibid.* p. 197–8.

29 For one of the most thorough discussions of available source materials see Yamada Ryūjō "Mappō shisō ni tsuite" in *Indogaku Bukkyōgaku Kenkyū* Vol. IV, no. 2 (March 1956) pp. 54–63.

30 The word appears in the earliest texts. Cf. *Dhammapada* verse 38; *Sutta nipāta* 1020, DN III, 252.

31 SN V, 173.

32 AN I, 69 trans. by F. L. Woodward, *The Book of the Gradual Sayings* Vol. I, p. 65.

33 AN IV, 278–9 trans. by E. M. Hare, *The Book of the Gradual Sayings* Vol. I, p. 65.

34 T. Vol. 27, p. 918.

35 SN II, 224. trans. by Mrs. Rhys-Davids in *The Book of the Kindred Sayings* Vol. II, p. 152.

36 DN III, 58–77.
37 S. Beal, *Buddhist Records of the Western World* p. xv–xvi.
38 Yamada, "Mappō shisō ni tsuite" p. 55.
39 T. Vol. 44, p. 786.
40 The Five Existences consist of: Hells, preta, animals, man, deva. When the Asura are added, Six Existences are formed.
41 Itabashi Tomoyuki ed. *Nippon Reiiki* (Tōkyō: Kadokawa, 1967) p. 71–2.
42 J. Hackin, *Asiatic Mythology* (N. Y.: Thomas Crowell, 1963) p. 40.
43 *Mahābhārata* I, 13–14 and 45–48.
44 *Nippon Reiiki* p. 153.
45 Hackin, *op. cit.* pp. 248–50; 363–8.
46 Vol. 19 story 24.
47 Cf. Matsunaga, *The Buddhist Philosophy of Assimilation* p. 236.
48 During the Muromachi, the cult to Jizō as the saviour of children from the riverbed of *Sai* (*Sai no kawara*) developed, which still exists in popular folklore.
49 Godhika SN I, 121–23 and Vakkali, SN III, 124.
50 I-tsing in his *Record of the Buddhist Religion as Practiced in India and the Malay Archipelago* (*AD 671–695*) trans. by J. Takakusu (Delhi: Munshiram Mahoharlal, 1966) p. 81, states that members of the Buddhist sangha can properly entertain such a hope.
51 *Milindapañha* p. 80 line 18–19.
52 For the Chinese versions see T. Vol. 11 p. 97c and T. Vol. 12 p. 272b and 350a.
53 T. Vol. 38, p. 327.
54 T. Vol. 39, p. 658.
55 See Matsunaga, *Buddhist Philosophy of Assimilation* p. 214–6.
56 For their description see Manabe Kōsai, *Jizōson no Sekai* (Tōkyō: Aoyama shoin, 1959) pp. 166–78.
57 The Five Myō-ō consist of:

Fudō	(Acalanātha)
Gōsanze	(Trailokya)
Gundari	(Kuṅḍalī)
Daiitoku	(Yamāntaka)
Kongō Yasha	(Vajra yakṣa)

Trailokya is occasionally divided into two deities: Gōsanze and Shōsanze. Also an independent deity is Aizen Myō-ō (Rāgārāja).
58 See H. Byron Earhart, *A Religious Study of the Mount Haguro Sect of Shugendō* (Tōkyō: Sophia Univ. 1970) p. 18.
59 During the Heian period mountain temples often acted as mortuaries as described in the story of "Yūgao" in the *Genji Monogatari*.

60 He is considered in esoteric Buddhism to represent a manifestation of Shaka belonging to the Shaka-in of the *Taizōkai mandara.*

61 *Mishōtai* literally means 'true body' and the practice is derived from the Shintō concept that the mirror captures the spirit of the individual and was used to symbolize the presence of an deity. With the development of the *honji-suijaku* theory, it become a popular Heian and Kamakura practice to engrave *mishōtai* with the figures of the *honji* Buddha, bodhisattva or deity.

62 Murayama Shūichi, *Shinbutsu Shūgō Shichō* (Kyōto: Heirakuji, 1961) pp. 79–80.

63 In modern times Shugendō practice on Mt. Hiei consist of a 700 day pilgrimage across the three stupas of the mountain finalized by an eight day retreat at the Myō-ō-in temple.

64 This sect later became known under the title of Sambō-in, the name of the Daigoji sub-temple established by Shōkaku, 14th abbot of the Daigoji in 1115. This became the headquarters of Tōzan Shugendō.

65 His life is found in the *Honchō Kōsōden* in *Dainippon Bukkyō Zensho* Vol. 102, pp. 142 ff.

ABBREVIATIONS

Mvy	*Mahāvyutpatti*, Mirnow (Bib. Buddhica XIII) 2 vol., 1910
T	*Taishō Shinshū Daizōkyō* 85 vol., 1922–33

Pali Text Society Series (London)

AN	*Aṅguttara Nikāya* 5 vol., 1885–1900
DN	*Dīgha Nikāya* 3 vol., 1967, 1966, 1960
SN	*Saṃyutta Nikāya* 5 vol., 1887–1902

SELECTED BIBLIOGRAPHY

Andō Kōsei. *Ganjin Daiwajōden no Kenkyū*. Tōkyō, 1960.

Andō Kōsei and Kamei Katsuichirō ed. *Ganjin Wajō*. Tōkyō, 1963.

Barua, B. *A History of Pre-Buddhist Indian Philosophy*. Delhi, 1970.

Bendall, C. and W. Rouse ed. *Siksha Samuccaya, A Compendium of Buddhist Doctrine*. Delhi, 1971.

Bharati, Agehananda. *The Tantric Tradition*. London, 1965.

Bhattacharyya, B. *The Indian Buddhist Iconography*. Calcutta, 1958.

Bukkyō Gakkai ed. *Hasshū Kōyō Kōgi*. Kyōto, 1967.

Chang, Garma C. *The Buddhist Teaching of Totality*. University Park, 1971.

Conze, Edward. *Buddhist Thought in India*. Ann Arbor, 1970.

Daitō Shuppansha pub. *Kōza Bukkyō*, 6 vol. Tōkyō, 1968–9.

Dasgupta, S. *A History of Indian Philosophy*. London, 1922.

Dayal, Har. *The Bodhisattva Doctrine in Buddhist Sanskrit Literature*. Delhi, 1970.

Dutt, N. *Early History of the Spread of Buddhism and the Buddhist Schools*. London, 1925.

Dutt, N. *Early Monastic Buddhism*. Calcutta, 1971.

Dutt, S. *Buddhism in East Asia*. Bombay, 1966.

Dutt, S. *Buddhist Monks and Monasteries of India*. London, 1962.

Earhart, H. Byron. *A Religious Study of the Mount Haguro Sect of Shugendō*. Tōkyō, 1970.

Eliot, Charles. *Japanese Buddhism*. New York, 1969.

Emmerick, R. E. *The Sutra of Golden Light*. London, 1970.

Frauwallner, E. *On the Date of the Buddhist Master of the Law Vasubandhu*. Serie Orientale Roma III, Rome, 1951.

Frauwallner, E. *Philosophie des Buddhismus*. Berlin, 1956.

Fridell, Wilbur M. "Notes on Japanese Tolerance", *Monumenta Nipponica* Vol. XXVII no. 3 (Autumn 1972) pp. 253–271.

Fujita Kōtatsu. *Genshi Jōdo Shisō no Kenkyū*. Tōkyō, 1970.

Fukui Kōjun "Sangyōgisho no Seiritsu o Utagau", *Indogaku Bukkyōgaku Kenkyū* IV, 2 (1956) pp. 308–20.

Funahashi Issai. *Genshin Bukkyō Shisō no Kenkyū*. Kyōyo, 1962.

Funahashi Issai. *Gō no Kenkyū*. Kyōto, 1961.

Fung, Yu-lan. *A History of Chinese Philosophy*. Princeton, 1953.
Glasenapp, H. von. *Buddhism, A Non-theistic Religion*. London, 1970.
Govinda, Anagarika. *The Psychological Attitude of Early Buddhist Philosophy*. London, 1961.
Guenther, H. V. *Buddhist Philosophy in Theory and Practice*. Berkeley, 1971.
Guenther, H. V. *The Tantric View of Life*. Berkeley, 1972.
Gundert, W. *Japanese Religiongeschichte*. Stuttgart, 1935.
Hakeda Yoshito, *Kūkai: Major Works*. New York, 1972.
Hanayama Shinshō. *A History of Japanese Buddhism*. Tōkyō, 1960.
Hanayama Shinshō. "Sangyōgisho ni tsuite" *Indogaku Bukkyōgaku Kenkyū* IV, 2 (1956) pp. 321–30.
Hashikawa Tadashi. *Gaisetsu Nippon Bukkyōshi*. Kyōtō, 1929.
Hattori Masaaki. *Dignāga on Perception, being the Pratyakṣaparicheda of Dignāga's Pramāṇasamuccaya*. Cambridge, 1968.
Herbert, Jean. *Shintō at the Fountain-head of Japan*. London, 1967.
Hirakawa Akira. *Genshi Bukkyō no Kenkyū*. Tōkyō, 1964.
Hirakawa Akira. *Ritsuzō no Kenkyū*. Tōkyō, 1960.
Hori Ichirō. "Mountains and Their Importance for the Idea of the Other World in Japanese Folk Religion." *History of Religions*, Vol. 6, no. 1 (Aug. 1966) pp. 1–23.
Hori Ichirō. *Wagakuni Minkan Shikō no Kenkyū*, 2 vol. Tokyo, 1953.
Ienaga Saburō. *Jōdai Bukkyōshi Kenkyū*. Kyōto, 1966.
Ienaga Saburō. *Nippon Bunkashi*. Tōkyō, 1962.
Ienaga Saburō ed. *Nippon Bukkyōshi* Vol. I, Kodaihen, Kyōto, 1967.
Ienaga Saburō. *Nippon Shisōshi ni Okeru Hitei no Ronri no Hattatsu*. Tōkyō, 1940.
Inaba Enjō. *Tendai Shikyōgi Shinshaku*. Kyōto, 1967.
Inada, Kenneth. *Nāgārjuna, A Translation of His Mūlamadhyamakakārikā with an Introductory Essay*. Tōkyō, 1970.
Inoue Kaoru. *Gyōgi*. Tōkyō, 1959.
Inoue Kaoru. *Narachō Bukkyōshi no Kenkyū*. Tōkyō, 1966.
Ishida Mizumaro. *Ganjin—Sono Shisō to Shōgai*. Tōkyō, 1958.
Ishida Mizumaro. *Jōdokyō no Tenkai*. Tōkyō, 1967.
Ishida Mosaku. *Tōdaiji to Kokubunji*. Tōkyō, 1959.
Iwamoto Yutaka. *Mokuren Densetsu to Urabon*. Kyōto, 1968.
Kadokawa Shoten pub. *Bukkyō no Shisō* Vol. II, III, IV, V, VI, IX. Tōkyō, 1968–70.
Kamstra, J. H. *Encounter or Syncretism*. Leiden, 1967.
Kashahara Kazuo et al. *Shūkyōshi* in *Taikei Nipponshi Sōsho* XVIII. Tōkyō, 1964.
Kawada Kumataro and Nakamura Hajime. ed. *Kegonshisō*. Kyōto, 1960.
Keith, A. B. *Buddhist Philosophy in India and Ceylon*. Oxford, 1923.
Keith, A. B. *The Religion and Philosophy of the Veda and Upanishads*. 2 vol. Delhi,

1970.
Kidder, J. E. *Early Buddhist Japan*. London, 1972.
Kino Kazuyoshi. *Hokekyō no Tankyū*. Kyōto, 1964.
Kitagawa, Joseph M. *Religion in Japanese History*. New York, 1966.
Lamotte, Etienne. *Histoire du Bouddhisme Indien*. Louvain, 1958.
Lamotte, Etienne, ed. *Sandhinirmocana sūtra*. Paris, 1935.
Luk, Charles. *The Vimalakirti Nirdesa Sutra*. Berkeley, 1972.
Mc Govern, W. M. *An Introduction to Mahayana Buddhism*. Varanasi, 1968.
Manabe Kōsai. *Jizōson no Sekai*. Tōkyō, 1959.
Matsunaga, Alicia. *The Buddhist Philosophy of Assimilation*. Tōkyō, 1969.
Matsunaga, Daigan and Alicia. *The Buddhist Concept of Hell*. New York, 1971.
Matsunaga, Daigan and Alicia. " The Concept of *Upāya* in Mahāyāna Buddhist Philosophy," *Japanese Journal of Religious Studies*. Vol. 1 no. 1 (March 1974) pp. 51–72.
Michibata Ryōshū. *Chūgoku Bukkyōshi*. Kyōto, 1965.
Miyamoto Shōson ed. *Bukkyō no Konpon Shinri*. Tōkyō, 1957.
Miyamoto Shōson. *Daijō Bukkyō no Seiritsushiteki Kenkyū*. Tōkyō, 1957.
Mizuno Kōgen. *Genshi Bukkyō*. Kyōto, 1961.
Müller, Max ed. *Vinaya Texts*, Sacred Books of the East, Vol. 20, 23, 25. Delhi, 1968.
Murayama Shūichi. *Shinbutsu-shūgō Shichō*. Kyōto, 1957.
Murti, T. R. V. *The Central Philosophy of Buddhism*. London, 1960.
Nanjio Bunyiu. *A Catalogue of the Chinese Translation of The Buddhist Tripiṭaka*. Oxford, 1883.
Nakano Gishō. *Kūkai* in *Gendai Bukkyō Kōza* 5. Tokyo, 1965.
Nakamura Hajime. *Ways of Thinking of Eastern Peoples*. Honolulu, 1964.
Narada. *A Manual of Abhidhamma*. Kandy, 1968.
Nippon Bukkyō Gakkai. *Shōtoku Taishi Kenkyū*. Kyōto, 1964.
Poussin, L. de La Vallée. "Bodhisattva," *Hastings Encyclopaedia of Religion and Ethics*. Vol. 2, pp. 739–753.
Poussin, L. de La Vallée. *L'Abhidharmakośa de Vasubandhu*. Paris, 1923–5.
Rahula, Walpola "Asaṅga," *Encyclopaedia of Buddhism* Vol. II pp. 133–46.
Rahula, Walpola. *History of Buddhism in Ceylon*. Columbo, 1956.
Ramanan, K. V. *Nāgārjuna's Philosophy*. Tōkyō, 1966.
Reischauer, Edwin O. *Ennin's Travels in T'ang China*. New York, 1955.
Robinson, Richard H. *Early Mādhyamika in India and China*. Madison, 1967.
Sakurabe Hajime. *Kusharon no Kenkyū*. Kyōto, 1969.
Sarkar, A. *Changing Phases of Buddhist Thought*. Patna, 1968.
Satō Tetsuei. *Tendai Daishi no Kenkyū*. Kyōto, 1961.
Sawa Takaaki. *Art in Japanese Esoteric Buddhism*. New York, 1972.
Schuon, Frithjof. *In the Tracks of Buddhism*. London, 1968.

Shastri, D. N. *Critique of Indian Realism*. Agra, 1964.
Shigematsu Akihisa. *Nippon Jōdokyō Seiritsukatei no Kenkyū*. Kyōto, 1965.
Sonoda Kōyū and Tamura Enchō. *Heian Bukkyō*. Tōkyō, 1962.
Stcherbatsky, Theo. *Buddhist Logic*, 2 vol. New York, 1962.
Stcherbatsky, Theo. *The Conception of Buddhist Nirvana*. Leningrad, 1927.
Stcherbatsky, Theo. *The Central Conception of Buddhism*. Delhi, 1970.
Stcherbatsky, Theo. *The Soul Theory of the Buddhists*. Varanasi, 1970.
Streng, Frederick. *Emptiness, A Study in Religious Meaning*. Nashville, 1967.
Suetsuna Joichi. *Kegongyō no Sekai*. Tōkyō, 1967.
Suzuki Daisetsu. *Kegon no Kenkyū*. Kyōto, 1935.
Suzuki, D. T. *Outlines of Mahāyāna Buddhism*, New York, 1963.
Suzuki, D. T. *Studies in the Lankāvatara Sūtra*. London, 1968.
Suzuki Munetada. *Yuishiki Tetsugaku Gaisetsu Kenkyū*, Tōkyō, 1957.
Tajima R. *Les Deux Grands Maṇḍalas et la Doctrine de l'Esoterisme Shingon*. Tōkyō, 1959.
Takakusu Junjirō. *Essentials of Buddhist Philosophy*. Honolulu, 1956.
Tamaki Kōshirō. *Eien no Sekaikan Kegongyō*. Tōkyō, 1966.
Tamamuro Taijō. *Nippon Bukkyōshi Gaisetsu*. Tōkyō, 1951.
Taya Raishun et al. *Bukkyōgaku Jiten*, Kyōto, 1961.
Thomas, E. J. *A History of Buddhist Thought*. New York, 1961.
Toganoo Shōun. *Himitsu Bukkyōshi*. Kōyasan, 1959.
Toganoo Shōun. *Mandara no Kenkyū*. Kōyasan, 1958.
Toganoo Shōun. *Mikkyō Bukkyōshi*. Kōyasan, 1959.
Tokiwa Daijō et al. *Japanese Alphabetical Index of Nanjio's Catalogue of the Buddhist Tripiṭaka*. Tōkyō, 1930.
Tokiwa Daijō. *Shina Bukkyō no Kenkyū*, Tōkyō. 1944.
Tsuji Zennosuke. *Nippon Bunka to Bukkyō:* Tōkyō, 1965.
Tsuji Zennosuke. *Nippon Bukkyōshi*. 11 vol. Tōkyō, 1947–51.
Tsukamoto, Zenryū. *Shina Bukkyōshi Kenkyū, Hokugihen*. Tōkyō, 1942.
Tucci, G. *The Theory and Practice of the Maṇḍala*, New York, 1969.
Ueda Yoshifumi. *Daijō Bukkyō no Konponkōzō*. Kyōto, 1957.
Ui Hakuju. *Bukkyō Jiten*. Tōkyō, 1953.
Ui Hakuji. *Indo Tetsugakushi*. Tōkyō, 1927.
Ui Hakuji. *Nippon Bukkyō Gaishi*. Tōkyō, 1951.
Ui Hakuji. *Shina Bukkyōshi*. Tōkyō, 1939.
Verdu, Alfonso. "The 'Five Ranks' Dialectic of the Sōtō-Zen School in the Light of Kuei-Feng Tsung Mi's 'Ariyashiki' Scheme" *Monumenta Nipponica* XXI no. 1–2 (1966) pp. 125–70.
Visser, M. W. de. *Ancient Buddhism in Japan*. 2 vol. Leiden, 1935.
Wakamori Tarō. *Shugendōshi no Kenkyū*. Tōkyō, 1943.
Warder, A. K. *Indian Buddhism*. Delhi, 1970.

Watanabe Shōkō. *Nippon no Bukkyō*. Tōkyō, 1958.
Watanabe Shōkō. *Saichō to Kūkai*. Tōkyō, 1955.
Yamada Ryūjō. "Mappō Shisō ni Tsuite" *Indogaku Bukkyōgaku Kenkyū* Vol. IV, no. 2 (1956) pp. 54–63.
Yamaguchi Kōen. *Tendai Gaisetsu*. Kyōto, 1967.
Yamaguchi Susumu et al. *Bukkyōgaku Josetsu*. Kyōto, 1961.
Yamaguchi Susumu. *Daijō to Shite no Jōdo*. Tōkyō, 1963.
Yamaguchi Susumu. *Hannya Shisōshi*. Kyōto, 1951.
Yamaguchi Susumu and Nozawa Jōshō. *Seshin Yuishiki no Genten Kaimei*. Kyōto, 1953.
Yasui Kōsai. *Chūgan Shisō no Kenkyū*. Kyōto, 1961.
Yokota Kenichi. *Dōkyō*. Tōkyō, 1959.
Yūki Reimon. *Seshin Yuishiki no Kenkyū*. Tōkyō, 1956.
Zürcher, E. *The Buddhist Conquest of China*. 2 vol. Leiden, 1959.

INDEX

B

N

T